Constitutiona

Administrative

Constitutional and Administrative Law

I.N. Stevens

Senior Lecturer in Law, University of Buckingham

Second Edition

THE M & E HANDBOOK SERIES

Pitman Publishing
128 Long Acre, London WC2E 9AN

A Division of Longman Group UK Limited

First published in Great Britain 1982
Second edition 1993

©MacDonald & Evans Ltd 1982
©Longman Group UK Limited 1993

British Library Cataloguing in Publication Data
A catalogue entry for this book is available from the British Library

ISBN 0 7121 1041 0

Founding Editor: P.W.D. Redmond

Printed and bound in Singapore

Contents

Part one   General constitutional law

Part two Parliamentary democracy

Part three The individual

Part four Executive authority and its control: administrative law

Preface

In the ten years or so which have elapsed since the first edition of this book appeared, there have been years of tremendous growth and change in the fields of Constitutional and Administrative law. As well as an enormous volume of case law on subjects such as Judicial Review and the European Community, this period has seen the enactment of some major pieces of legislation involving (amongst other things), Official Secrecy, Police Powers, and the system of local taxation. Even some of our fundamental institutions have come under increased scrutiny, so that, for example, changes in the financing of the Monarchy, and the Queen's immunity from income tax, now seem likely in the not-too-distant future.

In the light of these, and many other developments, I have taken this opportunity of completely re-writing the text, rather than simply updating and revising it. At the same time, I have sought to provide fuller coverage with more explanation, of the law on those 'key areas' which tend to feature in college and university courses, especially first degree courses in Constitutional and Administrative Law. The consequence of this is that some material less likely to be met in academic courses in law has been reduced or omitted altogether. I trust that, despite this, the book will remain useful to the general reader who simply wishes to acquaint himself with the subject, as well as undergraduates and other students of law.

For enabling me to produce the second edition of this book I must thank Lizzie Horne who, assisted by Elizabeth Stewart, 'processed' my messy handwritten drafts into a decent typescript; and also the Publishers for their fine editorial efforts and patience.

In general, the law is given as at October 1992. I have, however, anticipated the new system of local taxation which will be in place around the time of publication, or shortly thereafter, in the interests of simplicity, as much as the need to be up to date.

I N Stevens
October 1992

Table of cases

Table of statutes

List of abbreviations

AG	Attorney-General
AJA	Administration of Justice Act
CA	Court of Appeal
CCA	Contempt of Court Act
DPP	Director of Public Prosecutions
EC	European Community
ECA	European Communities Act
HL	House of Lords
MEP	Member of the European Parliament
MP	Member of Parliament
PA	Parliament Act
PM	Prime Minister
PR	Proportional Representation
RPA	Representation of the People Act
RSC	Rules of the Supreme Court
SDP	Social Democratic Party
UK	United Kingdom
USA	United States of America

Part one

General constitutional law

1

Constitutional and administrative law generally: the principal features of the British Constitution

Introductory

1. Constitutional and administrative law

These are, in fact, two distinct branches of law, but the distinction between them is a fine one, and it is not really possible to understand one branch without having some understanding of the other. The following will suffice as definitions:

(a) *Constitutional law.* This is that branch of the law concerned with the constitution of a State. Every State must have a constitution, in the sense of a body of rules by which that State is governed: constitutional law is concerned with that body of rules.

(b) *Administrative law.* This is that branch of the law concerned with the system of rules whereby the exercise of governmental power is controlled. In particular, it is concerned with the means whereby such power can be controlled by a court of law. This is referred to as judicial review of administrative action.

As the above definitions imply, administrative law springs from constitutional law. One might say that constitutional law is concerned with the system of rules whereby governmental powers arise; administrative law is concerned with the means whereby such powers, having arisen and been put into practice, are checked. Thus, administrative law takes over where constitutional law leaves off.

Administrative law is dealt with in Part 4; in this and the following two parts, we are concerned with constitutional law.

2. Constitutions

As noted at 1 above, constitutional law is that branch of the law concerned with the constitution of a State. The term constitution has both a broad and a narrow meaning.

(a) *The broad meaning.* In this sense constitution simply refers to the entire body of rules whereby a State is governed. Such rules need not invariably be laws: in the United Kingdom, for example, the Constitution may be said to consist of laws, conventions, customs and usages. (These terms are discussed in 5, below.)

(b) *The narrow (or concrete) meaning.* In nearly all modern States (the UK and Israel being the only exceptions) the constitution, or at least the major part of it, is embodied in a single, written document, or a short series of documents. In its narrow (or concrete sense) the constitution refers to this written document, or series of documents.

The most famous written constitution (and the first to be established in 1786) is that of the United States of America. This consists of seven Articles and 26 Amendments. (These amount to new Articles, added later by special procedure.)

3. State

It was suggested at 1 above, that every State must have a constitution. In effect, State and statehood can be defined by reference to this fact. The concept of a State is an ancient one, and is nowadays a concept of international law. Statehood refers to the attributes of a State; there are three of these, according to international law.

(a) *A defined territory.* To be a State, a country must have distinct borders, whether natural (e.g. the ocean or a river) or artificial, thus establishing a defined territory.

(b) *A people.* Nowadays, the people of a State are normally defined in terms of nationality (or, more traditionally, citizenship, as in 'American citizen').

(c) *A system of organised government.* At the very least, a State must employ some system whereby outside interference (military or otherwise) can be resisted, and order maintained internally. This last requirement, in particular, gives rise to the fact that a State *must* have a constitution, at least in the broad sense given at 2, above.

Varieties and classification of constitutions

4. Written constitutions

As stated in **2**, above, virtually all modern States have written constitutions – that is, the body of rules whereby the State concerned is governed is wholly, or at least largely, to be found in one written document. Even those States whose systems of government were established by the UK (such as former colonies) or which modelled their systems on the British one, all (with the exception of Israel, and of course the UK itself) have written constitutions, e.g. Canada, Australia, India and Sri Lanka. Two questions therefore arise:

(1) Why, and in what circumstances might a State acquire a written constitution? and

(2) What sort of rules will such a constitution contain?

These questions are answered below.

5. Acquisition of a written constitution

It is generally accepted that a written constitution will normally be acquired by a country either when that country first acquires statehood or if, for one reason or another, a State is obliged to form a new type of government.

(a) *Acquisition of statehood.* This is normally associated with the transition of a country from being the colony of an imperial power to becoming an independent State in its own right. Thus, for example, the USA (1786), Sri Lanka (1947) and Nigeria (1961) were all formerly colonies of Great Britain: they became independent and therefore acquired statehood.

On reaching statehood, after independence, it is normal for a State to introduce a written constitution. In some cases, however, this will actually replace an existing written constitution, created by the colonial power concerned. Thus, for example, the British North America Act 1867, passed by the UK parliament, established the Constitution of Canada. It was only after Canada became entirely independent (Canada Act 1982) that the Canadian Parliament was itself able to introduce changes to that constitution.

(b) *A fresh start.* Many states have been obliged to form a new type of government for one reason or another, and have at the same time acquired a written constitution. Such a fresh start may occur after a revolution (as in France in 1789) or after defeat in war (as in

Germany and Japan in 1945): in the latter case, the constitution may well be imposed on the State concerned by the victorious power.

The question is often posed: Why has the UK never acquired a written constitution? After all, England has been conquered (by William of Normandy in 1066), and Britain has suffered a revolution in the seventeenth century.

In fact, for a short while, a form of written constitution, known as the Instrument of Government, did exist, and was the legal basis of Oliver Cromwell's period as Lord Protector from 1653–60.

The usual explanation for the absence of a written constitution in the UK is that our institutions evolved gradually over a number of centuries, and this process began at a time when the writing down of anything was a rarity. Thus, in the UK, the principal organs of government – parliament, the Crown and the courts – were already established by the thirteenth century, and whilst they have been re-shaped by important written instruments and Acts of Parliament (such as the Magna Carta in 1215, and the Act of Settlement in 1700), these are too diverse, and omit far too many fundamental rules concerning government, to amount to a written constitution. On the other hand, since many of the rules concerning the government of the UK are to be found in such instruments and Acts, it would be wrong to describe the British constitution as unwritten. It is probably safest to simply say that the UK has no written constitution.

6. Rigid and flexible constitutions

The terms rigid and flexible refer to the ease with which a constitution can be changed or amended.

(a) A rigid constitution is one which is impossible, or at least difficult, to change. If change is possible, this will normally involve some special procedure, quite distinct from the procedure whereby laws are generally passed or changed. For example, a change in the constitution might require a referendum of all the electorate as in Australia: a larger than normal majority in the legislature (or Parliament) as in some European countries; or, in a federal system (*see* 12, below), ratification by the authorities in the component elements which make up the federation. In the USA an amending proposal must be passed by a majority of two-thirds in each of the Houses of Congress (the US legislature) and then ratified by at least three-quarters of the legislatures in the individual states which make up the USA.

(b) A flexible constitution, on the other hand, can legally be changed quite readily, so that in order to change the constitution, the same procedures are involved as in changing or passing any other law.

Thus, for instance, every major Act of the UK Parliament which deals with constitutional issues (such as elections, individual rights and police powers, etc) may be said to change the constitution itself. Amongst such Acts in recent years, some of the most significant have been the European Communities Act 1972 (incorporating EC law into the UK: *see* 5:15); the Police and Criminal Evidence Act 1984 (dealing with police powers and rights of suspects: *see* 11); and the Representation of the People Acts 1983 and 1985 (dealing with parliamentary elections).

In fact, it is not only Acts of Parliament (legislation) which can change the British constitution or add to it. In the UK, the following factors must also be considered.

(*i*) Common law. This refers to the body of 'judge-made' law, or judicial precedents. Many principles of constitutional law derive from judicial decisions, thus prompting Dicey to describe the British Constitution as, to all intents and purposes, 'judge-made' (*see* 17, below).

(*ii*) Non-legal rules. In the UK, a major contribution to the constitution is in the form of non-legal rules. These include custom, usages and, most important of all, conventions. Conventions are dealt with in chapter 3 of this book.

7. The status and contents of a constitution

These questions are closely related. Generally speaking, the constitution of a State is (amongst other things) the legal basis for governmental power. This is most obvious in the case of a written constitution, such as that of the USA. Article 1 of the American Constitution begins, 'All legislative power herein granted shall be vested in a Congress of the US', and Article 2 begins, 'The executive power shall be vested in a President of the USA', and so on.

Thus, the first two Articles of the American Constitution are, in effect, the legal sources of legislative and executive powers respectively. In other words, it is the Constitution which empowers congress to legislate, and the president to govern. As such, it follows that the constitution occupies a special place, legally, and is far more significant than other laws (a point reflected in the USA by the fact that the constitution is also rigid).

(a) *Status.* In the majority of cases, some special place is occupied by the constitution of a State. This is especially true of written constitutions, which may usually be described in the following terms.

(*i*) Fundamental law. As noted above, the very power to make laws enjoyed by, say, the Congress of the USA is established in the constitution. It is the constitution which establishes the principal organs of government, and determines what they can and cannot legally do. Thus, the constitution is fundamental to all other laws: without it, government could not lawfully proceed at all.

(*ii*) Superior law. It follows from (*i*) that the conduct of any agency or person is authority which is contrary to the provisions of the constitution has no legal basis, and is therefore unlawful. Taken to its logical conclusion, this means that, in a State having a constitution of this kind (i.e. written and rigid) it would be possible for even legislation enacted by the Parliament (or legislature) to be challenged in a court of law, on the grounds that it is repugnant to the constitution. Thus, in the USA, the Supreme Court (the court entrusted with the interpretation of the constitution) has ruled that it has the power to hold legislation passed by Congress to be invalid (or unconstitutional) on these grounds: *Marbury* v. *Madison* (1803).

The UK, on the other hand, has a constitution which is neither written nor rigid: one cannot really speak of the Constitution as a whole as fundamental or superior, since it can be readily changed, and there is no facility in the UK for a court to declare an Act of Parliament to be illegal (or unconstitutional). Indeed, according to O. Hood Phillips, the fact that the British Parliament can pass any laws it likes (including laws changing the constitution) which cannot be challenged is 'the one fundamental law in the British Constitution'. This principle (it is not exactly a law) is known as parliamentary sovereignty (or supremacy). It is dealt with in chapter 4.

(b) *Contents.* Generally speaking, every constitution will contain the following:

(*i*) Provision for the principal institutions (or organs) of government. There are normally three of these: the legislature, the executive and the judiciary. These reflect the three main categories of functions of government (*see* 8, below).

(*ii*) A system whereby the above are selected. This might involve election or some other form of appointment: in most countries, it is normal for at least the legislature to be elected.

(*iii*) A statement of the scope of the powers available to these organs of government.

In addition, most constitutions (at least if they are written) nowadays contain the following:

(*iv*) A statement of those rights enjoyed by all citizens which are considered to be fundamental (i.e. worthy of protection in the constitution itself). Such a statement is sometimes known as a Bill of Rights or Charter of Rights.

The above are more obvious in the case of a written constitution. In the UK, of course, there is no written constitution and, therefore, no Bill of Rights. The sorts of provisions which are to be found in a written constitution are, in the UK, to be found in constitutional law generally, and in those non-legal rules which are so important in the working of the British Constitution. Thus provision for the British prime minister is not laid down in any law at all, but is, in fact, a convention (*see* 3).

Government

8. Government

We saw at **2**, above, that a constitution may be defined as the body of rules whereby a State is governed. We must now look at the idea of government in greater detail. In the context of the above definition, the term government means the organisation and administration of all of the State's affairs. For analytical purposes, these are normally classified in three categories of functions.

(a) *Legislative.* This involves the enactment of new law and the repeal and amendment of existing laws.

(b) *Executive.* This involves the formulation of policy and its implementation in accordance with law.

(c) *Judicial.* This can be defined as the determination (final resolution) of legal disputes between individuals, or individuals and public bodies, in accordance with law.

9. The separation of powers

Since the functions of government can be neatly divided into three distinct categories, it is logical for an attempt to be made to allocate each of these functions to a separate body, or organ of government. This was the thinking which inspired the French eighteenth-century jurist and writer, Montesquieu, who wrote of the separation of powers in *The Spirit of the Laws*. Montesquieu saw a number of advantages which would result from allocating each function to a completely separate body. (The doctrine of the separation and its possible advantages are discussed in chapter 2.) For now, it is sufficient to state that in many countries three organs of government (namely the legislature; the executive; and the judiciary) are readily discernible. Whether each is completely separate from the other, however, is a matter which varies quite considerably from State to State. In the UK, they are not.

10. The government

In our definition of a constitution, we used the term government in the broad sense discussed in **8**, above, to denote a wide range of functions, all of which can be classified under one of three headings. Thus, government in this sense is used in the abstract, to describe such functions.

In popular parlance, however, the term the government is used in a more concrete sense: specifically to refer to that body of individuals concerned with the most important executive functions. There are a number of reasons for this, some of them (in the case of the UK in particular) historical.

(a) The head of the executive branch of the government is, in most cases, also referred to as the Head of State. Thus, the Head of State in the UK is Her Majesty the Queen and, in the USA the president (though, as we shall see, the US president wields far more political power than does the Queen).
(b) It is the executive which formulates the policy which will be incorporated in legislation enacted by the legislature. Thus, in the UK the executive shapes the programme of legislation during the lifetime of a Parliament, arguably to the extent of dominating it.

In the light of the above, and for purely historical reasons, the executive branch of government has become, of all three organs, that most closely associated with governing a country: this is especially apparent in the UK and to a greater or lesser extent in most constitutions, especially those (like Canada and Australia) based loosely on the so-called Westminster model. Thus, it is perfectly normal to speak of the government when referring to that body of persons who have the greatest responsibility and authority in connection with the executive functions. In the UK, this means the prime minister, other ministers of the Crown, and the Cabinet in particular (*see* 13).

Particular features of the British Constitution

11. The British Constitution

Mention has already been made of some of the chief features of the British Constitution: these will be merely summarised below. Other significant features, not hitherto discussed, are explained in more detail. Features which have already been discussed are:

(a) *No written constitution.* As mentioned at 4 above, the UK does not have a written Constitution.

(b) *Flexible constitution.* Again, we have already established that the British Constitution is flexible (*see* 6, above).

(c) *No system of fundamental or superior laws.* In the strict constitutional sense, there is no system of such laws in the UK, since the British Constitution is not a written one, and is flexible. However, there are certain principles which are regarded as fundamental to the British Constitution, in the sense that they hold some special significance. For instance, as mentioned at 7, above (and discussed further at 4), the doctrine of parliamentary sovereignty is considered fundamental in that the whole system of government as we know it in the UK is based on this principle, and could not proceed without it.

Another doctrine which is considered fundamental to the British Constitution (although arguably not quite as important as parliamentary sovereignty) is known as the rule of law: this is discussed at 16, below.

(d) *No true separation of powers.* This is discussed in detail in 2.

The following paragraphs deal with other important features of the British Constitution.

12. A unitary Constitution

Although the UK consists of several countries (namely England and Wales, Scotland and Northern Ireland), its constitution involves only one, centralised system of government. Thus, there is only one legislature, one executive and one judiciary for the whole of the United Kingdom of Great Britain and Northern Ireland (although these may have 'branches' in the various regions, and judges, for instance, may be assigned to particular areas). This can be contrasted with a federal system, such as that of the USA where there is a central government, comprising the federal authorities (Congress, the president and his government or administration, and the Supreme and Federal Courts), which has overall responsibility for the USA as a whole in most domestic and foreign affairs. However, each of the 50 states of the USA has its own independent legislature, executive and judiciary (as well as other authorities such as the police, etc.) which are responsible for the internal affairs of that state, and are, within their respective fields, autonomous. Thus, the government of, say, California proposes laws which, on being enacted by the Californian state legislature, become the law in that state, and are then applied by the California courts.

It is possible in a unitary constitution (such as that of the UK) to have some powers conferred upon local bodies. This takes two forms:

(a) *Power devolved upon regional assemblies.* The power referred to here is the power to legislate: such a power was, until 1972, enjoyed by an Irish assembly, sitting in Stormont Castle. (Plans to revive the system, and apply it to Scotland and Wales as well as Northern Ireland, have, at the time of writing, come to nothing.)

The legislative powers of such a regional assembly are usually very limited in scope, unlike those of the state legislatures in the USA.

(b) *Local government with delegated powers.* The UK has, for many years, had a system of local councils (local government). These are essentially executive and administrative bodies: to do their work, however, Parliament has granted them limited powers to make laws. These laws are known as delegated (or subordinate) legislation. They are, as it were, inferior or subordinate to an Act of Parliament, in that Parliament can grant or revoke the power to make such laws as it sees fit. Furthermore, such delegated legislation can be challenged in the courts (unlike an Act of Parliament) by the procedure known as judicial review (*see* 15).

As well as federal and unitary constitutions, it is possible for provision to be made for a Confederation of States. Here, each of the participating States is completely equal, and there is no central (federal) government having overall control (although the States may pool their resources for certain purposes, such as defence). The Confederation of Independent States, which is emerging as a replacement for the Soviet Union, appears to be being established on this basis: Switzerland, too, is a confederation.

13. Constitutional monarchy

(a) The word monarchy refers to a system where the Head of State (who would traditionally have ruled that State) is a monarch who becomes the Head of State by heredity (i.e. inheriting the position from his or her parent). This can be contrasted with a republic, where the Head of State is appointed by some process or other. (This might, for instance, involve an election.) The Head of State in a republic is usually known as the president. The USA is a republic. Its Head of State is a president who is elected every four years. The UK is a monarchy (as the title United Kingdom suggests).

(b) However, the UK is a constitutional monarchy. This means that the monarch, Queen Elizabeth II, does not rule absolutely, but is bound by the constitution, and subordinate to it. Other examples of constitutional monarchies are Japan (which has an hereditary emperor) and Sweden.

In the UK, it is the conventions of the constitution in particular, which limit the powers of the monarch (these are discussed in 3), and the monarchy (*see* 13:1–6).

14. Parliamentary democracy

(a) *Democracy.* This derives from a Greek word: it implies that government is conducted in accordance with the wishes of the people governed. The most effective way for this to occur is to provide for a system in which those who govern a country are responsible to the people, and accountable to them for their actions. This usually involves electoral responsibility: the most efficacious way of ensuring that the government is responsible and acts in accordance with the wishes of the people is to build in to the system regular elections at which the people can vote out a government of which they disapprove. Accordingly, democracy has for many people become almost synonymous with elections, and with the concept of 'one man (or woman!), one vote'. In the USA, a highly developed democracy, for instance, not only are members of both Houses of Congress elected, but so is the president. Indeed, in American states, not only are the governor and members of the legislature elected, but so are some judges.

(b) *Parliamentary democracy.* In the UK accountability of those involved in government takes a different form to that in, say, the USA. Specifically, of the three principal organs of government, only one (the legislature) is elected, and then not in its entirety. Members of the House of Commons must be elected at least every five years: members of the House of Lords are not elected at all, but obtain their places either by heredity or by appointment for life.

This does not mean that the UK is not a democracy: on the contrary, it is one of the oldest. In the UK, the government (executive) consists of Members of Parliament, who are elected (unless they are members of the House of Lords) and are by convention responsible and accountable for their actions to Parliament, and to the House of Commons in particular. Thus, the government is indirectly responsible to the electorate.

A democratic system can be contrasted with a dictatorship or a totalitarian system. In particular, what those systems lack is any choice available to the people as to the government: a dictatorship because a dictator is often self-appointed and will in any case not permit any alternative, and totalitarian system because it involves only one party, thus giving the electors no alternative policy from which to choose. The risks of dictatorship and totalitarianism can be avoided in several ways: Montesquieu, for instance, argued that a separation of powers was a safeguard against dictatorship. The UK has only a limited separation of powers (*see* 2): it does, however, have certain safeguards within the constitution. These include:

(*i*) The electoral system. By law, elections for the entire membership of the House of Commons must be held at least every five years.

(*ii*) Conventions. Mention has already been made of the convention of ministerial responsibility: conventions generally and their role in safeguarding parliamentary democracy are discussed later.

(*iii*) The party system. In the UK the party system is extremely important, since it is the political party which wins the most seats in the House of Commons at a general election which forms a government (another important convention of the constitution).

Sources of constitutional law

15. Sources generally

The most obvious source of constitutional law is, of course, the constitution itself. Thus, in a country having a written constitution, the constitution is, to all intents and purposes, the fundamental source of all law, providing as it does for the major law-making processes (legislation, etc.). This does not mean, however, that the constitution is the only source of constitutional law in such a country. It is quite common for a written constitution to be supplemented by other laws, usually in the form of legislation and judicial decisions. These supplementary laws (or organic laws as they are sometimes known) are essential to fill in gaps in the constitution, to interpret its provisions, and to confer further power on officials to implement the provisions of the constitution. Indeed, it is even possible for a written constitution to be supplemented by conventions (as in Canada and Australia, which share the conventional system of prime ministerial appointments with the UK). Thus, even where there is a written constitution (which is clearly the most important source) the actual sources of constitutional law – i.e. rules of a constitutional nature, or rules concerned with the system of government – can be quite diverse.

16. Sources of British constitutional law

The UK has no written constitution. Accordingly that particular source of constitutional law does not exist in the UK. However, all of those other sources mentioned at 14, above, as well as some others, do. Thus, in the UK, whilst we cannot speak of the constitution in the concrete sense of a written constitution, we can speak of constitutional law, the main sources of which are as follows:

(a) *Statutes (legislation).* Traditionally, this is the primary source of British constitutional law, deriving from the doctrine of parliamentary sovereignty (*see* 4). Every Act which deals with constitutional matters forms a part of constitutional law, and there are a very great number of these in force at the present time. Statutes take precedence over other sources (but note the discussion below and in 5 on European Community law).

(b) *Case law (judicial precedents).* This is also an important source of constitutional law in the UK. Many important principles of constitutional law, and of administrative law in particular, derive from such decisions. This fact was noted by Dicey, who included it in his formulation of the principle known as the rule of law (see 17, below). A judicial precedent, however, is overruled by a statute with which it conflicts, and to that extent, case law is secondary to legislation in importance. The system of case law as a whole is sometimes referred to as the common law.

(c) *European Community law (EC law)*. Since 1972, the UK has been a member of the European Community with the result that British courts have had to apply those parts of EC law which are said to 'take direct effect'. This is particularly so in the case of EC regulations which are 'directly applicable'. (These concepts are discussed in detail in 5.)

Although EC law is discussed herein after legislation and case law, this should not be taken to mean that it is necessarily subordinate to these. One of the novel features of EC law is that it is said to be 'part of our law, equal in force to any statute' (*per* Lord Denning).

(d) *Custom*. Historically, custom was a significant source of English law generally. This is no longer the case, however, and custom is not a significant source of modern British law, except for constitutional law. Here, many rules and principles are customary in origin, although one might describe them as forming part of the common law, in so far as the courts of law recognise them and determine their scope, although they do not actually enforce them. In particular, the following are customary in origin:

(*i*) The 'law of Parliament' and, in particular, parliamentary privilege. These are rules which Parliament has decided for itself, and which it alone can enforce (see 8).

(*ii*) The royal prerogative. This is that 'residue of arbitrary and discretionary authority' which is left in the hands of the Crown, and which operates by virtue of the common law, but outside its ordinary course (*see* 13).

In addition to the above, custom plays an important ceremonial role in British constitutional affairs, e.g. the State Opening of Parliament; the Queen's Speech.

(e) *Literary sources*. Very occasionally, where the law cannot be ascertained by reference to any statute or decided case etc., the courts may resort to the writing of famous authors in the field of constitutional and administrative law to clarify the law. Foremost amongst these is A.V. Dicey whose book, *An Introduction to the Study of the Constitution,* has been cited with approval in a small number of cases involving difficult points of constitutional law. Such writings are very much a subordinate source, however, and are really only used by the courts as a last resort.

The rule of law

16. The rule of law
The concept of the rule of law is an ancient one. The idea is that the rule of law is preferable to the rule of man, since the latter might be abused, and lead to dictatorship. In more modern times, the rule of law has come to be associated with the notion of respect for the law and, in particular, with law and order. However, an excessive concern with these can also be repressive, particularly in a country such as the UK, which as no written constitution or Bill of Rights embodying fundamental rights or laws of any kind. Thus, the rule of law, if it is to be relied upon to provide a suitable balance between authority and the freedom of the individual, must mean something more. Accordingly, the rule of law, as analysed by Dicey, assumes a uniquely British flavour, when applied to the British Constitution.

17. Dicey's analysis
Dicey regarded the rule of law as consisting of three limbs:

(a) No one should be punished except for a distinct breach of the law, established in the ordinary legal way in the normal courts of law. (The 'absence of arbitrary power'.)
(b) No one is above the law: everyone is subject to the jurisdiction of the ordinary courts.
(c) The constitution is 'pervaded by the Rule of Law'. Thus, the general principles of the constitution (including such things as the right to personal liberty) derive from judicial decisions determining the rights of individuals bringing their disputes before the courts, and not from a written constitution, as in some other countries. In other words, constitutional law is judge-made.

Thus, whilst the rule of law is a concept known to most countries and constitutions, it is, as formulated by Dicey, uniquely British.

18. Examples of the rule of law in practice
(a) *The 'absence of arbitrary power'.* In *Entick* v. *Carrington* (1765) the

Secretary of State issued a warrant for the search and seizure of the plaintiff's property. No offence was specified in the warrant, but the Secretary, Lord Carrington, claimed that since subversive activities were suspected, the normal procedures did not apply. The court rejected this argument; it was the law of the land that a warrant must indicate the offence in question. As for the distinction between 'ordinary' crimes and crimes involving the State, *per* Lord Campbell, ' . . . the common law does not understand that kind of reasoning, nor do our books take notice of any such distinction'.

A more recent case on the point is *Congreve* v. *Home Office* (1976). The applicant (amongst many others) decided to take out a new television licence before the expiration of his current licence, in order to avoid an increase in the licence fee. The Home Secretary threatened to use his powers under the Wireless Telegraphy Act 1949 to revoke the applicant's licence. The Court of Appeal held that such a threat, if carried out, would be unlawful. In taking out a new licence prematurely, the applicant had not broken any law, and could not lawfully be punished by the revocation of his licence. Furthermore, the 1949 Act did not authorise revocation in such circumstances, and in using the threat of revocation to force the applicant to buy a new one at the increased price, the Home Secretary was, in effect, attempting to levy an unauthorised charge, contrary to the Bill of Rights 1689.

(b) *'No one is above the law'*. The cases discussed in (a) above also illustrate this principle in the following ways:

(*i*) The courts were not prepared to allow the Home Secretary, in either case, to exceed the powers granted him by statute or at common law; and

(*ii*) They did not accept claims that the conduct of a government minister was outside the courts' jurisdiction.

Another case on this limb of the rule of law is *Conway* v. *Rimmer* (1968). Here, the Home Secretary objected to the production of certain documents as evidence in a case (not involving the government) claiming Crown Privilege. The House of Lords held that the question whether or not documents should be given in evidence was for the court to decide, not the Minister (though the court would, of course, listen to his argument that production might be prejudicial to the public interest in confidentiality (*see* 19:15)).

(c) *Constitutional law is judge-made*. There are many instances of important constitutional principles deriving from judicial decisions in the UK. In *Burmah Oil Co. Ltd* v. *Lord Advocate,* (1965), the House of Lords established the important principle that, whilst the government can order the wilful destruction of a British subject's property in time of war, it must pay compensation: the Crown's power, therefore, is a limited one.

In *Ridge* v. *Baldwin* (1964) the House of Lords established that a person who had been dismissed from a public office held under statutory provisions was entitled to know the reasons for his dismissal, and be given an opportunity to challenge them if he felt they were wanting.

In *Council of Civil Service Unions* v. *Minister for the Civil Service* (1984), the principle was established that where a body of workers have a legitimate expectation to be consulted in matters relating to their terms of employment based on a prior practice of consultation, they are entitled to such consultation, even where their employer is the Crown, acting under its prerogative powers (although the House accepted there would be exceptions: *see* 13:18).

The point here is that constitutional law (and especially administrative law) derives largely from such decisions, and that the Constitution is, indeed, shaped by judicial precedents.

One other feature of the rule of law, not addressed by Dicey, is that, in order for it to work, it is necessary that the individual has access to the courts. Thus, when we say that no one is above the law, and that no one should be punished except in accordance with the law, we must assume that a system exists whereby an individual can challenge the conduct of the government, or appeal against his treatment at the hands of the authorities. (Administrative law, and the important topic of judicial review, which addresses these issues, is dealt with in Part 4.)

19. Dicey's critics

As with his treatment of other matters, Dicey has been criticised for his treatment of the rule of law, which it is claimed, is riddled with exceptions. Thus, for example, one should not take Dicey's treatment of the 'absence of arbitrary power' *too* literally, since obviously officials (including government ministers) enjoy wide discretionary power in a modern society. Furthermore, there are clear examples of particular individuals who enjoy legal immunities and are, therefore, arguably above the law. Thus, for instance, Members of Parliament enjoy immunity from liability in respect of anything said in the course of parliamentary debates; the Queen and members of the Royal Family enjoy immunity from legal proceedings and from taxation, and so on.

Furthermore, it has been pointed out that, whilst we do not have a completely separate system of courts (like the French Conseil d'Etat) to deal with cases involving governmental authorities, we do have a system of administration tribunals (*see* 14), and special procedures where public law matters are concerned (*see* 17:8).

The fact that there are exceptions is accepted: the question is whether Dicey's analysis remains sufficiently accurate, taken generally and as a whole, to assist in an understanding of the British Constitution, and what makes it different from virtually all others. Provided one bears these exception in mind, the answer is – probably – yes.

Progress test 1

1. Define **(a)** constitutional law; and **(b)** administrative law; indicating the relationship between them. **(1)**

2. What is the 'Constitution' of a State? What types of Constitutions may exist and what will a Constitution typically contain? **(2, 3, 4, 6)**

3. What, in constitutional terms, is meant by 'government'? **(10)**

4. Outline the principal features of the British Constitution, indicating how it differs from some other Constitutions. **(11–14)**

5. What are the main sources of British constitutional law? **(15)**

6. Outline Dicey's analysis of the Rule of Law. Does this still apply today? **(16–19)**

2

The separation of powers: the independence of the judiciary and contempt of court

The separation of powers

1. The separation of powers

As we saw in Chapter 1, the work of government can be broadly divided into three types of functions, namely, legislative, executive and judicial. Since these functions are essentially different in nature, the case for assigning them to different persons or bodies arises, since not only could each body specialise in its own function (giving rise to greater efficiency in government) but the risk of concentrating too much power in any one body's hands could also be avoided.

Such a system, whereby each type of function is assigned to a completely separate body or organ of government, amounts to a separation of powers.

For the reasons stated above, this has proved attractive to many commentators and especially to the French jurist, Montesquieu (1689–1755), who advocated the separation of powers as a means of avoiding dictatorship, in *The Spirit of the Laws* (1748).

Perhaps more significantly, the separation of powers has been incorporated into the constitutions of several countries, and in particular that of the United States of America.

2. Separation in the USA

The constitution of the USA provides for a virtually complete separation of powers. In other words, the three main organs of government (the legislature, executive and judiciary) are as separate from each other as they possibly can be.

There are two aspects to such a separation of powers:

(1) Persons who are members of one organ of government are not, generally speaking, members of another; and

(2) Each organ of government is concerned only with its own functions and does not, generally speaking, exercise any of the functions of another.

Applying these aspects to the American Constitution, the following can be seen:

(a) Section 6 of Article 1 of the Constitution provides that no person holding office under the US may be a member of Congress (the legislature). Thus, the president and members of his administration (executive) are not members of Congress (legislature), nor may judges (judiciary) be members of Congress. The only (possible) exception is the vice-president, who is a non-voting chairman of the US Senate. However, the vice-presidency is not really an office as such: it is only in the event that a sitting president dies or leaves office for any other reason that the vice-president actually acquires any power.

(b) The constitution is quite clear, also, that each organ of government is separate as to its functions. For example, Article 1 states, 'All legislative powers herein granted shall be vested in a Congress,' and Article 2 provides, 'The executive power shall be vested in a President of the USA.'

Where each organ is separate as to its personnel, it will normally follow that functions can be similarly separated. This does not mean that there are no points of contact between the organs of government in the USA, however. Indeed, an elaborate system of checks and balances exists to ensure that there is interaction between all three on the one hand and effective controls on the other. The following are a few examples of these checks and balances:

(*i*) Ministers, ambassadors, consuls and Supreme Court judges are all appointed by the president. However, such appointments must be approved by Congress (normally on the recommendation of a Senate committee) before they can take effect.

(*ii*) The president (executive) has the power to make treaties between the USA and other countries. However, to take effect, such treaties must be ratified by two-thirds of the Senate. (Thus the legislature has a power of veto over executive action.)

(*iii*) Conversely, the president has a limited power of veto over legislation passed by Congress, and can refuse to sign a bill presented to him. However, this is only a limited power. If the president does refuse to sign a bill it goes back to the Congress, and if it is then passed by two-thirds of each House of Congress (the Senate and House of Representatives) it becomes law nevertheless.

3. Separation in the UK

Along with the absence of a written constitution, it is the absence of any real separation of powers which distinguishes the British Constitution from most others and from the American Constitution in particular. Thus, in the UK:

(a) *Members of one organ of government are often also members of one or more others.* For example,

(*i*) Legally and constitutionally, the Queen is head of all three organs of government; as 'the Queen in Parliament' (legislature), whose assent to a bill is necessary for it to become law; as Head of State (executive); and as 'Fount of Justice' (judiciary). In practice, however, the monarch exercises very little constitutional power personally.

(*ii*) The prime minister and other ministers of the Crown (executive) in the UK must be members of one or other of the Houses of Parliament (legislature). This is an important convention of the Constitution (these are explained further in 3).

(*iii*) Amongst the government's ministers (executive) are the law officers of the Crown (the Attorney-General and Solicitor-General for England and Wales, and Lord Advocate of Scotland). These officials have important judicial functions. The Lord Chancellor is head of the judiciary, as well as being a government minister and member of the House of Lords. Furthermore, the most senior judges in the UK, the Lords of Appeal in Ordinary (Law Lords) are also members of the House of Lords, and participate in its legislative functions.

(b) *Some of the functions of one organ are to some extent also exercised by another.* For example,

(*i*) **Legislation.** We tend to think of Parliament as the legislature. However, it should be remembered that Parliament includes government ministers (executive) and Law Lords (judiciary), who are therefore involved in legislation. Secondly, certain legislative powers are frequently delegated to ministers, local authorities and other executive bodies, who are thereby empowered to make laws (*see* 14). Furthermore, although not exactly legislation, judicial law-making occurs in the form of judicial precedents (*see* 1:15).

(*ii*) **Executive and judicial functions.** An interesting case in point here is that of the Privy Council (PC). The functions of the PC are mainly judicial – as far as it is the final court of appeal for Commonwealth nations who have opted to retain the system – and executive – in that it makes Orders in Council, grants Royal Charters to public bodies such as universities etc. In addition, the PC may make laws in the area of delegated legislation. The PC may also make laws in the form of delegated legislation (*see* 14). Even Parliament (the legislature) has certain judicial functions, including the enforcement of its own privileges (*see* 8).

The most that can be said for the UK, therefore, is that three separate organs of government can be identified, and that the three main types of governmental functions (legislative, executive and judicial) can be broadly identified within these organs. The amount of overlap between the three, however, is such that no clear separation of powers can be said to exist in Britain, unlike the USA. Despite this, one famous judge, Lord Diplock, once said, 'It cannot be too strongly emphasised that the British Constitution, though largely unwritten, is firmly based on the separation of powers': *Duport Steels Ltd* v. *Sirs* (1980).

4. Is a clear separation of powers desirable?

As was noted at 1, above, the main advantages of a clear separation of powers are: specialisation (intended to create efficiency) in government, and the avoidance of a concentration of too much power, which could lead to dictatorship. There are, however, certain disadvantages which must be addressed if a constitution is to work.

(a) If the powers were to be absolutely separate with no interaction, government would not be possible, since each of the organs of government could, if it wished, thwart the efforts of the others. Thus, for example, if the executive had no input into legislation, the government's policies could not be implemented. In the USA the system of checks and balances referred to in 2, above, ensures that this does not occur.

(b) In the UK, the fact that there is no clear separation of powers has been turned to advantage, and by means of **conventions**, the close relationship between the organs of government itself creates something like the American system of checks and balances. For example, as noted at **3**, above, British ministers must be Members of Parliament. This facilitates the convention of ministerial responsibility (*see* 3:11) by permitting MPs and peers immediate access to members of the executive, who can be called to account without the need for special inquiries and committees (which occur in the USA, since members of the executive, not being members of Congress, are unavailable for routine questioning). Again, in the UK the government must, by convention, command the support of the House of Commons. (This is not so in the USA, where one could, for example, have a Republican president but a Democrat majority in Congress.) Accordingly, in the UK, there is a good chance that the government's policies, which will have been approved by the electorate in a general election, will be implemented in the form of legislation by Parliament.

In short, it is arguable that a clear separation of powers such as that in the USA is not absolutely necessary to safeguard democracy and prevent dictatorship. Furthermore because of such things as the power of veto in the US there is a danger of stagnation and a lack of co-operation between the organs of government.

The independence of the judiciary

5. An independent judiciary

Whether a country has a clear separation of powers or not, it will (at least in the case of a developed democracy) in all probability have a judiciary which is relatively independent of the other organs of government, and from the executive in particular. In this regard the UK is no exception and, in theory at least, the judiciary is independent of the other organs of government.

The main reasons why an independent judiciary is considered desirable are as follows:

(a) Many cases brought before the courts involve public bodies, or members of the executive. In order that the law should be applied impartially without let or hindrance, it is essential that the judges are free from outside interference and therefore independent. This is becoming increasingly important in the field of judicial review (*see* Part 4). Here, the courts are concerned with examining the lawfulness of governmental action; it is, therefore, clearly essential here that they be independent.

(b) In the UK, constitutional principles, including those relating to individual liberties, are decided in courts of law (since there is no written constitution setting them out). (This is an aspect of the rule of law, according to Dicey.) An independent judiciary is an integral feature of this process. It is different in many continental countries, such as France, which have written constitutions, and special courts (the French Conseil d'Etat) deal with matters involving the administrations.

(c) The fact that the judiciary is relatively independent has certain other advantages, which are exploited in the UK. For instance, it is not unknown for an inquiry to be held after some major civil unrest or other event of a controversial or sensitive nature. In the UK, a member of the judiciary will often be asked to hold such an inquiry, on the grounds that a judge, being independent of the executive, will command respect, and will also bring his or her legal training to bear in gathering and hearing the evidence scrupulously and impartially. For instance, two such inquiries in recent years were those into the Brixton riots of 1981, by Lord Scarman, and the Strangeways Prison riots, chaired by Lord Justice Woolf, in 1991.

6. The basis of judicial independence

The independence of the British judiciary does not rest on one single law or other principle. As with so many other matters concerning our unwritten constitution, judicial independence is based on several factors.

(a) *Tenure.* Judges in the UK are appointed by the Crown on the advice of the prime minister (PM) who takes advice, in turn, from the Lord Chancellor (LC) as head of the judiciary. Only the Lord Chancellor himself may be described as a political appointee, since he is a member of the government (though obviously the role of both the PM and LC in appointing judges is a significant one).

Once appointed, however, judges enjoy a high degree of security of tenure. The Act of Settlement 1700 established the principle that, subject to good behaviour (*quamdiu se bene gesserint*), superior judges could only be removed from office by an address to the Crown by both Houses of Parliament. This principle now applies to all judges of the Supreme Court of Judicature, except for circuit judges and recorders, who may be removed by the Lord Chancellor for misconduct or incompetence: section 11, Supreme

Court Act 1981. Law lords have enjoyed similar security since the enactment of the Appellate Jurisdiction Act 1876 (*see* section 6). Judges must retire, however, at the age of 75, with the exception of those appointed before 1959: Judicial Pensions Act 1959.

The 'address' procedure referred to above is seldom, if ever, invoked though a small number of circuit judges have been removed for misconduct by the Lord Chancellor in recent years. Magistrates can be removed by the Lord Chancellor as he sees fit.

(b) *Immunity.* In general, judicial proceedings are privileged, in the same way as debates and proceedings in Parliament.

(*i*) Accordingly, a judge enjoys immunity from any civil or criminal liability in respect of things said or done by him in the course of proceedings presided over by him. Until recently, this immunity only applied to judges in superior courts: in *Sirross* v. *Moore* (1975), however, it was extended to judges in all courts, provided they honestly believe themselves to be acting within their juridsdiction.

(*ii*) As far as the law of defamation is concerned, this privilege extends not only to judges, but also to the parties, counsel and witnesses. Persons other than judges, however, do not enjoy a total immunity from other kinds of liability; in addition, a person may be found to be in contempt of court in respect of certain kinds of conduct in a court room (*see* **8**, below).

(*iii*) Magistrates enjoy a similar immunity when they are acting in a judicial capacity: *Law* v. *Llewellyn* (1906). No immunity is enjoyed by magistrates in their administrative capacity (e.g. licensing), however: *Attwood* v. *Chapman* (1914).

(*iv*) Barristers enjoy immunity from liability in respect of their presentation of a case in court, and matters 'intimately concerned with the conduct of a case in court': *Saif Ali* v. *Sydney Mitchell & Co.* (1978). They cannot, therefore, be sued in negligence by a client who claims his conviction was the result of poor presentation of his case by his counsel: *Rondel* v. *Worsley* (1969).

(c) *Freedom from criticism.* Judges do not enjoy any general immunity from criticism: just like any other public figures, their activities can be criticised. However, certain rules govern the circumstances and extent of such criticism.

(*i*) Comment which goes beyond the bounds of reasonable criticism, so as to amount to a scurrilous or abusive attack on a judge or his decision, may amount to contempt of court (*see* **8**, below).

(*ii*) Rules of both Houses of Parliament forbid discussion of certain matters relating to judges and to judicial decisions. Firstly, it is established that the conduct of a judge should not be the subject of a debate in Parliament, except on a substantive motion such as one for the judge's removal. Secondly, matters awaiting or under adjudication may not be debated in Parliament. This is known as the *sub judice* rule and whilst (like much of the law of contempt of court) it is designed to avoid prejudice to judicial proceedings, it does limit discussion of judges' conduct and comments.

7. Judicial impartiality

In return for the considerable immunities they enjoy, judges are required to be impartial. This does not simply mean not taking sides in any case before them (which might be grounds for review or appeal – *see* 16). It also means that judges must be politically impartial, and thus independent of the government of the day. Accordingly, judges may not sit in the House of Commons: section 1, House of Commons Disqualification Act 1975. (At common law all persons holding office under the Crown, which included judges, were in any case disqualified.) Additionally, judges are expected to refrain from party-political activities and statements, at least in their judicial capacities. There is nothing to prevent a judge from belonging to a political party, nor from voting as he pleases in a general or by-election, except in the case of Lords of Appeal in Ordinary who, being life peers, are incapacitated from voting: section 1, Representation of the People Act 1983. (As mentioned earlier, the constitutional impartiality of judges is exploited for some matters other than strictly judicial ones.)

Contempt of court

8. Contempt

The law of contempt is one of the means whereby the administration of justice is protected from undue interference. (As well as contempt, there are the related offences of perjury and perverting the course of justice.) Proceedings for contempt of court are unusual in that they are dealt with summarily, i.e. by a judge, sitting without a jury.

There are two broad categories of contempt: civil and criminal. Of these, criminal contempt is the largest category, and is itself divided into various sub-categories (*see* 10, below).

9. Civil contempt

This may be defined as the failure to comply with an order duly made by a superior court. A typical example would be where a defendant fails to comply with the terms of an injunction made against him.

In *Times Newspapers Ltd and another* v. *Attorney-General* (1991) the House of lords held that, where an injunction had been granted against one newspaper prohibiting it from publishing certain material, it was contempt for another newspaper knowingly to publish the same material. (In fact, such conduct was held to amount to criminal contempt insofar as it also impeded the administration of justice in the original case in which the injunction was granted: *see* 10, below.)

In *Home Office* v. *Harman* (1982) it was held that a solicitor was guilty of civil contempt when she allowed a journalist access to documents which had been disclosed to her during a trial. Despite the fact that the documents had been read out in open court, her conduct was a contempt, since it was in breach of her undertaking as a solicitor and officer of the court that she would use the documents only for the purpose of the trial itself.

10. Criminal contempt

At common law there were four categories of criminal contempt (as well as a fifth, residual category of offences which included perjury and perverting the course of justice). These were:

(1) Scandalising the court;
(2) Contempt in the face of the court;
(3) Publications prejudicial to fair civil proceedings; and
(4) Publications prejudicial to a fair criminal trial.

Of these (3) and (4) are now largely covered by the Contempt of Court Act 1981 and are, therefore, dealt with separately (*see* 10–14 below).

(a) *Scandalising the court.* An abusive or scurrilous attack upon a judge, or upon judicial proceedings or decisions, amounts to scandalising the court, and can be dealt with summarily by the judge being attacked.

An allegation that a judge is biased may amount to scandalising the court: *McLeod* v. *St Aubyn* (1899); *R.* v. *New Statesman Editor*

(1928). However, criticism of a judicial decision is not, in itself, contempt, provided it is reasonable. As Lord Russell CJ put it in *R. v. Grey* (1900), 'judges and courts are alike open to criticism, and if reasonable argument is offered . . . no court could or would treat that as a contempt.'

(b) *Contempt in the face of the court.* This covers a multitude of sins, ranging from a witness's refusal to answer questions, on the one hand, to a demonstration calculated to disrupt judicial proceedings (*Morris* v. *Crown Office* (1970), on the other. It includes any conduct which interferes with judicial proceedings. It has been held that 'in the face of the court' need not be taken literally. In *Balogh* v. *St Alban's Crown Court* (1975), it was held that the senior judge in a court complex could deal with this kind of contempt, even though the actual court where the alleged contempt had occurred was presided over by another judge.

The Contempt of Court Act 1981

11. The Contempt of Court Act 1981

This Act (CCA) was passed in response to growing criticism of the law on contempt of court, and particularly after the European Court of Human Rights decision in *Sunday Times* v. *UK* (1979), where English contempt laws were found to contravene provisions of the European Convention on Human Rights dealing with freedom of speech. The Act deals principally with publications prejudicial to fair civil and criminal proceedings (where, at common law, liability was strict). In addition, it deals with certain ancillary (but important) matters, such as the confidentiality of the jury room.

The following paragraphs summarize the main provisions of the CCA, drawing on pre-Act law for purposes of comparison, and discussing the main cases to have been decided since the Act by way of illustration.

12. The strict liability rule

The CCA retains the strict liability rule which, prior to 1981, existed at common law. It modified it, however, in the following ways:

(a) The strict liability rule applies only to publications: section 2(1).

(b) It applies only to a publication which creates a substantial risk that the course of justice in particular legal proceedings will be seriously impeded or prejudiced: Section 2(2).

(c) If applies only to proceedings which are active. This is defined in Schedule 1. Criminal proceedings are 'active' from the time of arrest, issue of warrant, summons, notice of indictment or charge, whichever occurs first. They cease to be active when acquittal, sentence or other verdict is reached, or when proceedings are discontinued, e.g. by means of a *nulle prosequi*, entered by the Attorney-General. Civil proceedings are active from the time a date, or other arrangements, for a hearing are made: they remain active until proceedings are compromised or discontinued, or until judgment, whichever occurs first. Controversially, (because juries are not involved) appellate proceedings are active for the purpose of the strict liability rule.

(d) An important provision is section 5. This states:

> A publication made as or as part of a discussion, in good faith, of public affairs or other matters of general public interest is not to be treated as a contempt of court under the strict liability rule if the risk of impediment or prejudice to particular legal proceedings is merely incidental to the discussion.

The effects of this section are discussed at 14, below.

13. Cases on the strict liability rule

The central question is, what is meant by 'substantial risk that the course of justice . . . will be seriously impeded or prejudiced'?

(a) *Criminal proceedings.* Prior to the Act, it was clear that a publication which pre-judged the particular issues in a criminal trial, and which might therefore have influenced jurors, incurred liability under the strict liability rule: *R. v. Bolam, ex p. Haigh* (1949). This remains true since the CCA was passed.

Where a newspaper article contains comments critical of a defendant's character or lifestyle, however, the position is unclear. A recent decision seems to suggest that some connection between the comments made and the issues involved in the proceedings in question must exist. In *Attorney-General v. Times Newspapers and others* (1983), five national newspapers were accused of contempt over articles published by them, concerning a man, F, who had allegedly illegally entered Buckingham Palace and, whilst inside, helped himself to a glass of wine. In connection with this, and other incidents, he faced charges of burglary, taking a car without consent, and assault. Newspaper A alleged that F was a drug addict and a liar. This was not a contempt, since these allegations were too remote from the issues under trial to create a 'substantial' risk to those proceedings. Newspaper B, on the other hand, alleged that F was having an affair with a Palace guard, and described F in unflattering terms. Since this established a link between F and the Palace, it was found to create a 'substantial' risk, as did an article in newspaper C, which alleged that F had admitted stealing the wine (and was therefore guilty of the burglary charge). This case also shows that it is possible for a publication to be in contempt if it creates a substantial risk of prejudice to the prosecution's case, though in most cases it is the defendant who is prejudiced.

(b) *Civil proceedings.* Such proceedings do not normally involve juries and, therefore, the sorts of things which create substantial risks of impediment or prejudice to the administration of justice in civil proceedings will usually differ from those which do so in relation to criminal trials.

A good example of this category is *Attorney-General* v. *Times Newspapers Ltd* (1974). Here, a newspaper published articles which severely criticised the conduct of the distributor of a drug, against whom civil actions had been begun, and effectively advised litigants and potential litigants not to accept the sum of money offered by the company by way of settlement for all claims. This was a contempt since it tried to influence the outcome of the proceedings in question by putting pressure on the parties to act in a particular way in relation to the proceedings.

In *Attorney-General* v. *Hislop* (1991), an article which was clearly designed to prevent a person from proceedings with her civil action was held to be a contempt. Since the action was one for defamation, unusually (in civil actions) it involved a jury: accordingly the publication also gave rise to the risk that jurors might be influenced, and therefore created a 'substantial risk' on that score, too.

14. The effects of section 5

The substance of this section has already been given (*see* 11, above).

The leading case on section 5 is *Attorney-General* v. *English* (1982). Whilst a doctor, A, was being tried for the murder of a child by neglect, an article appeared in a national newspaper, purportedly in support of a candidate for a parliamentary election. This candidate was standing as a 'pro-life' (i.e. anti-abortion) candidate. The A-G claimed that this created a substantial risk of prejudice in Dr A's trial, contrary to section 2(2), CCA. The House of Lords held that, by virtue of section 5, the publication was not a contempt. Furthermore, section 5 was not like a normal defence, which had to be established by the defendant on a balance of probabilities. Rather, where the publication was, *prima facie*, concerned with a discussion on public affairs (and no clear connection with the legal proceedings in question was made in the publication) then the onus was on the prosecution to show that the risk of prejudice to those proceedings – in this case, Dr A's trial – was more than merely incidental to the discussion. This the A-G had failed to do.

This decision was followed in *Attorney-General* v. *Times Newspapers Ltd* (1983) (see **13**, above) where newspaper D was not guilty of contempt when it published an aritcle dealing with security at the Palace generally.

15. Defences to the strict liability rule

The CCA contains certain standard defences, the burden of proof being on the defendant to establish them. These are:

(a) Section 3(1) provides that a person is not guilty under the strict liability rule if, having taken all reasonable care, he does not know and has no reason to suspect that the relevant proceedings are active;

(b) Section 3(2) provides that a person is not guilty under the rule if, having taken all reasonable care, he does not know and has no reason to suspect that the publication made by him contains offensive matter; and

(c) Section 4(1) provides that a person is not liable under the rule in respect of a fair and accurate report of legal proceedings, held in public, published contemporaneously and in good faith.

However, section 4(2) empowers the court to order the postponement of any such report where it appears to be necessary for avoiding a substantial risk of prejudice to the administration of justice in those proceedings, or in any other proceedings which are pending or imminent, for such period as the court thinks necessary for that purpose.

(d) It should be noted that section 6 of the CCA preserves common law liability for publications other than under the strict liability rule. Thus, a publication which amounts to a deliberate interference with the course of justice remains a common law contempt, as in *Raymond* v. *Honey* (1983) where a prison governor refused to forward a prisoner's letter relating to possible future proceedings to the prisoner's solicitor. However, any defences to the strict liability rule which existed at common law are also preserved.

(e) It should also be noted that proceedings under the strict liability rule can only be brought by or with the consent of the AG (other than Scottish proceedings) or on the motion of a court having jurisdiction: section 7, CCA.

Other matters

16. Other matters

As well as the strict liability rule, the CCA deals with the following matters:

(a) *Jury-room deliberations.* Section 8 provides that it is a contempt of court to obtain, disclose or solicit any particulars of statements made, opinions expressed, arguments advanced, or votes cast by members of a jury in the course of their deliberations in any legal proceedings.

(b) *Tape-recordings.* Section 9 provides that the use of such devices in court, or the publication of any report made with such a device, is contempt except when done by leave of the court.

(c) *Disclosure of sources.* Section 10 provides:

> No court may require a person to disclose, nor is any person guilty of contempt of court for refusing to disclose the source of information contained in a publication for which he is responsible, unless it is established to the satisfaction of the court that disclosure is necessary in the interests of justice, or national security, or for the prevention of disorder or crime.

In *Secretary of State for Defence* v. *Guardian Newspapers Ltd* (1984), a clerk at the Ministry of Defence leaked confidential information to a newspaper relating to the siting of missiles in Britain. Initially, the newspaper refused to identify their source. The House of Lords held, however, that they were obliged to do so, notwithstanding section 10, since the clerk's conduct was clearly criminal and had security implications (she was later prosecuted, and eventually imprisoned, for an offence under the Official Secrets Act). Here, disclosure was necessary in the interests of national security and the prevention of crime.

(d) *Withholding of names.* Section 11 provides that a court may require that a name or other matter may be withheld from the public, and may give such directions prohibiting publication of that name or other matter as appear necessary. (Failure to obey such directions is, of course, contempt: *Attorney-General* v. *Leveller Magazine Ltd* (1979).)

(e) *Penalties for contempt.* At common law, no fixed penalties for contempt were laid down. The CCA has rectified that, and provides that where a court has power to commit a person to prison for contempt, then the committal shall be for a fixed term which shall not exceed two years in the case of a superior court, and one month in the case of an inferior court: section 14.

17. Contempt by a government minister

Until very recently it was thought that the Crown enjoyed immunity from proceedings for contempt of court. In *M* v. *Home Office and others* (1991), it was established that ministers and civil servants alike were amenable to the court's jurisdiction in contempt, even when acting in their official (as opposed to private) capacity, provided that the necessary intention was established. In this case, the Home Secretary ignored a court order to the effect that an immigrant from Zaire who had come to the UK seeking political asylum should not be returned to Zaire. In so doing, the Court of Appeal held, he was guilty of contempt.

Progress test 2

1. What is meant by the 'separation of powers'? What advantages and disadvantages might result from the employment of a full separation of powers? **(1–4)**

2. To what extent can the judiciary in the UK be regarded as 'independent'? What factors give rise to this independence? **(5–6)**

3. Outline the main varieties of contempt of court, both civil and criminal. **(8–10)**

4. What were the main effects of the Contempt of Court Act 1981, on the 'strict liability rate'? **(11–15)**

5. Other than those provisions affecting the strict liability rule, what are the main provisions of the Contempt of Court Act 1981, and to what extent do these change the old common law rules? **(16)**

3
Conventions of the Constitution

General

1. Convention

The term convention, as applied to the British Constitution, was coined by Dicey in *An Introduction to the Study of the Law of the Constitution* (1885). Dicey pointed out that there were two kinds of rules, both important, which could be discerned in relation to the British Constitution:

(a) *The laws of the constitution.* These, according to Dicey, are those rules which are enforceable in a court of law.

(b) *Conventions.* These are rules which are not enforceable in a court of law. As the name suggests, conventions are based on consent or acquiescence, rather than enforcement, just like everyday conventions of behaviour. What makes conventions of the constitution significant is the role they play in shaping the conduct of those who are actually involved in government and in the working of the constitution.

2. The nature of conventions

As we saw in 1, above, conventions (whether relating to the constitution or not) are based on acquiescence or consent, rather than on some actual system of enforcement. However, the conventions of the constitution are of tremendous importance in the UK, and are more than mere customs or practices.

(a) Conventions are regarded as actually binding upon those to whom they apply: in that sense they are somewhat closer to laws than to customs. Furthermore, conventions usually have some distinct constitutional role to play, unlike most customs, which are often of historical or ceremonial value only (e.g. the ceremony surrounding the State Opening of Parliament, or the ritual whereby the Chancellor of the Exchequer supposedly carries his budget speech to the House of Commons in a rather battered red briefcase!)

(b) From (a), above, it follows that the observance of most conventions is a serious matter, and if a convention is not observed, the consequence will frequently be quite significant, often leading to a breach of the law. (This is discussed further at, **6**, below.)

3. Conventions in the UK

It is probably fair to say that conventions have a far greater importance in the British Constitution than in virtually any other. There are several reasons for this, partly historical. The single most important reason is the absence in the UK of a written constitution and separation of powers. If we take a country having both of these, such as the USA, we will find that conventions play a much smaller role, since the constitution itself provides the necessary rules and checks and balances which are provided for by conventions in the UK. This does not mean, however, that conventions are completely unknown in the USA. For example, it was considered to be a convention that a person could only serve for two successive terms as president of the USA. However, in 1940 Franklin Roosevelt was elected for a third term (albeit in the somewhat unusual circumstances resulting from war), and in 1945 for a fourth term. (In consequence of this Congress promoted the 22nd Amendment to the American Constitution, with the result that it is now constitutionally impossible for a President to serve for more than two terms). Again, the detailed procedures relating to the election of the president are partly dealt with by conventions, as is the American Cabinet system.

4. The functions of conventions

According to Hood Phillips in his well-known book *Constitutional and Administrative Law*, conventions are a 'means of bringing about constitutional development without formal changes in the law'. This statement must be understood in an historical context since many conventions are now just as well established (and in some cases more so) than laws. Indeed, since laws can be easily be changed by a simple Act of Parliament it may not be going too far to suggest that conventions deal with that part of the constitution which is too important to be enacted in laws. This is not so strange as it sounds: because conventions are distinct from laws, it means that the area with which they are concerned does not, strictly speaking, fall within the jurisdiction of the courts to interpret and apply. Underlying this, then, is the key to the real purpose of conventions, which is twofold:

(1) To preserve the balance of power between the persons who wield authority in the British Constitution, and between the three main organs of government in particular.

(2) To ensure accountability in government, either directly or indirectly.

5. The establishment of conventions

In general, most conventions come to be established by usage. This does not mean, however, that to become a convention, a practice must have existed for a very long time: conventions are not like customs (in the sense of 'customary' law) in that respect. Indeed, most conventions began after the 1688 Revolution, and many did not come into existence until the late nineteenth or early twentieth century. Some are still emerging.

On the other hand, conventions do not necessarily arise on the basis of a single precedent, unlike rules of common law. There may be some element of uncertainty surrounding a practice before it becomes sufficiently well established to be considered to be a convention. According to the well-known writer Sir Ivor Jennings, there are two requirements for the establishment of a convention:

(1) The fact that a rule is generally accepted as being binding (or obligatory) by those to whom it applies; and

(2) Some constitutional purpose which can be discerned from the context in which the rule arises. An example of how this occurs is the convention that the prime minister (PM) must be a member of the House of Commons. This is a relatively recent convention, which probably did not become fully established until 1963. Indeed, it was only during the nineteenth century that the convention that there should be a PM at all became established! At that time, it was quite possible for the PM to be a member of the Lords. In 1923, however, King George V was advised not to appoint Lord Curzon as PM, partly because he was a peer. The principle was not fully tested until 1963, however, when, in order to become PM, Lord Home felt obliged to take advantage of the newly enacted Peerage Act and renounce his peerage, thus making him eligible to stand for the Commons.

In this case, we can see both of Jennings's requirements in that, by 1963, all of those concerned (including the PM himself) felt that the principle that the PM should not be a peer had become obligatory and, second, we can see how the mood of the country, and the shift in importance away from the Lords and in favour of the democratically elected Commons, had become established.

6. Why are conventions observed?

It has already been pointed out that one factor which differentiates conventions from other non-legal rules, such as customs, is the fact that conventions give rise to certain obligations, and are, therefore, binding on those to whom they apply. However, this sense of obligation is not without foundation: a study of constitutional history shows that there are two very specific reasons why, in practice, conventions tend to be observed:

(a) *Breach of the law*. One view, espoused by Dicey, is that if a convention (or at least an important convention) is violated, then, sooner or later, this will in turn lead to a breach in the law. For example, it is only by convention that Parliament must meet at least once in each year (in practice, of course, it sits for much of the year). There is a law that a Parliament cannot last for longer than five years (section 7, Parliament Act, 1911), but no legal requirement as to the minimum. However, if Parliament did not meet on at least one day in each year, it could not pass the annual Finance Act, giving effect to the government's budget proposals, or pass the annual resolutions necessary to implement the Armed Forces Act, with the result that the government could not lawfully raise money by taxation or maintain the armed forces.

(b) *Change in the law*. Another view is that, if an important convention is not observed, Parliament will change the law to prevent a recurrence of this breach. Thus, in 1909, when the House of Lords disobeyed the convention that the Lords should yield to the wishes of the House of Commons (since that is the elected House), the Commons promoted the Parliament bill (under threat of swamping the Lords with new peers, sympathetic to the new legislation). This was passed in 1911 and became the Parliament Act, the effects of which were to remove the Lords' power to prevent bills passed by the Commons from becoming law, and substituting for it a delaying power only.

7. Why are conventions not enacted as laws?

This is an understandable question. If conventions are so important – indeed, fundamental in the British constitution – why are they not simply enacted into laws, or better still codified into a comprehensive system of legal rules?

In fact, a number of advantages result from the system of conventions, which would be lost if these were transformed into laws. These include the following:

(a) *Flexibility.* The British Constitution is sometimes described as flexible as opposed to rigid. Part of this flexibility lies in the system of conventions, whereby (as Hood Phillips points out) constitutional development and changes can occur without the need for formal changes in the law. This can be seen at its most obvious by a comparison with the American Constitution, where any change in the Constitution can be achieved only through the procedures laid down in Article 5 of the Constitution itself.

(b) *Balance of power.* As noted at 4, above, the fact that certain rules are conventions rather than laws means that the courts have little authority as to their application and meaning. This may be felt to be desirable in preventing the judiciary (which is not, in the UK, responsible to the electorate) from acquiring too much power.

(c) *Democracy* It has already been noted that, in the UK, conventions are an important aspect of the democratic process, in that they help to ensure that government is accountable, albeit indirectly, to the populace. In the absence of a separation of powers, it is at least arguable that they are the most effective means of achieving this.

To achieve the same ends by legal means would entail, in effect, a complete re-working of the British Constitution. For example, it is a convention that the leader of the political party which wins a general election should form the government (i.e. act as PM). However, the existence of political parties is not itself a legal requirement: accordingly, the convention could not be made a law without the introduction of many further changes, not all of which would be felt desirable.

Conventions and the courts

8. Conventions and Laws

As noted above, Dicey drew a clear distinction between conventions and laws: specifically, he pointed out that laws are enforceable in the courts, whereas conventions are not. This has led to the further distinction, whereby (according to some writers) laws are based on some enforcement machinery or sanctions, whereas conventions are based on consent and acquiescence. On the other hand, some writers, including Sir Ivor Jennings, have suggested that this is not entirely convincing, for the following reasons:

(a) Certain laws (e.g. parliamentary privilege: see 6) are enforced not in the courts, but in some other forum (in the case of parliamentary privileges, by Parliament itself).

(b) Laws, like conventions, depend on consent for their efficiency. If a sufficient number of people ceased to acquiesce in a law, and simply failed to observe it, it would in all probability not be enforced, and may well eventually lapse or have to be changed (the Sunday observance laws are an example of this).

(c) Conventions, though not actually enforced in courts of law, are at least recognised, both by the courts and in some statutes. (This is discussed below.)

9. Recognition of conventions

As mentioned in 8, above, some conventions, if not enforced, are at least recognised in statutes and even by the courts.

(a) *Statutes.* Whilst conventional rules have not been included in legislation, the existence of some conventions has been presumed in subsequent Acts, and the conventions concerned thus recognised and acknowledged as part of the constitution. For example, the Parliament Act 1911, limiting the Lords' power to prevent money bills (financial measures) which have been passed by the Commons from becoming law, presumed that such measures would be introduced by the government in the Commons, a purely conventional rule.

Similarly, legislation dealing with the Chequers estate (one of the residences of the PM) and with ministerial salaries, presumes the existence of the PM and other ministers; again, these are conventional in nature.

(b) *The courts.* In a large number of cases, the courts have recognised the existence of conventions, such that their decisions on the law have been occasionally influenced thereby. The following cases, provide examples of this:

(*i*) *Liversidge* v. *Anderson* (1942). A man was interned (imprisoned without trial) during World War II, on the orders of the Home Secretary, who was empowered by regulations made under the Defence of the Realm Act 1939 to intern persons whom he 'had reasonable grounds for believing to be of hostile origin or association'. The man challenged this order, on the grounds that the Home Secretary had failed to inform him of the grounds for his belief. The majority of the House of Lords held (Lord Atkin dissenting) that the regulations did not specifically require that the Home Secretary divulge his reasons, only that he had them. It was up to Parliament to require him to explain his decision, if they wished, in accordance with the convention of ministerial responsibility.

(*ii*) *Carltona Ltd* v. *Commissioners of Works* (1943). A civil servant issued an order requisitioning the plaintiff's factory. The Act of Parliament under which the order was purportedly issued empowered the Commissioner (a government minister) to issue such orders. The plaintiff challenged the order on the grounds that the Commissioner had not personally issued it. The Court of Appeal held that it was perfectly lawful for a civil servant to act on behalf of a minister for, as Lord Greene MR put it: 'Constitutionally, the decision of such an official is, of course, the decision of the Minister. The Minister is responsible. It is he who must answer before Parliament for anything that his officials have done under his authority.' Thus, the court recognised the convention of ministerial responsibility.

(*iii*) In *Attorney-General* v. *Jonathan Cape Ltd* (1976) the court arguably went further, coming very close to actually enforcing a convention, albeit indirectly. The publishers, Jonathan Cape, had agreed to allow the memoirs (the notorious *Crossman Diaries*) of a former Cabinet minister to be published in serialised form. Because these memoirs included details of Cabinet meetings which the former minister (Mr Crossman) had attended, the Attorney-General sought an injunction restraining the defendants from allowing publication. The court held that the convention of collective cabinet responsibility (*see* 7 and 12) placed upon ministers a duty of confidentiality: to publish details of Cabinet meetings in breach of this duty might amount to the tort of breach of confidence, and so an injunction could, in such a case, be ordered. This would not be appropriate in every case, so that where, as here, the Cabinet meetings in question had occurred more than 10 years earlier, there was no risk of prejudicing the responsibility of the Cabinet, and no reason, therefore, why publication should be prevented. Nevertheless, this case shows that, in effect, a legal duty of confidence can arise from the convention of confidentiality.

Classification of conventions

10. Classification

In practice, most conventions involve a number of persons or bodies. Most of these conventions are discussed in the chapters of this book where the constitutional roles and functions of these bodies are covered in detail. Accordingly, the classification which follows in the next paragraph does not go into details as to the workings of the conventions, but merely lists the most important ones.

11. The main conventions classified

(a) *Conventions governing the exercise of the royal prerogative.* These include the following:

(*i*) The sovereign should act on the advice of her ministers, given by the prime minister.

(*ii*) The sovereign should invite the leader of the political party which enjoys the support of the House of Commons to form a government. (i.e. act as prime minister).

(*iii*) The sovereign should appoint as ministers those persons the PM nominates.

(*iv*) The sovereign should always give her assent to any bills presented to her.

(*v*) The sovereign should normally grant a dissolution of Parliament at the request of the PM.

(b) *Conventions governing the Cabinet system and ministerial responsibility.*

(*i*) The Cabinet must be unanimous in its advice to the sovereign, and should present a united front to Parliament. A Cabinet member who is unable to agree with his Cabinet colleagues and maintain such a united front should resign, rather than publicly disagree with the collective decision of the Cabinet.

(*ii*) The Government must command the support of a majority of the House of Commons: if they cease to do so, the PM should request a dissolution of Parliament so that a general election can be called and a new government formed.

(*iii*) A minister must accept responsibility for the authorised conduct of officials in his department of ministry (and, of course, for his own decisions). He is accountable to Parliament for such conduct, and should protect the officials concerned (who should not even be personally mentioned). In a serious case, he should offer his resignation (*see* **9(b)(ii)**, above).

(c) *Conventions governing the Houses of Parliament.*

(*i*) The Lords should always yield to the will of the Commons as the democratically elected House.

(*ii*) Financial measures must be introduced in the Commons by a government minister (this is recognised in the Parliament Act 1911: see **9** above).

(*iii*) It is the task of the Speaker of the House of Commons to ensure that minorities are not swamped by the major parties, and are therefore given time to put their views.

(*iv*) MP's should have access to the Crown (i.e. should be permitted to question ministers, or put views to them) through the Speaker.

(*v*) All political parties are represented (normally in proportion to their representation in the House of Commons as a whole) in parliamentary committees.

(*vi*) Parliament must meet at least once a year (*see* **6**, above).

(d) *Conventions governing the judicial process.* There are, arguably, a small number of conventions here.

(*i*) Judicial proceedings (undergoing trial) should not be debated in Parliament. (In fact this is a rule of the House in any case.)

(*ii*) A judge's professional conduct should not be criticised in Parliament except on a substantive motion (such as one for his dismissal).

(*iii*) Peers who are not actually Law Lords should not participate in judicial decisions of the House of Lords. (Curiously, whilst the existence of Lords of Appeal (Law Lords) is a matter of law (Appellate Jurisdiction Act 1876) the above rule is not.)

(e) *Conventions governing the relationship between the UK and Commonwealth nations.*

(*i*) The UK Parliament should not legislate for an independent commonwealth nation, even where that country was once a colony, except where that nation requests and consents to such legislation. (This was enacted with respect to some countries in section 4 of the Statute of Westminster: *see* 4).

(*ii*) The sovereign acts on the advice of the government of an independent Commonwealth nation. Such advice is tendered to the Governor-General of that nation, as the Queen's representative, by the prime minister or premier of the nation concerned. The choice of Governor-General is itself a matter on which the Queen takes the advice of that country's government.

12. Interaction between conventions

From 11, above, it can be seen that conventions are of different varieties, and serve very different functions. It is hardly surprising, then, that some appear to be rather more important than others. Thus, if the Speaker of the House of Commons permits a minority party to be stifled, this may be undemocratic, but it would not lead to a breakdown in government, or confrontation with the law, unlike, say, breach of the convention that Parliament meets once a year.

It is probably fair to say that the function of some conventions, and the reason they came into existence in the first place, is to ensure observance of some other, more important convention. For example, we have already discussed the relatively recent convention that the PM should be a member of the House of Commons, and not a peer. This convention did not exist during the nineteenth century and the first signs of it having applied in practice were not until 1923 (*see* 5, above). The point is that, by 1923, it was becoming clear that a member of the House of Lords might experience difficulty in controlling the Commons. In other words, it was in order to ensure that the government of the day could command the support of the Commons – itself an established convention – that the convention that the PM should be a member of the Commons came into existence.

Progress test 3

1. What is a 'convention' of the constitution? What are the main functions of conventions in the British Constitution? (1-4)

2. Why are conventions observed, and why have they not all been enacted into laws? (5-7)

3. To what extent do the courts acknowledge the existence of conventions, and to what extent do they act on them? (Give examples.) (8-9)

4. Outline the main conventions of the Constitution by reference to the persons or bodies to whom they apply. (10-11)

4

The sovereignty of Parliament

Sovereignty generally

1. Parliamentary sovereignty

This refers to Parliament's capacity to make whatever laws it wishes, by means of legislation. It is also sometimes referred to as Parliament's 'legislative supremacy', thus emphasising the fact that legislation is the highest (supreme) source of law – including constitutional law – in the UK.

2. The significance of parliamentary sovereignty

Where a country has a written constitution (such as the United States of America), that constitution is generally also supreme or fundamental. In other words the constitution is the legal source of governmental power, including the power to legislate. Thus, Article 1 of the American Constitution provides, 'All legislative power herein granted shall be vested in a Congress of the US' (the legislature).

The UK, of course, has no written constitution. Accordingly, as Hood Phillips puts it in his book *Constitutional and Administrative Law*, the sovereignty of Parliament is 'the one fundamental law of the British Constitution'. In other words, whilst any other law (or legal principle) can be amended or dispensed with, the sovereignty of Parliament is indispensable, since without it, there would be no legal basis for the Constitution itself.

The classical theory of sovereignty

3. Dicey's analysis

The classic analysis of parliamentary sovereignty is that of A.V. Dicey, first published in 1885. He said that sovereignty consisted of two concepts, one positive and one negative:

(1) Any Act of Parliament which makes new law or which repeals or

amends existing law will be obeyed by the courts. (The positive concept.)

(2) There is no person or body known to the British Constitution which can make rules which will override or derogate from an Act of Parliament. (The negative concept.)

4. Proof of Dicey's analysis

Dicey's analysis (3 above) can be tested by an examination of judicial decisions and statements.

(a) *The positive concept.* There are a number of judicial statements which indicate that the courts accept Acts of Parliament as the law, and do not regard the courts as competent to challenge an Act of Parliament. One of the best known is that of Lord Campbell, in *Edinburgh and Dalkeith Railway Co.* v. *Wauchope* (1842):

> . . . all that a court can look to is the Parliamentary Rolls: they see that an Act has passed both Houses of Parliament and that it has received the Royal Assent, and no court of justice can inquire into the manner in which it was introduced into Parliament, what was done previously to its being introduced, or what passed in Parliament during the various stages of its progress through both Houses of Parliament.

In other words, once an Act has been passed, the courts must apply it, and cannot inquire into how it became law. This principle was followed in *British Railways Board* v. *Pickin* (1974) where the House of Lords held that a claim that the House of Commons had been misled during the passing of an Act could not be entertained by the court and that, it having been passed, it was the duty of the court to give effect to the Act. The principle was again followed in *Martin* v. *O'Sullivan* (1982): 'if the statute has been passed, it is the business of the courts to see that it is complied with, and not to go behind it'.

[Note: Since 1849, legislation has ceased to be recorded on parliamentary rolls, as referred to above. The court will now have regard to authenticated copies of Acts, which are kept in the House of Lords and the Public Record Office in London.]

(b) *The negative concept.* To establish whether Dicey was correct in asserting that no rules can override an Act of Parliament, one must examine judicial decisions where such rules have conflicted with Acts of Parliament. If Dicey was right, then Acts should always prevail.

5.   Cases where Acts have conflicted with other rules

(a) *Common law.* It is well established that an Act prevails over a rule of Common law, even one allegedly protecting a fundamental right. Thus, in *R* v. *Jordan* (1963) it was held that, even if the defendant was correct in asserting that at common law he had the right to freedom of speech, that right was in any case curtailed by the Race Relations Act 1967.

It has even been held that an Act of Parliament can change the common law with retrospective effect. Thus, the War Damage Act 1965, retrospectively changed the rule laid down in the *Burmah Oil* case (1965) (*see* 13:18). This would be impossible in the USA, since Article 1, section 9, provides that ' . . . no ex post facto law shall be passed'.

(b) *International law.* It was held in *Cheney* v. *Conn* (1968) that the UK's international treaty obligations could not be invoked so as to depart from an Act of Parliament. The Act must prevail. The general rule was stated by Lord Denning MR: 'We [the courts] take no notice of treaties until they are embodied in law enacted by Parliament, and then only to the extent that Parliament tells us': *Blackburn* v. *Attorney-General* (1972).

(c) *Executive action.* This can arise either under the royal prerogative (see 13) or under statutory authority (often in the form of delegated legislation: *see* 14).

In *Attorney-General* v. *De Keysers Royal Hotel Ltd* (1920), it was held that where a statute conflicted with or limited a prerogative power (in this instance by requiring the Crown to pay compensation to the owners of a hotel it had requisitioned in time of war) the statute must be applied, and should prevail over the prerogative.

In *Attorney-General* v. *Wiltshire United Dairies Ltd* (1920) it was held that the executive could not use the powers delegated to it by the Defence of the Realm (Consolidation) Act 1914 for the purpose of imposing a tax, since that was not authorised by the Act itself, and was contrary to the general principle (found in the Bill of Rights 1689) that the Crown may not impose taxation without Parliament's authority. A similar ruling was applied in *Congreve* v. *Home Office* (1976).

(d) *Parliamentary resolutions and other rules.* The best known case is *Bowler* v. *Bank of England* (1913). In April 1912 the House of Commons resolved to impose income tax on stock dividends. An Act of Parliament giving effect to this resolution was passed in August. The court held that the Bank were not entitled to deduct income tax between April and August, since a resolution of the

House did not make new law. Only the Act did that.

In fact, there are a large number of rules, including parliamentary privileges, (*see* 8) which are enforced in Parliament, but not in the courts. These can be readily amended or abolished by an Act of Parliament. As we have seen (**4**, above) the procedures observed within Parliament are no concern of the courts.

6. Where two Acts conflict

One possibility, not specifically referred to by Dicey, was that one Act should conflict with an earlier Act. It was held in *Ellen Street Estates Ltd* v. *Minister of Health* (1934) that, where one Act conflicted with another Act, then the one which was most recently passed prevailed over the earlier one. Furthermore, the earlier Act should be treated as having been impliedly repealed, to the extent that it was inconsistent with the later Act. This doctrine of implied repeal has come to be regarded as an important adjunct to parliamentary sovereignty.

7. Criticism of Dicey

The first major critic of Dicey was Sir Ivor Jennings: his views attracted much support amongst academics. The central 'plank' in this criticism was that Dicey's views were based on concepts dating back to a time when the sovereign (the king) held absolute authority. Even Parliament, they argued, did not have absolute authority, since in practice, there were limits on Parliament's powers. Accordingly, it was suggested that the term 'legislative supremacy' was a better one than 'sovereignty', since it suggested that Parliament was not necessarily unlimited in its powers, but that its legislation formed the highest source of law in the UK. The question, therefore, is whether any limitations on Parliament's sovereignty could, or do, exist.

Possible limitations on sovereignty

8. A limited legislature

In constitutional theory, it is perfectly possible to have a limited legislature – that is one which cannot legally do certain things, or pass certain kinds of legislation.

Generally, this situation might arise in three ways:

(a) *A written constitution.* Where a country has one, a written constitution is normally the supreme, fundamental source of law, and the legislature derives its authority to make laws from the constitution. This might limit the legislature by forbidding it to do certain things. For example, the American Constitution provides that Congress may not pass any *ex post facto* laws (*see* 5(a), above). Also, the First Amendment provides that Congress shall make no law abridging freedom of speech or of the press.

(b) *Colonial legislatures* Many colonies, particularly well-established ones, have their own legislatures. In the case of the British Empire, these included Canada, Australia and New Zealand (until these countries acquired virtually complete independence in 1931). In these countries, the legislatures could not pass certain kinds of laws unilaterally, particularly Acts changing their constitutions, since such powers had not been given them by the British Parliament when establishing the colonial legislatures in the countries concerned (*see* 14 and 15, below).

(This could work the other way round, so that one legislature could, at the same time as creating a new legislature, transfer to the latter some or all of its legislative powers (*see* 12 below).)

(c) *International law and organisations.* It is possible for international law to take primacy over local legislation. In particular, it has been contended that certain laws passed by the European Community take priority over national legislation, including Acts of the UK Parliament, thus limiting the latter. (This topic is discussed in detail in 4.)

9. The nature of such limitations

Whichever of the three situations described in 8, above, apply, any limitations will fall into one of two categories:

(a) *Limitations as to the subject-matter in respect of which the legislature may pass Acts.* We have seen two example of this in the case of the American Constitution (*see* 8(a), above).

(b) *Limitations as the manner and form which legislation must take.* The best-known example of this is again found in the American Constitution, this time Article 5. This provides that the Constitution can only be amended with the approval of two-third of both Houses of Congress, and three-quarters of the State legislatures. (This is what makes the American Constitution rigid, and Article 5 entrenched: *see* 1:6.)

10. The position in the UK

Since the UK has no written constitution, is not a colony, and (subject to very recent developments concerning the European Community, which are dealt with separately) does not give priority to international law or organisations, none of the situations referred to in **8**, above, applies here. Accordingly, in theory at least, if any of the limitations described in **9**, above, were to arise, it could only be because Parliament itself had brought about such a situation. A paradox therefore arises. In traditional constitutional theory, there are no limitations on the legislative competence of Parliament, and Parliament can make any laws it likes, including laws repealing earlier statutes. But if Parliament can make any law it likes, then it should be able to pass a law which cannot be repealed by a later Parliament. Its inability to do so is therefore an obvious limitation on Parliament's sovereignty, but at the same time is an example of it, being an inevitable feature of it.

The question, therefore, is can Parliament bind its successors? In other words, can it pass an Act which cannot be simply repealed by a subsequent Parliament or which can only be repealed in accordance with some special procedures or requirements which the Act itself lays down.

11. Limitations as to subject matter

In practice (again, leaving the EC aside for the time being) our courts have had to consider the possibility that such limitations have been created by the UK Parliament. These arise in two ways:

(1) Acts of Union; and
(2) Grants of independence.

12. Acts of Union

As noted earlier, the UK is a union of several countries, namely England and Wales, Scotland and Northern Ireland. All were formerly independent. England and Wales were united militarily in 1284. Scotland was united with England and Wales in 1707, to form Great Britain, and Ireland was united with Great Britain in 1800. In the cases of Scotland and Ireland, union was achieved by treaties between the national governments concerned, followed by Acts passed by the various parliaments. These Acts of Union provide us with some interesting examples of parliamentary sovereignty.

(a) *Union between England and Scotland.* When the English and Scots Parliaments respectively passed Acts of Union, they effectively abolished themselves as separate entities, handing over their sovereign powers to a new, British Parliament. Clearly, it is possible for Parliament to place limitations on its own sovereignty by taking the drastic steps of giving its sovereignty to another Parliament.

(b) *Britain and Ireland.* The Acts of Union purported to bind the various countries together for all time. Whilst England and Scotland remain united, the fact is that the 1800 Act of Union uniting Great Britain and Ireland was repealed by an ordinary Act of Parliament which created the Irish Free State: Irish Free State (Agreement) Act 1922. As a consequence, Southern Ireland (later to become Eire) became independent.

13. Grants of independence

During the twentieth century most of the countries which formerly made up the British Empire have become independent. This has been effected in two ways:

(a) *The Statute of Westminster 1931.* This gave independence to those colonies which had been longest established, and which were known as dominions. They were Australia, New Zealand, Canada, New Foundland, South Africa and the Irish Free State.

(b) *Independence Acts.* These were passed so as to confer independence upon individual countries on an *ad hoc* basis (e.g. India in 1947, and Nigeria in 1960). With the passage of such Acts, the UK Parliament lost its competence to pass laws in the countries concerned.

14. The Statute of Westminster

Section 4 of this Act supplements the established convention that the British Parliament will not pass an Act which applies in a dominion, unless the dominion wishes it. It provides that, 'No Act [of the UK Parliament] shall extend to a Dominion, unless it is expressly declared in that Act that the Dominion has requested and consented to the enactment thereof.' As a consequence of this, the British Parliament irretrievably lost its ability to pass laws in the dominions of its own initiative. As Lord Denning put it in *Blackburn* v. *Attorney-General* (1971): 'We have all been brought up to believe that, in legal theory, one Parliament cannot bind another, and that no Act is irreversible. But take the Statute of Westminster . . . Can anyone imagine that Parliament could or would reverse that statute?'

15. Limitations as to manner and form

The phrase 'manner and form' comes from the Colonial Laws Validity Act 1865. This provided that colonial legislatures were limited ones, in that, should they wish to enact certain kinds of laws, they were obliged to observe the 'manner and form' requirements in force at the time.

Thus, in *Attorney-General for New South Wales* v. *Trethowan* (1932) the Privy Council held that a bill passed by both Houses of the New South Wales Parliament could not be given the royal assent and become law, since it had not proceeded in accordance with the Constitution Act of 1902. This Act, which was the basis of the New South Wales Constitution, required that bills involving constitutional change were subject to a referendum procedure (vote by all the electors). Since the bill sought to abolish the Upper Chamber, it was subject to that procedure. Not having followed it, the bills could not become law.

Such limitations as this occur in countries having a written constitution, or in colonial legislatures which can pass certain laws only in accordance with some prescribed 'manner and form'. In English law, such limitations do not normally exist. However, the following paragraphs show how, in practice, they have to be considered by English courts.

16. The Canada Act 1982

Whilst the Statute of Westminster 1931 ended the power of the UK Parliament to legislate in Canada, except at the request of the Canadian government, there were still certain things the Canadian legislature could not do, owing to the provisions of the British North America Act 1867, which created the Canadian legislature and federal system. In particular, it could not change the Canadian Constitution without an Act of the UK Parliament being passed. (A similar but not identical situation existed in Australia: *see* 15, above.) Proposals were made that it should be given that power. Accordingly, once it had obtained sufficient support in Canada, the Canadian government requested that the Canada bill be passed by the UK Parliament and be given the royal assent. The resulting Act (Canada Act 1982) repealed section 4 of the Statute of Westminster, so far as Canada was concerned (thus ending the British Parliament's power to legislate for Canada altogether) and gave the Canadian legislature the power to amend the Canadian Constitution. (A similar Act was passed for Australia in 1986: Australia Act 1986; New Zealand had already been given complete control over its own Constitution in 1947: New Zealand Constitution (Amendment) Act 1947.)

17. *Manuel* v. *Attorney-General* (1983)

Whilst the Canada bill was before Parliament, an attempt was made to challenge it, on the grounds that the Canadian people as a whole had not requested and consented to the enactment of the bill, so that it did not comply with the requirements in section 4 of the Statute of Westminster. The Court of Appeal held in *Manuel* v. *Attorney-General* (1983):

(a) It was not necessary (to comply with section 4) that the people of a dominion actually requested and consented to an Act; it was sufficient that the government of that country did so.

(b) Furthermore, section 4 required only that the Act concerned contained a statement to that effect. Provided such a statement appeared in the Act, the court would not enter into an inquiry as to whether the statement represented the wishes of the majority of the people in the dominion concerned.

Thus section 4 of the Statute of Westminster gave rise to a variety of 'manner and form' limitation, as well as one relating to subject matter. However, since it has been repealed with respect to Canada and Australia and therefore no longer applies to any of the dominions it has ceased to have any further practical significance.

The Parliament Acts

18. The Parliaments Acts 1911 and 1949

It has been suggested that all Acts of Parliament have a particular manner and form, i.e. they must be authorised. To become an Act, a bill must have received the royal assent. It will normally also have been passed by both Houses of Parliament and will therefore contain the words, 'Be it enacted by the Queen's most excellent Majesty, by and with the advice and consent of the Lords spiritual and temporal and Commons in the present Parliament assembled . . .'

However, it is possible for a bill to be given the royal assent having been passed by the Commons alone: sections 1 and 2 of the Parliament Act 1911 and 1949. In the case of a money bill (a financial measure) this can occur if the Lords refuse to pass it for one month. In the case of any other public bill (except one to extend the duration of Parliament), this can occur if the Lords refuse to pass it in two successive sessions of Parliament (a year and a month). Thus, an alternative manner and form arises. However, these provisions are not true manner and form limitations. They are discussed further at 7:14-15.

Legal sovereignty

19. Conclusions – sovereignty as a legal concept

It is important to understand parliamentary sovereignty, as defined by Dicey and discussed in books on constitutional and administrative law, as a legal concept. It is not the same thing, for example, as national sovereignty, which is a concern of international law. (*See* 1:3.) In other words, it does not seek to explain questions of political power or practice. As Lord Sankey put it in *British Coal Corporation* v. *R* (1935), 'As a matter of abstract law, Parliament could even repeal or disregard section 4 of the Statute of Westminster . . . but that is theory and has no relation to realities.'

At the end of the day, therefore, the question for the student of British constitutional law is not whether or not Parliament could or would, by passing an Act, do certain things (since there may be various reasons, not necessarily legal ones, why it would not), but rather what would a British court do when asked to consider such an Act.

For example, as far as Sir Robert Megarry VC (in the *Manuel* case) was concerned, there was no difference between a country which had become independent under the Statute of Westminster, and one which had never been under British rule, since, if Parliament passed an Act which purported to apply in either country, 'it would no doubt . . . be ignored by the foreign state and would not be enforced by it.' However, 'that would not invalidate the Act in this country [i.e. the UK] . . . sitting as a judge in an English court, I owe full and dutiful obedience to (an) Act.': *Manuel* v. *Attorney-General* (1983).

In other words, the general view seems to be that if Parliament chooses to pass an Act which cannot, for practical reasons, be actually enforced (such as one which purportedly applies in a foreign land), that is up to Parliament. Such an Act would still be the law of the UK and, so far as possible, be enforced in British courts. It is this recognition that comprises parliamentary sovereignty.

However, this conception of parliamentary sovereignty has recently come under its most serious threat yet, namely the impact of European Community law. That subject is dealt with in the following chapter.

Progress Test 4

1. What is meant by 'parliamentary sovereignty'? What is its significance in the UK? **(1-2)**

2. Outline Dicey's analysis of parliamentary sovereignty. How might one establish whether or not Dicey's analysis was correct? **(3-7)**

3. In what circumstances might a legislature be 'limited' as to its law-making powers, and by what? **(8-9)**

4. Given that arguably the normal limitations on its law-making capacity do not apply to the British Parliament, what factors (practical as well as legal) may be said to impose limits of Parliament's sovereignty? **10-17)**

5. Distinguish: **(a)** limitations as to subject matter; and **(b)** limitations as to manner and form; in relation to legislation. **(11-17)**

6. What is meant by 'sovereignty as a legal concept'? **(19)**

5
The European Community

The Community generally

1. The European Community

After World War II, there was much debate as to the desirability of creating a sort of 'United States' of Europe, in order to foster greater co-operation and friendship between the European nations, and to discourage the sorts of developments which might lead to a recurrence of war. This movement took various forms, including the creation in 1950 of the Council of Europe, and the adoption by the major European States of the European Convention on Human Rights and Fundamental Freedoms.

A separate development (which must not be confused with the above) was the establishment of the European Community (EC), which also began in 1950. In 1951, a Treaty was signed in Paris by Germany, France, the Netherlands, Belgium, Luxembourg and Italy (known as 'the Six') establishing a European Coal and Steel Community. This was followed by the creation of a European Atomic Energy Community and finally, in 1957, by the European Economic Community (Treaty of Rome 1957).

In 1965, a treaty of merger was signed, as a result of which the functions and institutions of all three communities were effectively combined into one European Community. Britain joined that Community by means of a separate treaty of accession in 1971.

2. The nature and functions of the Community

The European Community is a complex body, rather different from other international organisations such as the United Nations Organisation (UN) or the North Atlantic Treaty Organisation (NATO). In particular, it is recognised that the EC has authority to make laws which transcend national law, and in some cases form part of it. As far as the UK is concerned, this is wholly novel, and may be said to represent something of a threat to traditional notions of parliamentary sovereignty (*see* **23–25**, below.) However, such authority as it does have is not all-embracing, and must be seen in the context of the main purpose and functions of the Community. This can be understood when one considers the colloquial title sometimes given to the EC, namely, the 'Common Market'.

Basically, the first objective of the Community was to establish a customs union, with free trade amongst member states. This means that there should be no barriers to trading between member states and that member states should adopt a common policy on such matters as tariffs, duties, etc. with regard to non-members. Ultimately, the intended policy is for all trade negotiation with non-members to be done by the Community, rather than by member states themselves, and for the Community to regulate not only tariffs and duties, but standards, subsidies and even interest rates throughout the Community.

The institutions of the EC

3. General

Like a state, the EC has a system of government of its own. Thus, the Treaty of Rome (as amended) may be said to be its (written) constitution, providing for the fundamental powers of the organs of government thus created. As with a state, three broad functions can be discerned, namely legislative, executive and judicial. At least two of these (the executive and judicial functions) can be identified with a distinct organ of government: the third function (legislative) is rather more complicated since three separate bodies (or institutions) are involved.

The principal institutions invested with power by the Treaty are:

(1) The Commission;
(2) The Council of Ministers;
(3) The European Parliament; and
(4) The Court of Justice.

The work of these bodies is discussed below.

4. The Commission

The functions of the European Commission are broadly comparable to those of the executive in a national system.

The Commission, as presently constituted, was established by a separate Treaty of Brussels, Article 9 of which empowered it to make proposals for legislation; and to exercise such powers as are conferred upon it by the Council (*see* 4, below) for the implementation of EC law. This latter function includes the bringing of proceedings for violations of EC law by member states in the Court of Justice. It is also the civil service of the EC. At present, there are 17 commissioners, including the president of the Commission, (currently Jacques Delors). The Commissioners are assigned particular areas of responsibility (rather like British Cabinet ministers). There are 23 such departments (known as 'Directorates-General'). One of the two British commissioners, Sir Leon Britten, is Director-General of Competition.

Commissioners are nominated for appointment by the governments of the member states: however, commissioners are required to further community interests, rather than national ones. The Commission is based in Brussels.

5. The Council of Ministers

The Council of Ministers consists of government ministers from each of the member states. It is not a fixed membership, however, since a different minister will attend council meetings, depending upon what area of community business is under consideration. Thus, for example, if the Council is discussing agricultural policy, then the minister with responsibility for that area (in the case of the UK the Minister for Agriculture, Fisheries and Food) will attend. If very high-level policy matters are discussed (particularly if this has constitutional implications for member states) a Council meeting might become a sort of summit between heads of government.

The main function of the Council is that of final decision-maker. In a sense, this makes the Council the most significant body where EC legislation is concerned: it would be wrong to describe it as the Community's legislature, however, since that function is shared, to a greater or lesser degree, with the Commission and Parliament (*see* 10, below).

In order to ensure permanent representation of member states, the Council is supported by a Committee of Permanent Representatives. Such representatives normally have ambassadorial status, and are sometimes referred to as 'ambassadors to the EC'.

6. The European Parliament

Despite its title, the European Parliament (EP) is not like the British Parliament. In particular, the EP cannot really be described as sovereign, in the sense that that word is understood in the UK, since the EP is not the principal legislative body in the Community (*see* 10, below). It *is* like most national parliaments, however, in that it consists of elected members, each of whom represents a special constituency. There are currently 518 members (referred to in Britain as MEPs: Members of the European Parliament), of whom 81 are from the UK. In all member states except the UK, MEPs are elected by means of a proportional representation system of voting: the UK adheres to its traditional voting method, as used in elections to the British Parliament (known as 'first past the post'). Like most national Parliaments, the EP is an important debating chamber. It also calls the Commission (the executive) to account, rather like the British Parliament. To this end, MEPs may ask questions concerning the Commission's conduct. Furthermore, a system of committees (similar to the British parliamentary committees) also exists to scrutinise the work of the Commission. Regarding proposals for community legislation (Acts), the EP has a power to amend, or even reject those proposals falling within the scope of the 1992 Single Market procedure (this is dealt with below).

7. The European Court of Justice (ECJ)

The ECJ sits in Luxembourg. It consists of 13 judges (one from each of the 12 member states, plus one extra to ensure an odd number, in case of majority rulings). In addition to the judges, there are important officials known as advocates-general, whose job it is to present the Community's view. One of the judges is elected President of the Court. The European judges do not necessarily hold (or previously have held) judicial office in their own countries, but they must have similar qualifications to those who do.

The jurisdiction of the ECJ is derived from Article 177 of the Treaty of Rome, and is basically two-fold:

(a) It decides cases referred to it by the Commission of alleged violations of their Treaty obligations by member states, including the obligation to implement Community law domestically.

(b) It makes preliminary rulings on matters of Community law referred to it by national courts before whom such matters arise. Such matters are identified in Article 177 as:

(*i*) The interpretation of the Treaty;

(*ii*) The validity and interpretation of Acts made by the Community's institutions; and

(*iii*) The interpretation of any statutes of bodies established by an Act of the Council.

The court cannot, except in a few very exceptional cases, hear matters referred to it by a private individual: however, some Community laws are directly applicable, meaning that an aggrieved individual can pursue his Community rights in the courts of his own country. (See below.) On the other hand, individuals may complain directly to the Commission of a member state's non-implementation of Community law, with a view to action by the Commission in the court.

Community law

8. Community law

The first, and most significant, point to make about Community law is that it is unlike general international law. The EC is not merely an international organisation; it has been described also as a supra national organisation. In other words, membership of the EC does not merely place obligations on member states, as between themselves, at governmental level. It also imposes obligations upon them, and rights upon their citizens, which can actually be enforced in member states' domestic courts. (This is discussed further below.)

To summarise the differences between Community law and general international law :

(a) Community Law is said to form part of the domestic law of each member state, unlike general international law.

(b) Certain rights, duties and obligations arising under Community law are enforceable in the domestic courts of member states.

(c) Furthermore, such rights, duties and obligations can be enforced by an individual. This is quite different from international law generally, where even though an individual might be the victim of a breach of international law, only a state or international organisation can enforce the law in the International of Justice at the Hague (or, in the case of the European Convention on Human Rights, the European Court of Human Rights in Strasbourg).

9. Sources of Community law

There are three sources of Community law, all of which may give rise to obligations as between member states, but which may also form part of the domestic law of member states. These are:

(1) The treaties;
(2) 'Acts' of the Community institutions (mainly the Council); and
(3) Decisions of the European Court of Justice.

10. The Treaties

As mentioned at 3, above, the treaties (and in particular, the Treaty of Rome) are in effect, the written constitution of the Community, and therefore the fundamental source of Community law. Thus, the power of the Community's institutions (the Council, Commission and Assembly) and jurisdiction of the court derive from the Treaty of Rome, as do the principal obligations which member states are bound by. Thus, breach of a member state's Treaty obligation will be actionable in the court at the instance of the Commission (or where another member state is affected, that member state). Over and above this, however, the Treaty of Rome is an important source of law within each member state, since certain of its provisions can be enforced in the domestic courts of member states. Thus, for example, the requirements of Article 48 (free movement of workers) and Article 119 (equal pay) 'take direct effect' (*see* 13, below). Accordingly, certain provisions of the Treaty form part of the law of all member states, including the UK, and are thus a source of British law.

11. Acts of the Community institutions

As noted at 3, above, it is the Council of Ministers which is the final decision-maker where it comes to Community legislation. However, as well as the Council, the Commission and EP are also involved in the law-making process. There are two distinct procedures, namely, the consultation and the co-operation procedures. Which of these procedures is involved depends upon whether or not the proposals fall within the scope of the 1992 Single Market programme: if they do, then the co-operation procedure is adopted. (The details of the law-making process is discussed below.)

Acts take two main forms: regulations and directives. In addition to these, Article 189 of the Treaty of Rome empowers the Council and Commission to take decisions and make recommendations: these are not binding upon member states, however, and are not, therefore, strictly speaking laws. (Regulations and directives are discussed at 13, below.)

12. The law-making process

As mentioned above, there are two procedures for creating Acts of the EC.

(a) *The consultation procedure.* This is the procedure established in the Treaty of Rome 1957, and which was, until 1992, the usual means whereby EC law (other than Treaty provisions and decisions of the court) were created.

(*i*) Proposals are made by the Commission. In formulating such proposals, the Commission may receive ideas from the EP, from member states, or from private interest groups, or it may simply formulate a proposal itself. However, proposals must emanate from the Commission if they are to become laws.

(*ii*) Proposals are put simultaneously to the EP and to the Council of Ministers. Having debated it, both generally and in Committee, the EP will then give an opinion, which is transmitted to the Commission for its consideration. Such an opinion will either be to accept the proposal, or to amend or reject it. However, the opinion of the Assembly is *not* binding on either the Commission or Council, which are meanwhile also considering the proposal.

(*iii*) The opinion of the EP is next transmitted to the Commission, which will re-consider the proposal, possibly amending it in the light of the EP's opinion. The Commission is not bound by the EP's opinion, and can ignore it, though that is actually rare.

(*iv*) Amended proposals are put to the Council of Ministers, who take the final decision as to whether the proposal should be adopted or not: If it is, then the Council will enact it by the issue of a Regulation or Directive (*see* 13, below).

(b) *The co-operation procedure.* This was introduced by the Single European Act 1986 which introduced the concept of a 'Single Internal Market' and which takes effect as of 1992 (hence the phrase 'Single Market proposal' or '1992 proposal'). The introduction of the co-operative procedure whereby EC laws can be made was designed to assist in the establishment of a 'full internal market' in the EC. The procedure is as follows:

(*i*) To begin with, the procedure is identical to the consultation procedure, in that ideas for proposals come from the same sources, and are made to the Commission, before being sent to the EP for consideration. Once again, the

Commission re-considers the proposals in the light of the EP's opinion.

(*ii*) However, after this, the procedure differs. Instead of simply adopting or rejecting such proposals, the Council of Ministers must arrive at what is called a 'common position'. A common position is a version of the proposal which is considered to be acceptable to the member states. It is arrived at by a vote, in which a 'qualified majority' will suffice. This is a complex procedure, in which each member state is allocated a set number of votes, which might differ from the number allotted to another member state (for instance, Germany and the UK have ten votes each, whereas Portugal has five and Luxembourg two). A qualified majority means 54 out of the total of 76 votes available.

(*iii*) The common position is then considered by the EP which has three months in which to give an opinion whether to accept it, amend it, or reject it. This opinion is arrived at by a vote, in which a simple majority will sufficed.

(*iv*) The EP's opinion goes next to the Commission, who may amend it, provided they do so within one month. A proposal (amended by the Commission or not) then goes back to the Council of Ministers for a final decision. The Council has three months in which to adopt a proposal or not: exceptionally, and with the EP's approval, this can be extended by a further month. The Council then votes on the proposal. A proposal which has been amended by the Commission can become law if a majority in the council vote in favour. The Council can refuse to accept such amendments, however, and may, if it wishes, adhere to its original 'common position'; however this requires a unanimous vote.

(A chart, showing the law-making procedures as well as how EC law is applied, both in the European Court and in domestic courts, appears on pages 65–6.)

13. Regulations and directives

These are the two main forms which laws promulgated by the Council of Ministers, in accordance with the procedures outlined above, may take.

(a) *Regulations.* These are rules which apply to all member states. By virtue of the principle of direct applicability they are a direct source

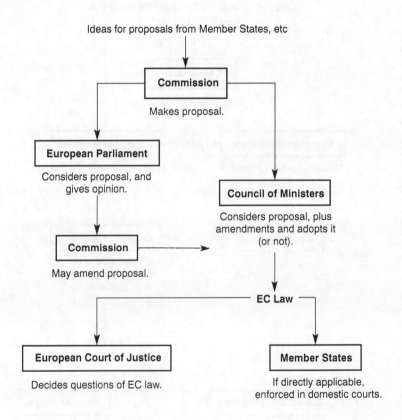

The making of Community law *(a)The consultation procedure*

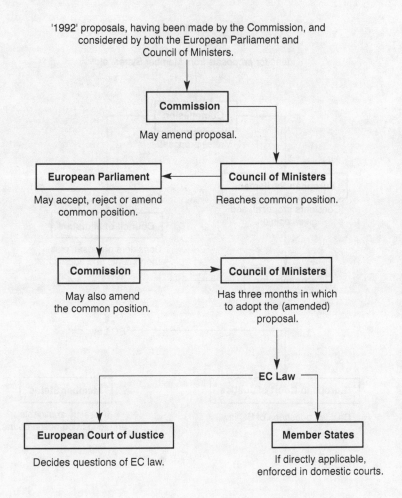

'1992' proposals, having been made by the Commission, and
considered by both the European Parliament and
Council of Ministers.

Commission

May amend proposal.

European Parliament   **Council of Ministers**

May accept, reject or amend   Reaches common position.
common position.

Commission   **Council of Ministers**

May also amend   Has three months in which
the common position.   to adopt the (amended)
proposal.

EC Law

European Court of Justice   **Member States**

Decides questions of EC law.   If directly applicable,
enforced in domestic courts.

The making of Community law *(b) The co-operation procedure* of law in all member states, irrespective of domestic law. Thus where a regulation counters any rights upon any persons, then that person can enforce his rights in a national court without having to wait for such rights to be ratified in domestic law.

The ECJ has held that, in the event that a national law is passed after a regulation has taken effect, and that law conflicts with the regulation, then a national court should nevertheless enforce any rights accruing under the regulation: *Amminstrazione delle Finanze del Stato* v. *Simmenthal SpA* (1978). This principle has been followed in the UK by the House of Lords in *Factortame* v. *Secretary of State for Transport* (1991) (*see* **24**, below).

Rights conferred upon a person by a regulation (known as 'enforceable community rights') can be upheld in the national courts of any member state, and not merely those of his own country. Thus, for instance, if a French citizen's community rights are denied him by the British authorities he may seek to enforce them in a British court.

(b) *Directives*. These are binding only on member states to whom they are addressed, unlike regulations. Furthermore, directives are not directly applicable, so that it is left up to each member state how to implement them.

Article 189 of the Treaty of Rome provides that 'a directive shall be binding as to the result to be achieved upon each member state to whom it is addressed, but shall leave to the national authorities the choice of form and method'. In the UK the favoured form and method is delegated legislation, and section 2(2) of The European Communities Act 1972 provides for this. Occasionally, implementation of a directive will require an Act of Parliament.

Nevertheless, directives are an important source of Community law, and are very numerous. For instance, by the end of February 1991, 150 directives concerning the Single Market had been issued. In practice directives are addressed to all member states simultaneously, so as to achieve uniformity throughout the community.

A time limit is set for the implementation of directives by member states. This can be enforced by the Commission in the ECJ. The ECJ has also held that where a directive confers any rights on an individual, then, on the expiry of the time limit, that individual can enforce them against the government in a domestic court: *Francovich* v. *Italian Republic* (1991).

14. Decisions of the Court

Decisions of the European Court of Justice (ECJ) are also an important source of Community law. As mentioned at **7**, above, such decisions may arise either from the following:

(a) *Cases brought by the Commission or by one member state* against a member state which has allegedly violated its treaty obligations (including its obligation to implement Community law); and

(b) *Points of Community law referred to the ECJ by national courts.* A reference may be made by any national court or tribunal at its discretion, but (according to Article 177 of the Treaty of Rome), a court or tribunal against whose decision no judicial remedy exists in domestic law must refer an unresolved point of Community law to the ECJ. Thus, in the UK, the House of Lords is obliged to refer such questions (unless of course, they have already been decided in previous cases).

According to Lord Denning in *Bulmer* v. *Bollinger* (1974) (a case involving a cider company's claim to refer to one of its products as 'Champagne Perry'), a UK court should refer a question of EC law to the ECJ in the following circumstances:

(*i*) The decision of the question is necessary to enable the UK court to arrive at its judgment.

(*ii*) The decision must be conclusive (i.e. determine the outcome of the case).

In any case, the UK court must also consider such things as the delay involved in referring such a question to the ECJ, as well as the expense and the burden on the ECJ, in exercising its discretion whether or not to refer.

In so far as Community law is concerned, decisions of the ECJ override those of national courts. However, the application of an ECJ decision to a case involving elements of both Community law and national law (as most do) is not always easy. (This is discussed below.)

Direct applicability and primacy of Community law

15. Direct applicability

This is the important principle whereby Community law becomes part of the national law of each member state directly, without the need for any adoptive process. Thus, in the UK, directly applicable Community law is part of British law without the need for any legislation by the British Parliament, or delegated legislation by the government. In so far as a piece of directly applicable community law confers rights upon any individuals then such an individual can enforce those rights directly in the national courts of a member state.

(a) Not all Community law is directly applicable. Strictly speaking, only regulations are directly applicable: these form part of the law of all member states throughout the Community, on being issued by the Council of Ministers.

(b) However, certain other Community laws can be enforced by an individual in national courts, and may therefore be described as 'taking direct effect'. Thus, for instance, the principle contained in Article 119 of the Treaty of Rome (equal pay) can be enforced by an individual in national courts. This is not directly applicable, however: it was only after the ECJ ruled that this was so that Article 119 could be thus enforced: *Defrenne* v. *Sabena* (1976). A distinction can therefore be drawn between directly applicable Community law, and Community law which takes direct effect. Only regulations are directly applicable: these also take direct effect. Other rules of Community law (such as certain parts of the Treaty) may take direct effect, but these are not, strictly speaking, directly applicable.

16. Primacy

As the term 'primacy' suggests, this principle implies that Community law overrides domestic law, and that, in the event of a conflict between the two, it is Community law which should prevail. (How this principle has been applied in the British courts is discussed below.) Certainly, the ECJ has upheld the principle, with the consequence that member states (including the UK) have not infrequently had to change their own laws to ensure compliance with Community law. Thus, in *Van Gend en Loos* v. *Nederlands Administrative der Belasingen* (1963), the ECJ pointed out that Community law constitutes a 'new legal order, for the benefit of which the member states have limited their sovereign rights' and the primacy of Community law was again upheld in *Costa* v. *ENEL* (1964). In the UK, comments by Lord Denning, presiding over the Court of Appeal in cases like *Application des Gaz* v. *Falks Veritas* (1974) and *Coomes (Holdings) Ltd* v. *Shields* (1978), appear to uphold the principle. In the former case, he said ' . . . In any transaction which contains a European element, we must look to the Treaty, for the Treaty is part of our law. It is equal in force to any statute.' In the *Coomes* case, Lord Denning went so far as to suggest that he would not apply an English statute if it clearly conflicted with directly applicable Community law.

Community law in the UK

17. The European Communities Act 1972

The UK joined the EC by means of a Treaty of Accession in 1971, negotiated by the then Prime Minister, Edward Heath. Signing the Treaty, however, was only the first step, since in the UK, as Lord Denning put it, 'We take no notice of Treaties until Parliament tells us, and then only to the extent that Parliament tells us': *Blackburn* v. *Attorney-General* (1971). In other words, Community law could not be implemented merely by signing a treaty of accession. Accordingly, Parliament passed the European Communities Act 1972. It was this Act which provided for the machinery whereby Community law became applicable in the UK. The Act came into force on 1 January 1973, and the relevant parts for present purposes of the Act are sections 2 and 3, and Schedule 2. These are as follows:

Section 2(1) All such rights, powers, liabilities, obligations and restrictions from time to time created or arising by or under the Treaties, and all such remedies and procedures from time to time provided for by or under the Treaties, as in accordance with the Treaties are without further enactment to be given legal effect or used in the United Kingdom shall be recognised and available in law, and be enforced, allowed and followed accordingly; and the expression 'enforceable Community right' and similar expressions shall be read as referring to one to which this subsection applies.

(2) Subject to Schedule 2 to this Act, at any time after its passing Her Majesty may Order in Council, and any designated Minister or department may by regulations, make provision –

(a) for the purpose of implementing any Community obligation of the United Kingdom, or enabling any such obligation to be implemented, or of enabling any rights enjoyed or to be enjoyed by the United Kingdom under or by virtue of the Treaties to be exercised; or

(b) for the purpose of dealing with matters arising out of or related to any such obligation or rights of it coming into force, or the operation from time to time, of subsection (1) above;

and in the exercise of any statutory power or duty, including any power to give directions or to legislate by means of orders, rules, regulations or other subordinate instrument, the person entrusted with the power or duty may have regard to the objects of the Communities and to any such obligation or rights as aforesaid.

(4) The provision that may be made under subsection (2) above includes, subject to Schedule 2 to this Act, any such provision (of any such extent) as might be made by Act of Parliament, and any enactment passed or to be passed, other than one contained in this Part of this Act, shall be construed and have effect subject to the foregoing provisions of this section; but, except as may be provided by any Act passed after this Act, Schedule 2 shall have effect in connection with the powers conferred by this and the following sections of this Act to make Orders in Council and regulations.

Section 3(1) For the purposes of all legal proceedings any question as to the meaning or effect of any of the Treaties, or as to the validity, meaning or effect of any Community instrument, shall be treated as a question of law (and, if not referred to the European Court, be for determination as such in accordance with the principles laid down by and any relevant decision of the European Court).

(2) Judicial notice shall be taken of the Treaties, of the Official Journal of the Communities and of any decision of, or expression of opinion, by, the European Court on any such question as aforesaid; and the Official Journal shall be admissible as evidence of any instrument or other act thereby communicated of any of the Communities or of any Community institution.

SCHEDULE 2.

PROVISIONS AS TO SUBORDINATE LEGISLATION.

1. (1) The powers conferred by section 2(2) of this Act to make provision for the purposes mentioned in section 2(2) (a) and (b) shall not include powers –

(a) to make any provision imposing or increasing taxation; or
(b) to make any provision taking effect from a date earlier than

that of the making of the instrument containing the provision; or

(c) to confer any power to legislate by means of orders, rules, regulations or other subordinate instrument, other than rules of procedure for any court or tribunal; or

(d) to create any new criminal offence punishable with imprisonment for more than two years or punishable on summary conviction with imprisonment for more than three months or with a fine or more than £400 (if not calculated on a daily basis) or with a fine of more than £5 a day.

(2) Sub-paragraph (1)(c) above shall not be taken to preclude the modification of a power to legislate conferred otherwise than under section 2(2), or the extension of any such power to purposes of the like nature as those for which it was conferred; and a power to give directions as to matters of administration is not to be regarded as a power to legislate within the meaning of sub- paragraph (1)(c).

2.(1) Subject to paragraph 3 below, where a provision contained in any section of this Act confers power to make regulations (otherwise than by modification or extension of any existing power), the power shall be exercisable by statutory instrument.

(2) Any statutory instrument containing an Order in Council or regulations made in the exercise of a power so conferred, if made without a draft having been approved by resolution of each House of Parliament, shall be subject to annulment in pursuance of a resolution of either House.

To summarise the effects of these important provisions:

Section 2(1) This provides for directly applicable Community Law to be enforced in British Courts.

(2) This empowers the government, or a minister, to make delegated legislation for the purpose of implementing Community law, with the exception of those topics mentioned in Schedule 2 (i.e. imposing taxation, creating criminal offences, etc.). This is important, since it means that a minister can, by means of delegated legislation, effect a change in statute law.

(4) This highly significant subsection provides, in effect, that future legislation shall take effect 'subject to the foregoing' (i.e. subject to section 2(1) and (2)). At the very least, this suggests that as a matter of construction, such legislation should be interpreted so as to be consistent with Community law. According to some commentators,

however, it goes rather further, and may itself be entrenched and therefore difficult, if not impossible, to repeal (*see* 4 and 22 below).

Section 3 (1) and (2) provides that questions of Community law, when they arise in a British court, should, if not actually referred to the ECJ, be decided in accordance with that court's decisions and, in any case, 'judicial notice' should be taken of EC law generally.

18. Community law in the UK
With the enactment of the European Communities Act 1972, Community law became a source of law in the UK. It can take three broad forms:

(1) Directly applicable Community law and 'enforceable Community Rights';
(2) Decisions of the ECJ; and
(3) Community law which has been implemented under section 2(2) of the 1972 Act.

19. Directly applicable Community law
Section 2(1) of the European Communities Act provides for the enforcement of directly applicable Community law (i.e. regulations) and 'enforceable Community rights'. Such rights include certain Treaty provisions, which take direct effect (such as Articles 48 and 119). They have been enforced in many cases in British courts (*see* 21–22, below).

20. Decisions of the ECJ
In practice, questions of Community law which arise in cases before national courts are frequently referred to the ECJ for a preliminary ruling, in accordance with Article 177 of the Treaty. The first such reference by a UK court took place in *Van Duyn* v. *Home Office* (1975). The plaintiff was a Dutch member of the Church of Scientology who sought to enter Britain to take up employment here. She was refused entry, on the grounds that Scientology was a creed which was considered contrary to the public good. She claimed this was contrary to her enforceable Community rights under Article 48 (free movement of workers). The question as to the scope of Article 48 was referred by the High Court to the ECJ, who ruled that Miss Van Duyn's rights were not unconditional, and that freedom of movement could be restricted on the grounds

of public policy. The first reference to the ECJ by the House of Lords was in *R* v. *Henn* (1981).

It should be noted that it is only the point of Community law which is referred to the ECJ by a national court. When the ECJ makes its ruling, the case is then returned to the court in question, where that ruling must be applied, before a final judgment is made. Any British court or tribunal *may* make a reference, whereas by virtue of Article 177, the House of Lords *must* (*see* 14 above). However, if the question has already been resolved by a higher British court, or by the ECJ itself, then the British court will not normally refer a matter, but follow that decision. Thus, decisions of the ECJ may be said to form precedents (as far as Community law is concerned) to be followed by British courts: this is actually provided for in section 3(1) of the European Communities Act.

British cases involving EC law

21. General

A complete picture of the impact of Community law on the UK can only be gained by a thorough study of the cases in which a European element has played a part. Such cases are now extremely numerous and wide-ranging in scope, involving such diverse topics as the rights to enter the country, restriction of imports of certain goods, tariffs, competition and so on.

One area where Community law has had a significant impact on UK law and which (unlike trade law and the like) is broadly within the field of constitutional law is that of equal pay. Article 119 of the Treaty of Rome provides that member states should uphold the principle of equal pay for workers, irrespective of their sex. Various directives have also been issued by the court to ensure compliance with this principle and further define its scope. Cases involving Article 119, in particular, have been heard in the Court of Appeal and the House of Lords. The ECJ have also ruled that Article 119 'takes direct effect' (*see* 13, above).

22. Court of Appeal cases

(*i*) In *Coomes (Holdings) Ltd* v. *Shields* (1979), the Court of Appeal held that an industrial tribunal had been wrong in rejecting the applicant's claim to the same pay as her male counterpart. Whilst the Equal Pay Act 1970 required that to qualify for the same pay as a man, a woman had to be engaged in 'like' work, this did not mean that her work had to be identical in every respect for her to qualify. Additionally (per Lord Denning) she was entitled to equal pay under Article 119.

(*ii*) In *McCarthy's* v. *Smith* (1979) a woman complained that, when she filled a job vacancy, she was paid at a lower rate than a man who had held that job some months earlier. The Court of Appeal held that under British law, her employers were acting quite lawfully: however, they referred the question as to the scope of Article 119 in such a situation to the ECJ, who ruled that the principle in Article 119 extended to the applicant, who was thereby entitled to the same rate of pay as her (male) predecessor. The Court of Appeal, applying this ruling, held that she had an enforceable Community right to equal pay.

23. House of Lords cases

(*i*) The House of Lords considered Article 119 in *Garland* v. *British Rail Engineering LA* (BREL) (1982), a rather complex case. The appellant, a woman, complained that on retirement, women ceased to enjoy certain valuable fringe-benefits (such as subsidised travel on trains for themselves and their families) which men were permitted to retain. BREL argued that under section 6(4) of the Sex Discrimination Act 1975 it was lawful for them to discriminate in this way when it came to benefits which applied after retirement and that, in any case, travel concessions did not fall within the scope of 'equal pay' as required by Article 119. The House referred the latter question to the ECJ, who ruled that the concept of equal pay did, in fact, extend to fringe benefits such as these.

This ruling posed a problem for the House, for the Court of Appeal had rejected the appellant's claim, holding that Section 6(4) of the 1975 Act disqualified her. However, rather than admit to a conflict between UK law and Community law, the House held that the Court of Appeal had been wrong in its interpretation of section 6(4), and that that section applied to benefits which arose only *after* retirement. Accordingly, since the benefits in question were enjoyed by both men and women prior to retirement, then the 1970 Act did make it unlawful discrimination for BREL to withdraw these from a woman on her retirement. The House was therefore able to steer a middle-course upholding both English and EC Law.

(*ii*) *Duke* v. *GEC Reliance Ltd* (1988) must be contrasted with

Garland v. *BREL* (1982). Here, a woman complained that she was required by her employers to retire at age 60, whereas men could continue working until 65 years of age. This, she claimed, was contrary to her rights under EC law, as well as the Sex Discrimination Act 1975. In this case (unlike *Garland*), the Court of Appeal held that the alleged discrimination only arose in connection with post-retirement matters, and was therefore permitted by virtue of Section 6(4). Regarding Community law, the only EC law specifically dealing with retirement age was Council Directive 76/207, and since a directive is not directly applicable, this did not conifer any enforceable community rights on the applicant, whose claim was therefore rejected.

(*iii*) The House next considered the effects of Article 119 in *Pickstone* v. *Freeman's Ltd* (1987). Some female warehouse operatives complained that they were being unlawfully discriminated against in that, though they were paid the same as male warehouse operatives, they were actually doing work of the same value as that done by male checkers, who received higher pay.

The employers contended that the women were engaged in like work to that of male operatives, with whom they shared equal rates of pay.

The Court of Appeal held that, although the applicants could not bring their claim under the Equal Pay Act, they could claim under Article 119. The House of Lords upheld this: whilst an applicant might not be afforded a right under English law, this did not debar her from pursuing a claim under Article 119. According to Article 119, as clarified by EC Council Directive 75/117, men and women were entitled to equal pay not only for the same work, but for work of equal value.

24. The *Factortame* case

The latest, and probably most significant, case decided by the House of Lords concerning Community law (though not Article 119) was *Factortame Ltd* v. *Secretary of State for Transport* (1991). In this case, the ability of the House to simply interpret British law in the light of EC Law and find that the latter merely added to the available rights under UK law was stretched to the limit. The case arose out of claims made by a fleet of Spanish fishermen (Factortame Ltd) to share in the UK's quota of fish stocks. The applicants had registered their vessels in the UK under existing

British Law, but a change in the law (the Merchant Shipping Act) in 1988 meant that they were no longer entitled to register and, therefore, ceased to be entitled to their share of the UK quota. This, they argued, contravened their Community rights under Article 7 of the Treaty (discrimination on grounds of race) and Articles 54 and 58 (freedom to engage in business throughout the Community).

Since their livelihood was placed in immediate jeopardy by the new legislation, the Divisional Court acceded to their request to grant an injunction against the Secretary of State, ordering him not to apply the provisions of the Merchant Shipping Act pending a final judgment on their claim. This was a controversial decision, in the light of the established principle that injunctions are not normally awarded against the Crown (*see* 13:4). The House of Lords restated that general principle, but referred the matter to the ECJ, since an important point of EC law was involved. The ECJ ruled that if a rule of national law was the sole obstacle to the granting of effective relief to an applicant claiming that his enforceable Community rights were being infringed, then that rule of national law should be set aside. Accordingly, the House held that, since this was the position regarding Factortame and, since Factortame's livelihood would suffer considerably if no relief was granted forthwith, then the injunction sought should be granted.

The *Factortame* case is a very important one, since, in effect, it establishes that an Act of Parliament can be 'dissapplied', at least insofar as it affects a particular person, where it has the effect of denying that person his enforceable Community rights. Furthermore, to that end, injunctions may seemingly be granted against the Crown, contrary to established principles of English law. Finally, in *Factortame* the House of Lords appears to have accepted the doctrine of the primacy of Community law (*see* 16, above).

Community law and parliamentary sovereignty

25. The problem

The main problem arising in connection with British membership of the EC is that, on the face of it, membership is incompatible with the traditional view of parliamentary sovereignty. (For a detailed discussion *see* 4.)

In particular, the doctrines of direct applicability, direct effect, and primacy of Community law, accepted by the House of Lords in the *Factortame* case (**24**, above) seem to pose a threat to established notions of sovereignty. According to the ECJ, the member states have 'limited their sovereign rights' (*Van Gend en Loos*: see **16**, above). However, it should be remembered that, in the Community, Britain is alone in that (as Hood Phillips puts it) the sovereignty of the UK Parliament is the only fundamental law of the British Constitution, whereas most European states have limited legislatures, having as they do written constitutions. (*See* 1:4–7.) Accordingly, it is necessary to approach this question in the same way that matters of sovereignty are normally dealt with in the UK law.

It will be remembered that, according to Dicey's analysis, parliamentary sovereignty consisted of two elements:

(1) Any Act of Parliament which creates new law or repeals old law will be obeyed by the courts.
(2) There is no body which can make rules which override an Act.

It follows from the above:
(3) Any Act passed by one Parliament can be repealed by a later Act : it is not possible to 'entrench' an Act of Parliament (i.e. pass an Act which cannot be repealed by a later Act), and
(4) If any limitations are to be placed on Parliament's competence to pass any laws it wishes, these must be self-imposed: it is not possible (in accordance with (b), above) for any outside body to do so.

26. The practical effects of EC membership

As usual, when 'testing' a theoretical statement, such as that contained in Dicey's analysis (**25**, above), one must look at the cases, to see what the courts have actually done. Thus, it will become clear that a re-appraisal – though not necessarily a rejection – of traditional notions of sovereignty must be made.
(a) The first, and least contentious, point is this. Clearly, the courts have now consistently applied Community law, which may now be said to be a distinct source of law in the UK. As Lord Denning put it 'Community law is part of our law. It is equal in force to any statute': *Application des Craz* v. *Falks Veritas* (1974). In itself, this does not threaten the traditional doctrine of parliamentary sovereignty. Indeed, if our courts do apply Community law, it is arguably only because Parliament has, in sections 2(1) and 3 of the European Communities Act 1972, directed them to do so. Thus, the courts are arguably actually *applying* the doctrine of sovereignty.

(b) However, some of the cases indicate the court's willingness to interpret UK legislation, both passed prior to 1972 and subsequently, 'in the light' of Community law. For example, the House of Lords decision in *Garland* v. *BREL* (*see* **23**, above) shows such a willingness.

Thus, according to some commentators, EC membership has, at the very least, brought about in British courts a 'new principle of interpretation' to the effect that the courts give effect to EC law when applying UK statutes.

Arguably, this does not necessarily pose a challenge to sovereignty as such, as analysed above. Furthermore, the courts can once again claim to be giving effect to section 2(4) of the European Communities Act 1972. It is, however, of great significance.

(c) It has been argued that the effects of the European Communities Act, and of British membership generally, do go further.

Specifically, it has been suggested that the ECA 1972 has received a degree of entrenchment – that is, it cannot be simply repealed by a future Act of Parliament. There are two versions of this view, one moderate, and the other somewhat extreme.

(*i*) According to the moderate view, the effect of section 2(4) is that the vital provisions of the ECA 1972 (mainly section 2) are protected against implied repeal, since legislation should, in accordance with section 2(4), be interpreted and applied so as to be consistent with Community law, and with the provisions of section 2 as a whole.

(*ii*) The extreme view has it that the effect of section 2(4) is to quite simply entrench section 2 as a whole: thus, Parliament cannot, even by express legislation, repeal section 2.

Whilst there is some evidence that the moderate view has been subscribed to, this extreme view has found little if any favour in the courts. As Lord Denning stated in *Macarthy's* v. *Smith* (1979):

In construing our statutes, we are entitled to look at the Treaty as an aid to its construction and even more, not only as an aid, but as an overriding force. If on close investigation it should appear that our legislation is deficient – or is inconsistent with Community law – by some oversight of our draftsmen – then it is our bounden duty to give priority to Community law. Such is the result of section 2(1) and (4) of the European Communities Act 1972.

Thus far I have assumed that our Parliament, whenever it passes legislation, intends to fulfil its obligations under the Treaty. If the time should come when our Parliament deliberately passes an Act with the intention of repudiating the Treaty or any provisions in it, or intentionally of acting inconsistently with it, and says so in express terms, then I should have thought that it would be the duty of our courts to follow the statute of our Parliament. Unless there is such an intentional and express repudiation of the Treaty, it is our duty to give priority to the Treaty.

27. Summary

From the discussion at **26**, above, the following conclusions can be drawn regarding the impact of EC membership on the sovereignty of the UK Parliament.

(a) There is no doubt that in passing the ECA Parliament authorised the Courts to apply EC law, which must therefore now be regarded as an important source of UK law.

(b) It is also equally clear that the courts have sought to interpret British statutes so as to remain consistent with EC law, which may therefore be said to have had an effect on statutes. However, this is not, in itself, the same thing as EC law overriding statutes: questions of interpretation are in any case always for the courts to decide, according to rules of their own devising.

(c) In at least one important case, on the other hand, a British court has held that a British statute should not be applied so as to negate a person's enforceable Community rights (*Factortame*). Accordingly, as far as its application to such a person is concerned, the courts have, as it were, 'dissapplied' a statute, and declined to enforce it. To that extent, traditional notions of sovereignty (and in particular the principle given at **26(a)**, above) is threatened.

(d) On the other hand, it seems clear that nothing arising from EC membership has affected Parliament's power to pass an Act which was expressly intended to conflict with or repudiate EC law. Thus, Parliament could, at least by express words, repeal or modify the ECA 1972, which is not (nor could it be) entrenched against such repeal.

Even if one accepts that the Act could not be accidentally repealed (as Lord Denning seems to accept), this would not seriously challenge Dicey's analysis of sovereignty. At most, it would require that the doctrine of implied repeal be re-examined; that doctrine was only established finally in 1934 in *Ellen Street Estates Ltd*

v. *Minister of Health* (1934), and played no real part in Dicey's original analysis.

Thus, it is submitted that, whilst the introduction of EC law has had an impact on British law, and upon parliamentary sovereignty, this has been limited in scope, in that, for the most part, the courts are merely following the provisions of the 1972 Act, and have been generally successful in preserving English law. Furthermore, since nothing in the 1972 Act is truly entrenched, Parliament could repeal it, and free the courts of any further obligation to apply EC law at all. Thus, any real effects on sovereignty are also conditional, the condition being the continuation in force of the ECA and with it, British membership of the Community.

Progress test 5

1. Briefly outline the historical background, nature and functions of the European Community. **(1–2)**

2. Describe the principal institutions of the EC and their main functions. **(3–7)**

3. Outline the main procedures and sources whereby community law arises. What is the 'status' of community law in domestic courts? **(8–14)**

4. What is meant by: **(a)** 'directly applicable' community law; and **(b)** community law which 'takes direct effect'? What are the differences, if any, between the two? **(15)**

5. Outline the main provisions of the European Communities Act 1972? **(17)**

6. Summarise the impact of community law as a source of law in the UK. **(19–24)**

7. To what extent, does the application of community law in the UK pose a threat to established views on parliamentary sovereignty? **(25–27)**

Part two

Parliamentary democracy

Parliamentary elections and Members of Parliament

Parliamentary democracy

1. Parliamentary democracy

It was pointed out at 1:14 that one of the chief features of the British Constitution is that it entails a parliamentary democracy. This can be taken to mean a kind of qualified democracy, in which the government of the day itself is not elected, nor accountable directly to the people. Instead, the government is accountable to Parliament, and members of the government must also be Members of Parliament. Furthermore, members of one of the two Houses of Parliament are, by law, elected at least every five years. Accordingly, the government is, in the UK, indirectly accountable to the people, by virtue of the important conventions of ministerial responsibility.

In this chapter, we shall be looking more closely at Parliament: the differences between the two Houses, how their members are appointed or elected, and at the workings of parliamentary democracy in practice.

We shall also be looking at the legislative side of Parliament's work, and at how Acts are passed.

2. The Queen in Parliament

It is important to note that, so far as legislation is concerned, one should speak of 'the Queen in Parliament'. Legislation is effected by the Queen in Parliament (though, of course, the sovereign does not actually sit in Parliament, or participate in debates in either House). Nowadays, the role of the Queen is limited to giving the royal assent to bills, and even here, she has no choice in the matter, by convention. However, whereas the sovereign is the head of state (head of the executive) and 'Fount of Justice' (head of the judiciary), she is not the head of the legislature, even in constitutional theory. This was established in the seventeenth century: the role of the sovereign in relation to legislation is as an equal participant, constitutionally, and not a head. In other words, the royal assent is a necessary feature of the legislative process, just as passage of a bill through the House of Commons is.

3. Historical background

The word Parliament probably derives from the same source as the word 'parley' – to talk, or discuss. Historically, Parliament originated as a forum for discussion, and for advising the king (who, at that time, had the power to make laws himself). To this day, Parliament remains an important forum for discussion and debate, though of course it has assumed prime responsibility for legislation (since the seventeenth century) and, more recently, for holding the government of the day accountable.

The specific origins of Parliament lie in the King's Council (Curia Regis) which was set up by William I on the Norman (French) model. It consisted of those advisers and military leaders whom the king turned to for advice. It also included the judges and was sometimes also known as the king's court, though by about 1215 (the date of Magna Carta) this term had come to be used for the judicial aspect of the work of the Council, and not its general debating and advisory functions. Nevertheless, the term 'the High Court of Parliament' is still sometimes used, and serves to remind us that Parliament still retains some functions of a judicial character (these are dealt with later: *see* **7:28**).

Quite early on in its history, Parliament became split into two 'Houses'. The background of these is as follows:

(a) *The House of Lords.* The original members of the King's Council were principally those military leaders and other advisers whom the king trusted. By way of rewarding them for their help and advice, King William I granted them large areas of land in England, which they held as the tenants-in-chief of the King. These tenants-in-chief were permitted to grant parts of their land to lesser tenants, thus establishing the system of land tenure known as the feudal system. As part of that system, each tenant had to pay 'dues' (originally services, but later rent) to his landlord. The tenants-in-chief (or barons, as they were also known) were obliged to provide the King with his army.

To ensure continuity in the system, a man's land automatically passed, on his death, to his eldest son, thus establishing the principle of inheritance of property.

By the early thirteenth century, the barons were becoming increasingly concerned that they should have a more permanent voice in affairs of state, and so in 1215, they forced the King to sign the Great Charter (Magna Carta), as a consequence of which the most important barons acquired the right to sit on the King's Council on an hereditary basis. Thus, a baron's son inherited his father's title to sit on the Council, on his father's death, and a permanent 'house' of Parliament, the House of Lords, became established, based on the same principle as land tenure, namely title by inheritance, or 'heredity'.

(b) *The House of Commons.* Not all the barons actually exerted their newly won right to sit in the King's Council (or House of Lords, as it became known). Some – particularly those who lived a great distance from Westminster, where the Council normally sat – were more concerned with running their estates. Accordingly, some of the barons, or Lords, sent knights to attend at Westminster, and report back to them on proceedings there. In 1265, a nobleman named Simon de Montfort organised this system, so that these knights met separately from the Lords to discuss matters of interest to them. In the de Montfort system, each shire (county) and borough (town) sent representatives (name knights and burgesses respectively) to Westminster: not being Lords (or 'peers') but 'commoners', they were not actually permitted to participate in the Council, but instead formed a separate House of Commons. They were not allowed to address the King or Lords personally either, so, in order to communicate with the Crown and Lords, they appointed one of their own number to do so. This person became known as the Speaker, whose function it still is to communicate the views of Members of Parliament (MPs) to the Crown (nowadays the government) and Lords.

Today, this is done somewhat formally, since many members of the government actually sit in the Commons, and an MP may be no more than a few feet away from a government minister.

Nevertheless, parliamentary procedure dictates that the Speaker acts as intermediary for all such communications, even to this day.

The Houses of Parliament

3. The Houses of Parliament today

The British Parliament is sometimes described as a bicameral Parliament, that is, one consisting of two chambers (or houses). The origin of these two chambers has already been discussed; their detailed composition and functions is discussed in the following paragraphs in this chapter.

It is important to note, however, that the two Houses are not equal partners and that, in effect, the historical position has been reversed. Thus, whereas the House of Lords originated in the King's Council itself, and therefore had the most significant role of the two Houses, this situation gradually changed, so that, by the nineteenth century, it was the Commons which had emerged as the dominant House, particularly where legislation was concerned. Thus, by the end of the nineteenth century the important constitutional convention that the Lords must always yield to the will of the Commons had become established.

Nevertheless, the historical superiority of the Lords has been preserved in a symbolic form, so that, even today, one may refer to the House of Lords as the 'upper' House, and to the Commons as the 'lower' House. (Though, somewhat whimsically, MPs, when speaking in the Commons, never refer to the House of Lords as the upper House, or even mention Lords; instead, they refer to the other chamber as 'another place' as do the Lords when referring to the Commons!)

4.   The House of Lords

At the time of writing, there are 1,195 members of the House of Lords (or peers as they are generally known).

(a) *Hereditary peers.* Not all members of the House of Lords are hereditary peers. Of the present membership, 758 (including 18 women) are hereditary peers; 19 of these are 'hereditary peers of the first creation' that is, they did not inherit their title from their father, but were actually made peers by the Crown, on the advice of the prime minister. As hereditary peers, of course, they are able to hand down their titles to their own sons. The practice of creating such hereditary peerages was discontinued in 1964 by general agreement; it was revived however by Margaret Thatcher PM from 1979–90 when she conferred hereditary peerages on two eminent politicians (Lords Whitelaw and Stockton) and on the retiring Speaker of the House of Commons (Viscount Tonypandy).

(b) *Life peers.* The possibility of a person's being made a peer for their own lifetime, and not being enabled to hand down the title to his son, arises under the Life Peerages Act 1958. Such peerages are granted by the Crown, on the advice of the PM.

At present, there are 373 such peers (including 59 women, who can be made life peers under the 1958 Act).

(c) *Lords Spiritual and Temporal.* The House of Lords includes, as well as hereditary and life peers of the kind described above, the Lords Spiritual. These are the Archbishops of Canterbury and York, the Bishops of London, Durham and Winchester, and the 21 most senior bishops of the established Church of England (in terms of length of time since their consecration). One may regard the Lords Spiritual as hereditary peers of a special kind.

(d) *Lords of Appeal in Ordinary.* Since the Appellate Jurisdiction Act 1876 reconstituted the judicial side of the House of Lords, making it the ultimate Court of Appeal in the UK, there has been provision for 20 Lords of Appeal in Ordinary (Law Lords) who, as the judges of that court, sit in the House of Lords. They are life peers.

(e) *The Lord Chancellor.* The Lord Chancellor is the head of the Judiciary and a government minister. He is also the chairman of the House of Lords, where he has a place on the Woolsack. Unlike the Speaker of the House of Commons, however, he does actually participate in debate, and particularly debate about the judicial system and administration of justice. In relation to these matters, the Lord Chancellor (LC) himself will introduce bills (proposals for legislation). The Lord Chancellor is a life peer.

(f) *Ranks of peers.* There are, in fact, five grades or ranks of peers.

(*i*) *Dukes.* The highest rank. These include three royal dukes (i.e. members of the Royal Family), namely the Dukes of Cornwall, York and Kent.

(*ii*) *Marquesses.* The next highest, there are currently 35 of these.

(*iii*) *Earls.* One of the hereditary peers created by Mrs Thatcher was the Earl of Stockton (former PM, Harold Macmillan).

(*iv*) *Viscounts.* There are 108 of this rank including Viscount Tonypandy, a peerage also created recently.

(*v*) *Barons.* There are 819 barons or baronesses presently in the Lords.

Of the above, life peers are invariably barons or baronesses. Hereditary peers may hold any of the five ranks discussed. However, new hereditary peerages are only made in the ranks of earls, viscounts and barons.

5. The Peerage Act 1963

Largely at the instigation of Viscount Stansgate (now Tony Benn) who had no wish to be a peer, and instead wished to remain a member of the Commons (which is not possible for peers: House of Commons Disqualification Act 1957, and now 1975) Parliament passed the Peerage Act in 1963. By virtue of this Act, a person may, on inheriting a peerage, disclaim if for his lifetime only, provided he does it within one year, (or in the case of a member of the House of Commons, like Mr Benn, one month: sections 1 and 2, Peerage Act 1963).

The number of peers who have disclaimed their peerages since 1963 is 11, including (as well as Mr Benn) Sir Alec Douglas Home (who disclaimed the title of Lord Home in order to become PM in 1964).

6. Female Peers

There are a small number of female peers currently in the House of Lords.

(a) *Hereditary peeresses.* There have for centuries been a small number of hereditary peeresses. Until 1963, however, they could not sit in the House of Lords. The Peerage Act 1963 (section 6) removed that anomaly, and hereditary peeresses may now sit. There are 18 of them.

(b) *Life peeresses.* The Life Peerages Act 1958, expressly provided that both men and women could be made life peers. There are 59 female life peers.

7. Attendance and political affiliation

(a) *Attendance.* In theory, every peer can be required to attend at the House. However, it is possible for peers to obtain leave of absence from the Lord Chancellor. Such leave is often granted to those hereditary peers, in particular, who do not wish to take part in the regular business of the House. Since they do not attend, such peers are sometimes known as backwoodsmen. They cannot be prevented from attending however. In 1989, for instance, a large number of 'backwoodsmen' were requested to attend at the Lords for the purpose of voting on the Local Government Finance bill (introducing the 'poll tax') which, the government feared, might otherwise be defeated.

(b) *Political affiliation.* There is no requirement that peers belong to any political party, indeed, it would be impossible, given the large number of hereditary peers, to ensure membership. In practice, however, those peers who do attend (known as working peers), and those life peers appointed by the Crown each year, do tend to belong to one or another of the major political parties. There are currently 465 Conservative peers, 114 Labour peers and 58 Liberal peers. As well as these, there are 263 peers known as cross-benchers (from the location of their seats in the chamber, which are on neither the government nor opposition sides). These are peers of no particular political affiliation. Since new life peers are created in proportion to the parties' existing standing, it can be seen that the Conservative Party has a built-in majority in the Lords. There is reason to believe that the hereditary peers also tend towards the Conservative Party in their sympathies, too.

The House of Commons

8. The House of Commons

The origins of the House of Commons (HC) has been dealt with (*see* **3**, above). Unlike the House of Lords, the HC is an elected chamber (the subject of elections is dealt with below). Members of the HC are known as Members of Parliament (MPs) to distinguish them from peers (members of the House of Lords).

9. Parliamentary Elections

(a) *General elections.* By law, an election for the entire membership of the House of Commons must be held at least every five years: section 7, Parliament Act 1911. Such an election is known as a general election. Accordingly, a 'Parliament' can only last for a maximum of five years. (This shows the dominance of the Commons over the Lords nowadays: although the Lords are not elected, and the same peers therefore return to the House after an election, we nevertheless speak of a 'new' Parliament which meets after a general election.)

(b) *By-elections.* From time to time, an individual MP retires or dies, and his seat falls vacant. His seat will be filled by a candidate elected in a by-election, i.e. an election in his constituency only. Such an election is held following the issue of a writ by the Speaker; the proposal that the writ be issued is usually made by an MP of the same political party as the outgoing member, and must be agreed by the House as a whole. The House is not obliged to call a by-election: this is one of the privileges (*see* **8**).

10. Parliamentary constituencies

It was noted at **3**, above, that in the De Montfort Parliament of 1265, a system was established whereby the shires and boroughs were represented by knights and burgesses. This is the historical basis for parliamentary constituencies. A parliamentary constituency is an area of the country which is represented in the Commons by one MP. Modern constituencies date back to 1832, when the 'single member' constituency was established (under the De Montfort model, which survived until 1832, each shire and borough was represented by two persons).

The theoretical basis behind the modern constituency system is that each constituency should contain, so far as possible, a similar number of electors. This is, of course, not really practicable, since some parts of the country (e.g. the Scottish Highlands) are so thinly populated that, if a highland constituency were to contain the same number of electors as a London one, it would be enormous. Nevertheless, given that impracticality, such is the aim. At present, there are 650 parliamentary constituencies in the UK, each entitled to be represented by one MP.

11. The Boundary commission

Since populations shift over the years, it is necessary to keep the situation under review, so as to ensure that (as far as possible) the aims of proportionality referred to in 10, above are met. This is the task of the Boundary Commission, a body which was established by Act of Parliament in 1944, and empowered to make recommendations regarding changes in parliamentary constituencies (boundary changes). These recommendations may be incorporated in Orders in Council and, once approved by Parliament, take effect: House of Commons (Redistribution of Seats) Acts, 1949–79. Once made, such an Order may not be challenged in court: section 4, Parliamentary Constituency Act 1986.

Whilst the Boundary Commissioners are public bodies, subject to the supervisory jurisdiction of the High Court, the Court of Appeal has acknowledged the virtual impossibility of their task of ensuring exact proportionality. In *R* v. *Boundary Commissioners for England & Wales, ex p. Foot and others* (1983), the Court held that that requirement was a guideline, which could not be enforced against the Commissioners. Provided that, in every other respect, the Commissioners acted according to the requirements of the Act, their recommendations could not be set aside by a court of law: the fact that such recommendations, if implemented, would benefit one political party more than others was insufficient ground on which to challenge the Commissioners' recommendations.

The franchise and elections

12. Universal franchise

In the UK, the franchise is said to be universal. That is, the right to vote in parliamentary elections is enjoyed by all citizens, irrespective of sex, race, colour or creed. In fact, the franchise is not truly 'universal', in that, whilst the old property requirements which once applied have been done away with, and the franchise has been extended to women as well as men, there are still a number of conditions and disqualifications.

(a) The modern law is contained in the Representation of the People Act 1983 (RPA). Section 1 of the Act provides that, in order to qualify as an elector in a parliamentary constituency, a person must:

(*i*) Be resident in that constituency on the qualifying date (10 October in England, Wales and Scotland, and 15 September in Northern Ireland);

(*ii*) Not be subject to any legal incapacity; and

(*iii*) Be of the voting age (18 years or more) on the date of the poll.

The Act goes on to provide that a person so qualified is entitled to vote only if registered in the register of electors in the constituency concerned. No person may vote more than once in a parliamentary election.

(b) The following are legally incapacitated from voting, either under the 1983 Act or previous law:

(*i*) Aliens;

(*ii*) Minors (persons under 18 years);

(*iii*) Peers (except Irish peers);

(*iv*) Convicted persons undergoing custodial sentences (section 4, RPA 1969); and

(*v*) Persons convicted of electoral offences or corrupt practices are disqualified for five years following conviction.

13. Particular points on the franchise

(a) *The residence requirement.* To qualify as a voter, a person does not have to reside in a constituency permanently. It is sufficient if he 'dwells there for a reasonable time': *Fox* v. *Stirk* (1970). Thus, a university undergraduate might qualify in his university constituency.

Furthermore, the status of a person's residence is immaterial. In *Hipperson* v. *Newbury Electoral Officer* (1985) the electoral officer refused to register a woman on the grounds that she did not satisfy the residence requirement, being a member of a 'women's peace-camp'. The women concerned lived in tents and other makeshift accommodation; as such, they would have been considered homeless had they applied for council accommodation under the Housing Act. Furthermore, they were technically trespassers on the site, which belonged to Newbury council. Nevertheless, the court held, the women did 'reside' at the camp for the purposes of the RPA 1983, and the applicant was therefore entitled to be registered to vote.

(b) *Non-residents.* Exceptionally, a person who does not meet the residence qualification or is otherwise unable to actually vote in person, may vote in the constituency concerned. This can arise in three ways:

(*i*) A person who is unable to attend a polling booth in his constituency on the day of the election may be entitled, on application to the registration officer, to vote by proxy (i.e. authorise someone else to actually cast his vote on his behalf): sections 19–22, RPA 1983. He is, therefore, an 'absent voter'.

(*ii*) A person who would be resident in a constituency, but, by reason of having a member of the forces or other servant of the Crown or British Council, is temporarily in a post abroad, may be entered in the register there and exercise their franchise as a 'service voter'. This also applies to the spouses of such persons.

(*iii*) A British citizen who is resident abroad may qualify to vote in a parliamentary constituency as an 'overseas voter'. To qualify, he must have been included in the constituency register not more than twenty years before the qualifying date: section 1, RPA 1983.

14. Electoral procedures

The basic procedure applicable to parliamentary elections dates back to the Parliamentary and Municipal Elections Act 1872 (the 'Ballot Act'). This provides for a secret ballot, whereby premises are designated as polling stations on the day of the election, and registered voters attend at the polling station to cast their votes. This is done by entering a polling booth, where the voter indicates his choice of candidate (*see* **15**, below) by writing a tick or cross beside that candidate's name on a slip provided. (It has been held that writing 'yes' is a valid vote.) He then folds the slip and places it in a sealed box; the boxes are opened at the end of the election, and the total votes cast for each candidate in the constituency is counted. The results of the election are then publicly announced by an official known as the returning officer (usually the mayor or similar local official). The victorious candidate is then 'returned' to Westminster to serve as MP for that constituency.

15. Parliamentary candidates

Subject to legal disqualifications, any person may stand as a parliamentary candidate in any constituency. He is not required to reside in that constituency, nor have any connection whatsoever with it (unlike candidates for local elections). Parliamentary candidates are not required to belong to any political party (*see* **16**, below), although membership of a party is clearly advantageous. Legal disqualifications derive from two sources.

(a) *Common law.* At common law the following are disqualified from candidacy.

(*i*) Aliens, who are defined as persons who are neither British citizens, Commonwealth citizens, nor citizens of the Republic of Ireland: section 37, British Nationality Act 1981;

(*ii*) Persons under 21 years of age;

(*iii*) Persons suffering from mental illness (as defined in section 141, Mental Health Act 1983);

(*iv*) Peers and peeresses (except Irish peers);

(*v*) Persons convicted of treason or (under section 1, RPA 1981) persons convicted of any offence and consequently undergoing a custodial sentence of 12 months or longer;

(*vi*) Undischarged bankrupts; and

(*vii*) Persons convicted of electoral offences or corrupt practices.

(b) *The House of Commons Disqualification Act 1975.* Under this Act, the following are disqualified:

(*i*) Holders of judicial office (including, as well as judges, stipendiary magistrates, but not JPs);

(*ii*) Civil servants;

(*iii*) Members of the armed forces;

(*iv*) Members of any foreign legislature;

(*v*) Members of specified bodies having some connection with government or Parliament (e.g. boards of nationalised industries, and the Law Commission);

(*vi*) Specified officials appointed by or connected with the Crown (e.g. Boundary Commissioners, ambassadors, the chairmen if certain tribunals); and

(*vii*) Section 2 of the 1975 Act goes on to provide that only 95 Ministers of the Crown may be members of the Commons. If a government is going to consist of a larger number of ministers (and a government of around 120 is the norm), the remainder must be peers. In theory at least, some of those to whom the 1975 Act applies could technically stand for election. However, none of those identified could take a seat in the House of Commons, being disqualified by law. A person belonging to any of the above categories would have to resign his position in order to do so.

16. Political parties

A political party is an organisation whose purpose it is to organise and provide support for parliamentary candidates and MPs of a particular political persuasion. The existence of such parties is not a legal requirement (as noted at 14, above a candidate – or for that matter, an MP – need not belong to a party). However, political parties are enormously important in the British Constitution for the following reasons:

(a) By convention, the PM is the leader of that party which enjoys a majority of seats in the House of Commons. The majority party, in other words, forms the government.

(b) The co-ordination of the election campaign is one of the tasks of political parties. This is obviously difficult and expensive. In practice independent (non-party) candidates have far less access to publicity, etc., and are unlikely to be returned. In England, the two dominant parties (in terms of seats in the Commons) are the Conservative Party (the present party of government) and the Labour Party.

It is somewhat different in Scotland and the provinces, where the Scottish Nationalist and Welsh Nationalist parties have some support. In Northern Ireland, the two main parties are the Ulster Unionist and Christian Democrat parties: these are broadly comparable to the Conservative and Labour parties respectively. In England and Wales, at least, the Liberal Party is the third largest party.

17. The conduct of elections

This is governed by the Representation of the Peoples Acts 1983-85.

(a) *Candidates.* Qualified candidates must submit their nominations to the returning officer within the time laid down. A nomination must be sponsored by a proposer, a seconder and at least eight other electors. It must be accompanied by a monetary deposit of £500; this is forfeited if the candidate fails to poll one-twentieth of the total votes cast: section 13, RPA 1985. A candidate must have an election agent, who is responsible for the conduct of his campaign (he may nominate himself as his own agent).

(b) *The election campaign.* It is the responsibility of an electoral agent to ensure that his candidate's campaign conforms with the legal requirements as to the electoral campaign. In particular, the law lays down the maximum permissible amounts that may be disbursed by way of election expenses; to exceed these amounts may amount to a corrupt practice, resulting in a candidacy being pronounced void, and the candidate disqualified from standing again for five years. Under section 76 of The 1983 Act there is a limit of £2,700. It should be noted that these requirements only apply to candidates at constituency level. There is no legal limit as to the amount of money which can be spent by a political party in promoting that party and its objectives generally, nor on the amount which can be spent by a party in the production of the Party Political Broadcasts (which are allowed) and which are broadcast on radio and television at election time. (Well-known film directors have, in recent years, been hired to assist in the production of such broadcasts.)

A candidate it permitted the use of a suitable room in a maintained school within the constituency for the purposes of holding public meetings to further his candidature: section 95, RPA 1983.

(c) *Election courts.* For the purposes of enforcing disqualification as to electors, dealing with allegations of illegal and corrupt practices, and resolving disputed elections, special election courts, consisting of two Queen's Bench judges, are established: Part III, RPA 1983. As a branch of the High Court, such courts enjoy the status and powers of that court; appeals from their decisions may be made to the Court of Appeal, but not to the House of Lords.

Corrupt practices include bribery, exerting undue influence and personation (e.g. using another elector's name to cast a vote). Illegal practices include unauthorised broadcasting or use of premises, making false declarations concerning candidacy and any failure to comply with the legal requirements as to candidacy.

18. Particular members and officers of the House

(a) *The House of Commons.*

(*i*) *The Speaker.* The role of the Speaker has already been discussed (*see* 2, and 7:4). He is an MP and must therefore stand successfully in an election before being elected Speaker by the House. Customarily, no candidate stands for election against the Speaker in his own parliamentary constituency. It is the Speaker's task to preside over the House, maintaining order in debate, and acting as the avenue of communication between members and the Crown. In addition, the Speaker rules on questions of procedure and privilege (*see* 8).

(*ii*) *The Chairman of Ways and Means.* Like the Speaker, he is an MP, who is elected to the post of Chairman of Ways and Means by the House at the beginning of each session. He deputises for the Speaker in his absence. He also acts as chairman of committees of the whole House (*see* 7).

(*iii*) *The Sergeant-at-Arms.* He is the policemen of the House. He is not an MP, but is appointed by the Crown. It is his task to implement the Speaker's (and House's) directions in maintaining order. He has the power, therefore, to arrest or eject persons offending against the House, and can keep such persons in custody at the direction of the Speaker.

(*iv*) *Whips.* The term 'whip' derives from the old hunting term 'whipper-in' (of the hounds). Both government and opposition parties employ whips. These are MPs whose task it is to ensure as many members of their party as possible turn up to vote in divisions.

(*v*) *The Leader of the House.* A Cabinet minister, his job is to represent the interests of the House, and of MPs. He is also involved (along with the Speaker, PM and leaders of the opposition) in arranging the agenda for parliamentary business.

(b) *The House of Lords.*

(*i*) *The Lord Chancellor.* A Cabinet minister, the Lord Chancellor (LC) is also head of the judiciary in England and Wales. He is, in effect, the Speaker of the House of Lords, but he does nor exert quite the same level of authority as does the Speaker of the Commons. It is the Lords itself which maintains order and is thus self-regulating, unlike the Commons.

Furthermore, the LC participates in debate, and has a vote, unlike the Speaker of the Commons. (He also has a number of ancient functions unconnected with the House, such as being chairman of the Privy Council, holder of the Great Seal, etc.)

(*ii*) *The Gentleman Usher of the Black Rod*. This officer has the customary function of summoning the Commons to attend at the Lords for the purpose of hearing the Queen's Speech at the commencement of a new Parliament. He is also the policeman of the Lords (rather like the Sergeant-at-Arms in the Commons), having the power to 'arrest' persons who offend against the privileges of the House, as directed by the Lords themselves. He is not, himself, a peer.

(*iii*) *The Chairman of Committees*. Like the Chairman of Ways and Means in the Commons, he deputises for the LC as Speaker, and is chairman of Committees of the whole House.

Progress test 6

1. Outline the historical origins and development of: **(a)** the House of Lords; and **(b)** the House of Commons. **(3)**

2. Briefly summarise the composition of the House of Lords. What are: **(a)** 'Lords spiritual'; **(b)** backwoodsmen; and **(c)** life peers. **(4, 5, 7)**

3 By whom is the Parliamentary franchise currently enjoyed? What categories of persons are disqualified from: **(a)** voting in general elections; and **(b)** taking a seat in the House of Commons? **(8, 12, 13, 15)**

4. Discuss the significance of political parties in relation to parliamentary elections and the British constitution generally. **(16)**

5. List some of the most important members and officers of both the Houses of Parliament, indicating their main functions. **(18)**

7

The functions and proceedings of Parliament

General

1. The meeting of Parliament

It has already been noted (at 3:6) that, by convention, Parliament must meet at least once each year. In practice, a parliamentary session (the period in each year when Parliament formally meets) usually lasts for around nine months, from October to July. The actual procedures involve the Queen, in the exercise of various of her royal prerogatives. (For a detailed discussion of the prerogative, *see* 8.)

(a) *Prorogation.* This is the procedure whereby a session of Parliament is ended. All parliamentary business ends with prorogation, so that (for instance) bills which have not been passed must be re-introduced in the new session.

(b) *The Queen's Speech.* A new session of Parliament is marked by the reading of the Queen's Speech (in fact prepared by the government). If the session is the first one of a new Parliament (i.e. following a general election) the Queen's speech is normally read by the Queen herself during the State Opening of Parliament; otherwise, it is read separately in each House (by the Lord Chancellor and Speaker in the Lords and Commons respectively).

(c) *Dissolution of Parliament.* This refers to the ending of a Parliament. It no longer requires any personal participation by the Queen, nevertheless, dissolution is a royal prerogative, exercised constitutionally by the Crown. It occurs automatically at the end of the five-year period laid down in section 7 of the Parliament Act 1911. If Parliament is to be dissolved sooner than this, it is done, by convention, at the request of the PM.

(d) *Summoning of Parliament.* A new Parliament is 'summoned' by the Queen, by means of writs of summons. In the case of peers, these are sent directly; in the case of MPs, writs of summons are issued to the returning officers, requiring them to return one member from each of the parliamentary constituencies (*see* 6: 14).

Upon the summoning of a new Parliament, each House assembles and, in the case of the Commons, appoints for itself a Speaker. This is done by election, although ordinarily, it is uncontested, the custom being that the post of Speaker rotates between the two major parties. The current Speaker is the first female one, Betty Boothroyd.

(e) One further prerogative in relation to parliamentary proceedings is the royal assent to bills: this is discussed below.

2. Parliament's main functions

The UK Parliament is, of course, the legislature. In the British (Westminster) model of parliamentary democracy, parliament exercises four functions, of which legislation is but one:

(1) General debate on issues of importance;
(2) Legislation;
(3) The scrutiny of the administration; and
(4) The control of national finance.

In connection with all of these, both Houses play a role, although not necessarily an equal one. The relationship between the two Houses, and the consequences of disagreement between them, are discussed at **13–14**, below.

Debate

3. Debate

Parliament remains a most important debating forum, where issues of importance can be discussed fully, without fear of recrimination (due partly to the protection afforded by parliamentary privilege). Not all debates in Parliament give rise to legislation: as well as the conduct of the government of the day (*see* **18–21**, below) such matters as foreign affairs, the conduct of the Church of England and even that of the media (amongst other matters) are not infrequently debated in Parliament.

4. Rules of debate

In each House, the rules of debate are essentially those of a typical debating society (for which Parliament is the model). The rules are designed to ensure orderly discussion, but also that the views of all parties, and not just the major ones, are aired. Briefly, debate proceeds as follows.

(a) *The motion.* All parliamentary debates begin with a motion. In general debate, this might take the form of a censure or other expression of view (as in 'This House deplores the conduct of . . .'). With regard to legislation, it may be that 'the bill be read for a second time'. (The detailed procedure on legislation is dealt with below.)

(b) *Detailed rules.* Debate on the motion is a matter of detailed rules. For example an MP wishing to speak must be invited to do so by the Speaker: in order to be so invited, he must 'catch the Speaker's eye'. Members are not referred to by name (a member refers to another MP as 'the Honourable Member', or, in the case of a Privy Councillor 'the Right Honourable Member') except by the Speaker. Members may speak only once in a debate, except to clarify points raised, and must do so through the Chair (i.e. comments must be addressed to the Speaker). The Speaker will call alternately on members who support the motion and who oppose it. Proceedings are somewhat similar in the Lords, except that the Chancellor does not exert the same controlling function as the Speaker of the House of Commons. The Lords are, as it were, self-regulatory, and a peer will address the House itself, as 'My Lords'.

(c) *The question.* At the end of a debate, the Speaker (or Chancellor in the Lords) 'puts the question'. This precipitates a vote on the original motion. In the Commons, a disputed motion is voted on by means of a division. Members divide into lobbies, according to whether they are voting for or against the motion, where they are counted. In the Lords, divisions are not normal, and peers express themselves as being either 'content' (i.e. in favour of the motion) or 'not content' (i.e. opposed to it).

(d) *The agenda.* The agenda for parliamentary debate is agreed in advance, with time being allocated both to the government and opposition (but favouring the government). In the Commons, these arrangements are made by the PM, the Leader of the Opposition, Leader of the House, and the Speaker.

Exceptionally, a member may introduce debate on an unscheduled topic, by way of an adjournment motion. On such a motion, the Speaker may, with the agreement of the House, permit debate on the matter at the commencement of the following day's business.

(e) *Members' interests.* There is no rule that MPs (unlike ministers) are prohibited from having 'outside interests' (such as investments, directorships in companies, etc.). However, if such an outside interest impinges on the matter under debate, a Member should declare his interest when speaking, and should not vote in the matter. The *Register of Members' Interests*, published every year, is kept wherein MPs can publicly declare their interests; it is not, however, obligatory for members to be entered in the *Register*, and several are not.

5. Order and time in debate

Whilst the Lords are largely self-regulatory, as far as order in debate is concerned, the Commons rely on the controlling function of the Speaker. It is undeniable that debate in the Commons is more adversarial in nature (largely due to the fact that the PM and most of the government ministers are members of the Commons), and the need for such a controlling influence is greater there than in the Lords.

(a) *Order.* By custom, and under the Standing Orders of the House, the Speaker has specific power to enforce the rules of the House in connection with debate. Thus, if an MP breaks any of the rules, or repeatedly makes offensive remarks, he is 'named' by the Speaker, and the House invited to consider a motion to punish him. This punishment normally takes the form of suspension.

(b) *Time.* To ensure that a debate does not go on for too long, several measures are available to the House:

(*i*) *The closure.* This involves a motion, put by an MP to the Speaker, that 'the question be now put' (i.e. debate ended and a vote taken). The closure motion must itself be voted on by the House, and at least 100 MPs must support it for it to take effect. The Speaker is not obliged to put a closure to the House, however, and should not do so if, for instance, it appears to be being used in a deliberate attempt to suppress open debate.

(*ii*) *The guillotine.* This is a motion, put and voted on at the beginning of a debate, that a specified period of time, and no more, be devoted to the debate in question. The guillotine applies only to debate in a bill, and must be put by a minister.

(*iii*) *The kangaroo.* This quaintly named device also applies to debates on bills. It amounts to a motion that only selected parts of a bill are debated, rather than the entire contents. The kangaroo applies only to the committee stage of a bill (*see* 11(d), below): Like the other motions, however, it must be agreed in advance by the House, and implemented by the Speaker.

6. The sources of rules of procedure

Parliament (and the House of Commons in particular) employs a vast number of rules relating to procedure and debate. These rules derive from a number of sources.

(a) *Practice and usage.* These are the oldest, customary rules. They remain the most numerous and important of parliamentary rules: the rules governing the readings of bills, for example, are of this kind.

(b) *Standing Orders.* Each House has its own Standing Orders. These are rules which are agreed by the House by resolution. They are less numerous than practices and usages, but increasingly important nowadays.

(c) *Precedents.* These are rulings by the Speaker on points referred to him for decision.

(d) *Statutes.* Somewhat surprisingly, these are not a major source of rules of procedure in Parliament. Unlike other rules, statutory rules are passed by, and apply to, both Houses of Parliament.

The most important factor to bear in mind concerning the detailed rules of parliamentary procedure is that, with the exception of statutory rules, such rules are the concern of each House itself. Each House is, by virtue of parliamentary privilege, the master of its own proceedings and it is up to each House to enforce its own rules (*see* 8 for a detailed discussion of parliamentary privilege).

Legislation

7. Legislation

This refers to the process whereby laws are enacted. It is also sometimes used to refer to enacted law generally, or to the body of enacted law on a particular topic (e.g. road traffic legislation). Legislation in the UK is effected ('passed') by the Queen in Parliament in accordance with the doctrine of parliamentary sovereignty (*see* 4). No other body can legislate as such. However, Parliament is not the only body with the capacity to make laws which can be enforced in a court of law. In particular, EC law is now enforceable in British courts. We also speak of 'delegated' or 'subordinate' legislation. Powers of delegated legislation are enjoyed by executive bodies (such as ministers and local councils). Such powers, however, are normally given to the bodies concerned, by Parliament (hence 'delegated'). Unlike Acts of Parliament, delegated legislation can be challenged in a court of law.

The fact that it is the Queen in Parliament who legislates is constitutionally very significant, for the following reasons:

(1) The royal assent is a necessary part of the legislative process; and

(2) It serves to remind us that, in the British model, government ministers (the Crown) who are, constitutionally, advisors to the Queen, are by convention Members of Parliament. The UK has no strict separation of powers; accordingly, it is not wholly accurate to speak of Parliament as the legislature without regard to this fact.

8.   The legislative process

Like any other items on the parliamentary agenda, a bill is subject to debate, and to that extent the normal procedures (discussed in 3–6, above) apply.

However, the passage of a bill through Parliament is the subject of certain particular procedures, not applicable to other matters. The main features (or stages) in the legislative process are as follows:

(1) Introduction of the bill;

(2) Readings;

(3) Committee and report stages; and

(4) The royal assent.

In general, the above apply in both Houses. If a bill is introduced in the Commons, then, having passed all of the above stages in that House, it is presented to the Lords to undergo similar stages there. It is quite possible for a bill (but not one involving financial measures) to be introduced in the Lords, in which case it is presented to the Commons having been passed by the Lords. In either case, both Houses must have had an opportunity to debate a bill (and, subject to the exceptions discussed at 14, below) will have passed it before the bill is presented for the royal assent.

9.   Bills

A bill is a parliamentary measure, which, on receiving the royal assent, becomes an Act of Parliament. There are two different categories of bills (and corresponding Acts): public and private.

(a) *Public bills.* These are measures of general public concern, normally applicable throughout the country (though sometimes separate measures are passed with respect to Scotland and

Northern Ireland). Public bills are themselves of two kinds, depending upon by whom they are introduced in Parliament.

(*i*) *Government bills.* A Government bill is one which is introduced by a government minister, normally that minister responsible for the area or topic concerned (e.g. measures affecting education are normally introduced by the Secretary of State for Education: the budget proposals or finance bill by the Chancellor of the Exchequer). These are the most numerous of public bills and have priority in terms of parliamentary time.

(*ii*) *Private members' bills.* These are public bills which are introduced by MPs who are not ministers. Such an MP may be a government supporter (i.e. member of the governing party) or member of the opposition. The chances of a private member's bill actually becoming law are slight, since a limited amount of time (Fridays in each session) is allocated for debate on private members' bills. To secure time for debate on his bill, a private member must succeed in a ballot, which occurs each session. Furthermore, if the bill is not passed by the House by the end of the session, it 'dies', and cannot be debated in the new session (unless, of course, the member succeeds again in the new ballot and re-introduces it).

(b) *Private bills.* A private bill is one which affects a limited class of people, or is confined in its scope to a particular area, e.g. the Liverpool Corporation Act. Such bills are introduced by the persons concerned or by a representative group which seeks to promote the objects of the bill.

10. Sponsorship of bills

A bill is sponsored by the person or body introducing it. It is the responsibility of that person or body to draft and publish the bill. This can be costly, and is another reason why private members' bills are less likely to become law than government bills. The government has public funds at its disposal, as well as a team of professional draftsmen, known as parliamentary counsel to the Treasury.

However, if the government is sympathetic to a private member's bill, it might make its resources available to the member: if such a private member's bill seems endangered by lack of time, the government may even allocate some of the time allocated to debate on government bills ('government time') to it, thus adopting the bill so as to ensure its success.

11. Procedure on public bills

The procedure adopted for the passage of legislation is broadly the same in both Houses. The following are the main stages as applied in the Commons:

(a) *Introduction of a bill.* The bill is formally presented to the House by the person (either a minister or member) introducing it.

(b) *First reading.* This is also a formality. It amounts to notice of the title of the bill.

(c) *Second reading.* This is the first really significant stage: the member who introduced the bill moves that it be read for a second time. If the bill is acceptable to the House as it stands, it then receives its second reading, and moves on to the next stage. If it is not, however, it is set down for debate at one of the times allocated for discussion of opposed bills. Most bills are, in practice, opposed. A few bills, particularly those designed to deal with emergencies or similar crises, or upon which a consensus exists, are not.

An opposed bill is subject to debate, before a vote is taken on the second reading. The vote must be favourable if the bill is to proceed to the next stage.

(d) *The committee stage.* Once a bill has undergone its second reading, it is referred to a standing committee (i.e. a permanent committee of the House, established for the purpose) to consider its contents in detail. The committee scrutinises the bill clause by clause, proposing amendments (including ones of both form and substance) as it sees fit.

(e) *The report stage.* The committee reports to the House. This involves a consideration of the bill, as amended in committee. Each amendment should normally be considered by the House, who may agree further amendments.

(f) *Third reading.* Finally, a bill is 'read' for a third time: in giving it its third reading, the House passes the bill, which is then sent to the House of Lords for its consideration.

12. The role of the Lords

As previously noted, bills (with the exception of money bills, i.e. financial measures) may be introduced in the Lords. In practice, however, the role of the Lords in relation to legislation tends to be somewhat circumscribed.

(a) *Initiation of bills.* In theory, any bill (other than a money bill) may be introduced in the Lords. In practice, however, the sorts of bills which originate in the Lords are as follows:

(*i*) Bills for which parliamentary time cannot be found in the Commons, and which are non-controversial (i.e. do not involve constitutional issues, such as electoral matters);

(*ii*) Bills involving the administration of justice (due to the presence in the Lords of the Lord Chancellor) or law reform (because of the Law Lords there);

(*iii*) Private members' bills. There is rather more scope for peers to introduce private members' bills than MPs. Additionally, private members' bills introduced in the Commons sometimes receive much more attention in the Lords.

(b) *Amending of bills.* It is not uncommon for insufficient time to be spent on a bill in the Commons, with the result that further amendments may occur in the Lords: these are not necessarily hostile to the bill, and may even be proposed there by a government minister, so as to improve or complete the eventual Act. (In recent years, it is as a 'reforming chamber' that the Lords has become best known.) If the Lords do make amendments to a bill, these must be considered by the Commons, who may accept or reject them (*see* 13, below).

(c) *Delaying of bills.* Since the Parliament Acts 1911 and 1949, the Lords has lost its power to veto a bill passed by the Commons. It can, however, delay the passage of a bill (this is dealt with more fully at 14, below).

In addition, the House of Lords retains a significant role in relation to delegated legislation, which must normally be approved by both Houses. Whilst the Lords does not enjoy such a significant role as the Commons in connection with government accountability (*see* 18–22, below), it does fulfil certain other functions, such as its judicial ones.

13. Commons and Lords in disagreement

It is an important convention of the Constitution that the Lords must yield to the will of the Commons, since the latter is the democratically elected chamber. Thus, a bill, having been considered by the Lords, must be returned to the Commons, where the Lords' amendments must be considered. If the Commons approve of the Lords' amendment, all well and good. If not, then there is only a limited amount which the Lords can do since, if it rejects the Lords' amendments, the Commons can ensure, by invoking (or threatening to invoke) the provisions of the Parliament Acts 1911–49, that the bill becomes law, subject only to the delaying power of the Lords.

14. The Parliament Acts 1911–49

In 1909, the House of Lords, contrary to established convention, refused to pass government measures which had been passed by the Commons. Accordingly, the government introduced in the Commons a further measure, the Parliament bill, and under threat of being swamped by newly created peers sympathetic to the government, the Lords passed this bill which, on receiving the royal assent, became the Parliament Act 1911.

(a) *The Parliament Act 1911.* Section 1 provides as follows:

(*i*) If a money bill having been passed by the Commons is sent to the Lords at least one month before the end of the parliamentary session is not passed unamended by the Lords within one month, the bill shall be presented for the royal assent and become an Act of Parliament notwithstanding the fact that it was not passed by the Lords. (A money bill is defined as a public bill certified as a money bill by the Speaker of the House of commons.)

(*ii*) If a public bill, other than a money bill or one to extend the maximum duration of a Parliament beyond five years, has been passed by the Commons in three successive sessions, and having been sent to the Lords at least one month before the end of each session, is rejected by the Lords each time, the bill may be presented for the royal assent, and become an Act of Parliament notwithstanding the fact that the bill was not passed by the Lords. (The five-year maximum life of a Parliament was fixed by section 7 of the 1911 Act.)

(b) *The Parliament Act 1949.* This Act remains controversial, not least because it was passed by the Commons using the procedure established in the 1911 Act (i.e. it was not passed by the Lords). The Act amended the 1911 legislation by further reducing the powers of the Lords in relation to public bills (other than money bills and attempts to prolong the life of Parliament, which are excluded). Section 3 of the 1949 Act provides that if any public bill (other than those mentioned above) is passed by the Commons in two successive sessions, and having been sent to the Lords at least one month before the end of each of those sessions, is rejected by the Lords, the bill shall, on the second rejection, be presented to the sovereign for the royal assent, and thereby become an Act of Parliament without having been passed by the Lords.

It was the Parliament Acts 1911–49 which reduced the Lords to the status of a 'delaying' chamber. Under these Acts, it is possible for an Act of Parliament to be enacted having been passed by the Commons alone. A recent example of this was the War Crimes Act 1991, where the Commons invoked the Parliament Act to secure the enactment of a bill which was rejected by the Lords.

15. Can the House of Lords be abolished?

The preamble to the Parliament Act 1911 contains a recitation to the effect that it was intended to replace the existing House of Lords (which at that time was based virtually exclusively on heredity), with a representative chamber of some sort. Since then the House of Lords has been reformed by the introduction of life peers and the admission of peeresses (Life Peerages Act 1958; Peerage Act 1983: *see* 6: 4–6).

Nevertheless, the preamble raises the possibility of the abolition of the House. In fact, there are two questions here:

(a) *Abolition by a normal Act of Parliament.* Clearly, if such a bill were passed by both Houses, it would, on receiving the royal assent, bring about the abolition of the House of Lords (such a thing has occurred in other countries, such as Australia, which changed from a bicameral to a single chamber Parliament some time ago).

(b) *Abolition by an 'Act' passed by the Commons alone, in accordance with the Parliament Acts 1911–49.* There is some dispute as to whether this would be possible. One view (held by Hood Phillips) is that only certain powers were granted to the Commons and sovereign by the 1911 Act. On the other hand, it can be argued that, applying normal principles of statutory interpretation to section 2 of the 1911 Act (which was passed by both Commons and Lords) the only exception to the powers of the Commons to legislate without the Lords' agreement is an attempt to prolong the life of Parliament.

16. The royal assent

It is only on receiving the royal assent that a bill which has been passed by both Houses of Parliament (or the Commons alone, if the provisions of the Parliament Act are invoked) becomes law. The royal assent is, in other words, an essential stage in the legislation process, and is constitutionally necessary.

The royal assent is nowadays given by means of 'letters patent', sealed with the Great Seal and signed by the sovereign: Royal Assent Act 1967. Traditionally, it was announced by the sovereign personally, in Parliament. This seldom occurs nowadays, and such notification is either made by Commissioners, in the Lords with the Commons in attendance, or by the Speaker and Chancellor in the Commons and Lords respectively. The royal assent falls within the scope of the royal prerogative. In legal theory, therefore, it could be refused by the sovereign. By convention, however, it is never refused; the last time a monarch refused to give the royal assent to a bill was in 1707, when Queen Anne did so. The theoretical possibility of refusal, however, gives rise to the same question as that which arises in connection with the House of Lords, namely, could the sovereign veto a bill, passed by both Houses of Parliament, for the abolition of the monarchy? The short answer is probably not, since refusal in any case is itself unconstitutional. There are those, however, who believe that such a radical change in the nature of the Constitution could only occur in practice if a sufficient number of the people supported it. In any case, the co-operation of the judiciary, in applying such a law, would be necessary.

17. Procedure on private bills

It has already been mentioned that private bills are introduced to Parliament by their sponsors. Whilst a private bill is subject to the same stages as a public bill (three readings, etc.), in practice, little time is given over for debate on a private bill by the House as a whole, and much of the work on private bills (discussion, amendment, etc.) takes place in committee. Such a bill must be read three times in the normal way, however.

An interesting variant, sometimes adopted, is the 'hybrid' bill. This is one which has elements of both public and private bills, in that it may involve matters of public concern, but is nevertheless sponsored by a private person or body, and dealt with largely in committee. A recent example of such a bill is the Channel Tunnel bill, sponsored by the consortium of companies which had successfully tendered for the contract to build the Channel Tunnel. Such a bill is sometimes used (as with the Channel Tunnel bill) to avoid the need for a large-scale public inquiry, which developments of this kind would normally require if they were to proceed under existing powers. With such a bill, the inquiry can take place within Parliament, making it cheaper and speedier.

The scrutiny of the administration

18. The scrutiny of the administration

This refers to the means whereby the government of the day is made accountable to Parliament, and to the House of Commons in particular. It is also the practical machinery whereby the important constitutional conventions of ministerial responsibility are put into effect. As such, this aspect of Parliament's work is central to our notion of Parliamentary democracy: indeed, some commentators regard this as the most important of all of Parliament's (and especially the House of Commons') functions.

There are three broad ways in which the government (the administration) is kept under scrutiny by the House of Commons (and to a lesser extent by the Lords):

(1) Questions;
(2) The raising of issues for debate; and
(3) The committee system.

These are dealt with separately below.

19. Questions

It is a feature of parliamentary procedure that questions may be addressed to ministers, either orally or in writing.

(a) *Oral questions.* About an hour of each day (except Fridays) is set aside by the House for the purpose of ministerial questions. Ministers attend according to a pre-arranged rota, so that questions concerning their areas of responsibility can be asked. (On Tuesdays and Thursdays, the prime minister is the subject of such questions.) Whilst questions are addressed orally, written notice must be given, so that a minister will have had time to prepare his answer: however, an MP can follow up a minister's answer to his original question with a supplementary question, which need not be notified and which might, therefore, catch the minister unawares. Such a device has, for obvious reasons, become extremely popular in recent years. If the MP is willing, the minister may respond to an oral question with a written answer: he may even refuse to answer a question altogether, usually on the grounds of public policy.

(b) *Written questions.* An MP may address a question to a minister at any time, provided it concerns his area of responsibility. This method is often used by MPs to convey grievances referred to them by constituents.

20. Raising of issues

As mentioned at **4**, above, the agenda for debate in the House is arranged by the Speaker, prime minister, Leader of the House, and Leader of the Opposition, with parliamentary time being allocated to both government and opposition jointly in proportion to size. Clearly, the opposition will take the opportunity to use much of their time in debate to scrutinise or criticise the conduct of the government. A particular example of this is the confidence motion (i.e. a motion, put by the opposition, that 'This House has no confidence in the government'). It was on losing such a motion that the Callaghan government fell in 1979. There is a limited amount of scope for an individual MP to raise issues in debate; in particular, he can employ the 'adjournment debate' (*see* **5**, above), to have matters relating to the conduct of the government debated, and therefore scrutinised, in the House.

21. The committee system

The system of parliamentary committees is used for a variety of functions, and not just for the scrutiny of the administration. However, that is one of the most important functions of the committee system. The most important Commons committees which are concerned with this particular task are the Select Committees assigned to particular government departments or other areas of activity. They include the Committee of Public Accounts (an old-established Commons committee), and the 14 select committees established in 1979, largely at the instigation of the then Leader of the House, Norman St John Stevas (now Lord St John of Fawsley).

These are departmental committees, i.e. each committee keeps the conduct of a particular government department under scrutiny, and reports to the House at regular intervals. Thus, there are committees concerned with home affairs, defence, trade and industry, and education (amongst others). Such committees are called 'select' because their members are selected personally, rather than on the basis of party affiliation. These committees are also known as standing committees, i.e. they are permanent committees, which do not vary with the government of the day, nor are they *ad hoc* committees (i.e. set up to deal with a particular topical issue, and disbanded afterwards).

As well as the committees discussed above, there are also a number of important committees concerned with other matters. For instance, the House has a number of standing committees for the scrutiny of bills (the committee stage: see **11**, above). As mentioned, an *ad hoc* committee may be set up to consider a matter of urgency, and occasionally, a joint committee (of both Houses) is employed to consider matters of interest to both Houses (e.g. constitutional reforms).

22. The authority of the select committees

Each select committee is authorised to 'examine the expenditure, administration and policy' of the department concerned: Commons Standing Order No. 130, 1979. As a committee of the Commons, it enjoys by way of delegation many of the powers of the House itself; these include the power to require persons to attend the committee's deliberations, and to have documents and other materials produced for scrutiny. (This is an aspect of the House's historical role as part of the High Court of Parliament (*see* **28**, below).

It is a moot point whether a committee can actually compel a person summoned to appear before it to answer questions under threat of contempt (*see* 8: **12**) in the same way that a court of law can compel a witness to answer.

Control of national finance

23. General

Obviously, the work of government requires the raising and spending of vast sums of money. Such sums as are required come from a variety of sources: these include hereditary income from Crown estates, income from nationalised industry and utilities and, of course, taxation (by far the largest source of governmental income). Nowadays, all such income is subject to parliamentary control and scrutiny. All money raised from the above sources is pooled in what is known as the Consolidated Fund; it is the responsibility of the Exchequer (headed by the Chancellor of the Exchequer) to administer the fund, subject to Parliament's approval and authorisation.

24. Taxation

There are many different kinds of taxation by means of which the government can raise money. The fundamental principle (established in *R* v. *Handen* (1637) case of Ship Money) is that the Crown may not impose any form of taxation ('charge on the public') without Parliament's approval. Thus, for the imposition of any new source of tax or duty (e.g. import duties) an Act of Parliament is necessary.

In the case of certain taxes, a once and for all Act is all that is required (i.e. the tax or duty remains in force until the Act's repeal). For others, however, an annual Act is necessary. In particular, the annual rate of general income tax must be fixed each year by means of the Finance Act.

25. Public expenditure

Like taxation, every item of public expenditure must be authorised by Parliament. Once again, some such expenditure is authorised by permanent Acts (e.g. to authorise the salaries of ministers, judges and other Crown servants). An annual Act of Parliament, however, is required to authorise continued expenditure in other cases, e.g. the Armed Forces Act.

26. General principles

There are a number of general principles applicable to all kinds of charges on the public or upon public funds (i.e. to both taxation and public expenditure). These are set out below.

(a) Unless already authorised by Parliament, no such charge can be made without an Act of Parliament.

(b) A proposal that such a charge be introduced must be made by a government minister, in the House of Commons.

(c) The House of Lords has no power to veto or substantially amend such a proposal: section 1, Parliament Act 1911.

27. Further controls on national finance

As well as fundamental principles discussed in 24–26, above, the House of Commons employs a number of other means of controlling national finance. These are not that different from the scrutiny of the administration (after all, it is the government which is actually concerned with the raising and spending of public money), and include the committee system (in this case special select committees, such as the Commons Expenditure Committee) as well as parliamentary debate and the questioning of ministers (e.g. the budget debate each year). In addition, some special procedures and officials are utilised to keep all governmental proposals involving public expenditure under review. In particular, an official known as the Comptroller and Auditor General has the power to scrutinise government accounts so as to ensure that any expenditure is specifically authorised by Parliament.

The High Court of Parliament

28. Parliament as a court

It was stated at **3**, above that the historical origins of Parliament lie in the King's Council, also known as the King's Court. Until the thirteenth century no real distinction was drawn between that body's judicial functions and its other functions, including legislation.

In practice, of course, most of the judicial functions once exercised by the King's Court fell to the common law courts. However, Parliament is still vested with some residual functions of a judicial character, namely:

(a) *The appellate jurisdiction of the House of Lords.*
(b) *The application and enforcement by both Houses of Parliament of its privileges* (*see* 8: **12**).
(c) *Impeachment.* This is the power to try a person for a State offence, such as high treason (e.g. Guy Fawkes, for the so-called Gunpowder Plot in 1603). In practice, this power has become obsolete, not having been exercised since 1805, when Lord Melville, Treasurer to the Admiralty was impeached (but acquitted). Recommendations have been made for its abolition.

As well as the specific functions listed above, a consideration of Parliament as a court serves to remind us of some of the powers it exerts in connection with its more everyday functions. For instance, a committee of the House of Commons (such as a select committee, or *ad hoc* committee of inquiry) can require the attendance of individuals to answer questions, in much the same way as a court of law can summon witnesses (*see* **22**, above).

Progress test 7

1. Summarise those royal prerogatives which have a bearing on the meeting and procedures of Parliament, showing how these operate. (1)

2. Describe the procedures in the House of Commons applicable to: (a) debate generally; and (b) legislation. (3–5, 7–11)

3. What are the principal sources of those rules of procedure observed in Parliament? **(6)**

4. Outline the main functions and procedures of the Lords in relation to legislation. In the event that the Lords do not approve of a Bill which has been passed by the Commons, what steps are open: **(a)** to the Lords, to amend the Bill; and **(b)** to the Commons, to ensure that it becomes law. **(12–14)**

5. Would it be possible for the House of Lords to be abolished, contrary to its wishes? **(15)**

6. Describe the procedure whereby the Royal assent is given, and a Bill becomes law. Could the Royal assent be refused? **(16)**

7. Summarise the main features of Parliament's: **(a)** scrutiny of the administration; and **(b)** control of national finance. **(18–27)**

8. To what extent does Parliament remain a 'court', constitutionally? **(28)**

8

Parliamentary privilege

Privilege generally

1. Parliamentary privilege

According to Lord Kilmuir LC, a legal privilege is 'a private advantage in law enjoyed by a person or association which is not enjoyed by others' (*The Law of Parliamentary Privilege* 1959). Parliamentary privilege consists of such advantages: they are enjoyed by each of the two Houses of Parliament and, incidentally, by their members. As usual with legal advantages, they may take the form of rights, powers or immunities. As such we may speak of several distinct privileges, some of which are enjoyed by each House corporately and others by members individually. These are classified below.

2. Origins of privilege

The basis of all parliamentary privileges is the requirement that each House of Parliament may conduct its business without interference. Orginally, this was asserted by the King, so as to ensure that his advisers (the King's Council) were able to attend his court. As the two Houses of Parliament began to separate themselves from the sovereign, they came to assert this right, and developed further privileges of their own.

Parliamentary privileges may therefore be said to form part of the laws and customs of Parliament, which each House has evolved for itself to expedite its work. They are not the product of legislation or of judicial decisions, though both of these have had an affect upon particular privileges (*see* **14** below). As Coke C J stated in the early seventeenth century in his Institutes; 'Just as every court of Justice hath laws and customs for its direction, so the High Court of Parliament hath laws and customs.' Parliamentary privileges are amongst the most important of these.

Privileges of the Commons

3. Classification of privileges

In general, both Houses of Parliament enjoy similar privileges. However, these take very different forms, as a result of the different composition and nature of each House. Accordingly, the privileges of the House of Lords are treated separately (*see* 14, below). In each House, the overall purpose of privileges is the same, namely to enable the House to conduct its own business effectively and without interference from outside. These requirements are mirrored in the two-fold classification of privileges enjoyed by the House of Commons.

(a) *Privileges enjoyed by the House in its corporate capacity.* These relate to the House's capacity to conduct its business effectively. The most important are as follows:

(*i*) The right to regulate its composition;

(*ii*) The right to regulate its proceedings; and

(*iii*) Penal jurisdiction.

(b) *Privileges claimed by the Speaker at the commencement of each session for the benefit of members.* These 'ancient and undoubted' privileges include:

(*i*) Freedom of speech in debate; and

(*ii*) Freedom from arrest.

These are explained further below.

4. Composition of the House

Whilst the House of Commons enjoys the privilege of regulating its own composition, it must be remembered that this matter is largely one of statute law, so that such things as elections, qualifications of parliamentary candidates and the franchise are all provided for by statutes such as the Representation of the People Acts 1983 and 1985. The privilege in question is therefore a residual one. It takes several forms:

(a) The House may impose its own rules and requirements for members. Thus, in *Bradlaugh* v. *Gossett* (1884) it was held that it was lawful for the House to order that a member (Charles Bradlaugh, an atheist) should not be permitted to take the parliamentary oath, and therefore not be permitted to take his seat.

(b) The House enforces legal disqualifications upon members. Thus in 1960, when Mr Anthony Wedgwood Benn succeeded his father as Viscount Stansgate, the House declared his seat to be vacant, since as a peer, Mr Benn was now legally disqualified from sitting in the Commons (*see* 6:5). (In fact, Mr Benn renounced his peerage in accordance with the Peerage Act 1963 and, on being re-elected, was thereby enabled to sit in the Common later.)

(c) The House may expel a member whom it considers unfit to sit. This can arise in connection with (a) or (b) above, or otherwise: e.g. if a member is convicted of a criminal offence. Under the Representation of the People Act 1981, any member who is imprisoned for more than a year for a criminal offence is legally disqualified. An expelled member may seek re-election, however, as did John Wilkes on several occasions in the 1770s.

(d) When a seat falls vacant due to the death or retirement of a sitting member, it is up to the House to decide whether and when to fill that seat. This it does by means of a warrant, ordered by the Speaker, for the issue of a writ ordering that a by-election be held.

Historically, the House also resolved disputed elections; this is nowadays done by a special Election Court, consisting of two High Court judges: Representation of the People Act 1983.

5. Proceedings

It has already been noted that the courts will not inquire into the procedure whereby the House has passed a bill which subsequently, on receiving the royal assent, becomes an Act: *British Railways Board* v. *Pickin* (1974).

The general rule is that the internal proceedings of the House are no concern of the courts, and are a matter solely for the House itself. This rule has been applied even to matters not directly concerned with the immediate business of the House, provided they are regulated by procedures laid down by the House itself. Thus in *R* v. *Graham Campbell, ex p. Herbert* (1955), it was held that no legal proceedings could be brought in connection with the sale of intoxicating liquor in a Commons bar contrary to the Licensing Act 1910, since the running of the bar fell within the responsibility of a Committee of the House, subject to internal procedures, and was therefore privileged. Many of the rules whereby the business of the House is conducted fall within the scope of this privilege, though many have now been codified in the Standing Orders of the House. These may be, and sometimes are, changed by the House; the power to do so is itself a matter of privilege.

Freedom of speech in debate

6. Freedom of speech

This is undoubtedly the most important of all parliamentary privileges. It was enshrined in the Bill of Rights 1689, Article 9 of which says ' . . . freedom of speech in debate or proceedings in Parliament ought not to be impeached or questioned in any court or place outside Parilament'. It is clear that MPs should not be prevented from attending and participating in debates and in other activities vital to their work and to that of the House both as legislative chamber and deliberative assembly. In practice, this means that MPs enjoy complete immunity from outside interference, including proceedings in the courts, in respect of what they say in the course of debate or proceedings in parliament: *Wason* v. *Walter* (1868). This immunity is particularly important where the law of defamation is concerned, but it also applies to all civil and criminal proceedings, such as breach of the Official Secrets Act 1989.

Any attempt by a person or body outside Parliament to interfere with freedom of speech is regarded very seriously by the House, and may be treated as a breach of privilege (*see* 12, below).

7. Proceedings in Parliament

The privilege declared in the Bill of Rights is confined to debate or proceedings in Parliament. However, this phrase has never been comprehensively defined in law, or by the House itself.

(a) Conduct which has nothing to do with proceedings or debate is not privileged, and an individual concerned is not protected from judicial proceedings. In *Rivlin* v. *Bilainkin* (1953), a man distributed defamatory leaflets within the precincts of the House, contrary to a court order. It was held that the order could be enforced, since his conduct had nothing to do with proceedings in the House and was not, therefore, privileged.

(b) Much of the work of an MP is of necessity done outside Parliament. Clearly, not everything done by a member, even in his capacity as an MP, is privileged. For example, statements made in constituency meetings, though part of an MP's work, are probably not privileged. On the other hand, it has been held by the Privy Council that the offer of a bribe to an MP was a breach of privilege: *Attorney-General for Ceylon* v. *de Livera* (1963).

One of the leading cases involving the scope of proceedings in

Parliament was *In, re Parliamentary Privilege Act, (Strauss's case)* (1958). Strauss, an MP, had sent a letter to a minister (the Paymaster General) complaining about the conduct of a local electricity board. The Board began a libel action against Strauss, who raised the question of privilege. By a majority, the House decided that the MP's letter was not within the scope of proceedings in Parliament, and was therefore not privileged. (In the event no libel action was brought, since the minister held an inquiry into the Board's conduct.)

The question having been raised, however, it was finally ruled by the Speaker that a communication by an MP to a minister in response to a matter actually arising in a debate would be a 'proceeding in Parliament'. (Clearly, a written question addressed by an MP to a minister in such circumstances would also be.)

(See **15**, below, for discussion of other aspects of the *Strauss* case.)

(c) Even if a legal cause of action arises in respect of something which occurs outside Parliament, unconnected with proceedings therein, nothing said in the course of parliamentary debate can be used as evidence. In *Church of Scientology* v. *Johnson-Smith* (1972), P sought to establish that what D had said in a television interview was motivated by malice, in order to defeat the defence of fair comment which D claimed in libel proceedings brought by P. It was held that what D had said during a parliamentary debate could not be used as evidence of malice, being absolutely privileged and therefore not subject to question in a court of law.

This was followed in *Rost* v. *Edwards* (1990), where it was held that details of appointments to Commons committees could not be given in evidence. In *R* v. *Secretary of State for Trade, ex p. Anderson Strathclyde* (1983) it was held that comments made by a minister in the House could not be used to support an application for judicial review of his decision.

8. The Parliamentary Commissioner Act 1967

In establishing the office of Parliamentary Commissioner for Administration ('the ombudsman'), this Act provided that communications between an MP and the Commissioner and between the Commissioner and other parties involved in the course of an inquiry by the Commissioner are privileged. Such an inquiry must begin with a written complaint, made by a member of the public to the MP, concerning administration in one of the government departments or other bodies included in the

Commissioner's jurisdiction: section 10(5), Parliamentary Commissioner Act 1967.

9. Reporting and Broadcasting of Parliament

(a) *Reporting.* In *Stockdale* v. *Hansard* (1839) (*see* 15, below) it was held that reports of parliamentary proceedings, even though authorised by the House, were not the subject of parliamentary privilege. Accordingly, Parliament passed the Parliamentary Papers Act 1840, which provided that no judicial proceedings should be brought in respect of any reports or papers published by order of either House, or on its authority. (Unauthorised reports are not privileged, though at common law a defence of qualified privilege exists with respect to defamatory statements contained in such reports: *Wason* v. *Walter* (1868). *see* 10, below.)

(b) *Broadcasting.* Since 1976, both Houses have permitted radio broadcasts of their proceedings, and since 1986, the Lords have permitted television broadcasts. All of these have been placed on a permanent footing. In 1990, the Commons agreed to television broadcasting on an experimental, temporary basis; in all cases, the broadcasts are monitored by select committees. These broadcasts will, in all probability, be treated in the same way as unauthorised reports, so that as far as the broadcasting bodies are covered the common law defence of qualified privilege, which applies only in respect of defamatory statements, may arise (*see* 10, below). Statements made by Members themselves, of course, remain absolutely privileged.

10. Qualified privilege

As far as defamatory statements are concerned there is a common law defence known as qualified privilege. This defence is available in respect of a range of publications, and in some cases is somewhat similar to parliamentary privilege, in that it covers proceedings in Parliament and/or statements or communication made by Members.

The most important differences between qualified privilege and parliamentary privilege itself are as follows:

(*i*) Qualified privilege only protects a person in respect of defamatory statements, whereas parliamentary privilege protects him from all liability for any wrong, whether criminal or civil.

(*ii*) Unlike parliamentary privilege, where motive is irrelevant, qualified privilege is only available to the maker of a statement who acts honestly and without malice.

The most important situations in which qualified privilege arises are as follows:

(*i*) Fair and accurate reports of parliamentary proceedings. This was established in *Wason* v. *Walter* (1868). Where newspapers and broadcasting are concerned, this is now incorporated in section 7 of the Defamation Act 1952.

(*ii*) Fair and accurate reports of judicial proceedings. This, too, is in section 7 of the Defamation Act 1952. (The section also covers certain other bodies such as local councils.)

(*iii*) Statements made by a person under a legal, moral or social duty to a person having an interest in receiving them. This is capable of protecting some statements made by, or to, members of Parliament and other officials. In *Beech* v. *Freeson* (1971), it was held that, where an MP wrote to the Law Society and to the Lord Chancellor furthering a complaint made to him by a constituent, the occasion was covered by qualified privilege, since he had a moral or social duty to further the letter to the proper authorities.

(*iv*) Where the maker and receiver of a defamatory statement have a common interest in the subject of the statement.

(*v*) Statements made to the proper authorities for the purpose of redressing a grievance. For the privilege to apply, it must be addressed to the appropriate person. However, a letter of complaint to an MP will clearly be an appropriate way in which to initiate the process since the MP has an interest in hearing his constituents' complaints and is well placed to further them to the appropriate authority. The MP's communication with that authority will itself be subject to qualified privilege: *R* v. *Rule* (1937).

Freedom from arrest

11. Freedom from arrest

In accordance with the fundamental requirement that members should be free to attend at the House (*see* **2, 8**, above), the House claims for its Members the privilege of freedom from arrest. Nowadays, however, this is confined to arrest in civil matters (which is in any case a rarity) for, since the Parliamentary Privilege Act 1770, Members' immunity from criminal proceedings (including arrest) has been removed. However, the House itself is privileged and the authorities would therefore not actually enter the House to arrest a Member there.

'Civil' arrest nowadays seldom occurs, since arrest and imprisonment for debt have been abolished. It might arise, where a judgment debt is not paid or a court order disobeyed, as part of the enforcement procedure. Members enjoy immunity from civil arrest only during a parliamentary session and for forty days before and after it (unlike peers, who enjoy this privilege continuously). The leading case, where the privilege was claimed by a member who had failed to obey a maintenance order, was *Stourton* v. *Stourton* (1963). (This case in fact involved a peer.)

Penal jurisdiction

12. Penal jurisdiction

As the High Court of Parliament (*see* 7:28), the House has the jurisdiction to enforce its own rules, including its privileges. In practice, this takes two forms: breach of privilege and contempt.

(a) *Breach of privilege.* This amounts to an infringement or interference with an established privilege. For instance, where a member of the public attempts to interfere with a member's freedom of speech in debate by initiating legal proceedings against him (e.g. *Strauss's case: see* 7, above).

(b) *Contempt.* Just like a court of law, the House can punish persons (whether members or 'strangers') whose conduct, whilst not necessarily interfering with an established privilege, amounts to 'an offence against its authority or dignity' (Erskine May, *Parliamentary Practice*). The best-known cases are those of Allighan, in 1947; and Profumo in 1963. Allighan, an MP, wrote a newspaper article suggesting that MPs had divulged confidential information to journalists. Profumo, a minister, lied to the House when making a statement concerning a person relationship which gave rise to a possible security risk. Allighan was expelled; Profumo resigned.

The House also has the power to control members who abuse their privileges (e.g. by exploiting freedom of speech in debate to air personal grudges). Recently, the extent of the House's jurisdiction has been questioned. In particular, doubt has been expressed about the House's power to compel individuals to appear before it and answer quetions, under threat of committal for contempt if they refuse. It has been contended that this power, if it exists, should only be used against government ministers so as to hold them to account. It should not be used against private individuals, whom it is argued, enjoy the common law right to silence (for example, the Maxwell affair, 1992).

(c) *Penalties.* The House has a wide range of penalties at its disposal. These range from a reprimand or admonition, to expulsion (in a serious case, such as Allighan's). Historically, the House could imprison a person guilty of breach of privilege. If he was a stranger, this would be in one of Her Majesty's prisons; if he was a member, the Clock Tower ('Big Ben'). The last member to be so imprisoned was Charles Bradlaugh in 1881.

13. The Committee of Privileges

Although it is the House itself acting as the High Court of Parliament which decides questions of privilege, in practice the Committee of Privileges actually considers such questions and recommends appropriate punishments if breach of privilege or contempt has occurred. The House normally follows its recommendation (but *see* 15, below).

The Committee has fifteen members, including one of the law officers. It considers questions relating to privileges or allegations of contempt referred to it by the House on the Speaker's proposal. Any recommendation made by the Committee must be considered by the House: only the House can punish offenders. One of the reasons why a committee, rather than the House as a whole, is used to investigate alleged breaches of privilege is that traditionally such matters take priority over other matters in the day's proceedings. Use of a committee allows the House to observe this tradition whilst getting on with its business.

Privileges of the Lords

14. The privileges of the Lords

Generally, the Lords enjoy similar privileges to those enjoyed by the Commons. Due to the different nature and composition of the Lords, however, these sometimes take a different form.

(a) *Composition.* Like the Commons, the House of Lords has the power to determine its membership, subject to the law. In the Lords, this takes the form of deciding questions as to the validity of peerages or concerning disputed peerages (e.g. the *Wensleydale Peerage* case (1856)).

(b) *Proceedings.* The Lords determine their own procedures.

(c) *Freedom of speech and freedom from arrest.* Like MPs peers enjoy these privileges. In the case of freedom from civil arrest however, peers enjoy the privilege continuously (*see* 11, above).

(d) *Penal jurisdiction.* The Lords also has a penal jurisdiction, though in practice this is less frequently invoked than that of the Commons. The Lords retain the power to impose fines on guilty parties, unlike the Commons.

As well as the above, the House of Lords also enjoys several ancient powers which might be regarded as privileges:

(i) Since the Law Lords are amongst its members, it may request their advice on legal matters.

(ii) It may secure, by means of a warrant, the release of a peer who has been improperly arrested. (Prior to the Criminal Justice Act 1948, The House of Lords had the power to try peers for all criminal offences itself.)

Privileges and the courts

15. Privileges and the courts

Parliamentary privileges are the concern of each of the two Houses of Parliament exclusively. It is the House (either the Commons or the Lords) which enforces its own privileges, and not the courts of law.

Two propositions follow:

(a) The function of the courts, when a privilege is claimed, is to determine 'whether the privilege arises, and if so its scope and effect', *per* Scarman J in *Stourton. v Stourton* (1963). If the matter in question falls within the scope of a privilege, then the court has no jurisdiction. However, questions as to the law of the land, including Parliament's enactments (i.e. statutes) *are* questions for the courts of law to decide.

The relationship between questions of law and privilege can be seen in *Strauss's case* (*see* also 7 above). The Privy Council, in its capacity as a court of law, was asked by the House of Commons whether the Parliamentary Privileges Act 1770 (which provides that no person shall be prevented from bringing proceedings in the courts against a Member of Parliament by any claim of parliamentary privilege) prevented the House from treating a letter from an MP to a minister as privileged. The Privy Council ruled that the 1770 Act only applied to Members in their personal, private capacity – in other words it underlined the principle that it was the proceedings in Parliament which are privileged, and not the person making the statement. However, the PC declined to express a view as to whether the letter written by an MP (Mr Strauss) to a minister was covered by parliamentary privilege at all, since they had not actually been invited to do so. That question was put to the Committee of Privileges (*see* **13**, above) which decided that the issue of a writ for libel against Mr Strauss in respect of his letter was a breach of privilege. Unusually, on a free vote, the House resolved not to follow the advice of the Committee, ruling that the letter was not a matter of privilege.

(b) On the other hand, neither House can create new privileges, nor extend the scope of existing privileges, so as to oust the jurisdiction of the courts. This was established in *Stockdale* v *Hansard* (1839) (*see* **9**, above). The only way new privileges can be created is by Act of Parliament (e.g. the Parliamentary Papers Act 1840, and the Parliamentary Commissioner Act 1967). This, of course, involves both Houses, and also requires the royal assent (*see* **7:16**). Accordingly, such privileges, though they might confer immunities similar to parliamentary privileges, are not parliamentary privileges as such, and do fall within the jurisdiction of the courts of law to rule upon, being questions of law.

Progress test 8

1. Define parliamentary privileges. What are their historical origins? **(1–2)**

2. To what extent is it correct to say that the House of Commons enjoys the privilege of regulating its own composition? What forms does this privilege take? **(4)**

3. Discuss the following situations, indicating whether the MPs (and others) concerned are protected by the parliamentary privilege of freedom of speech in debate or proceedings in Parliament.

(a) Shifty, MP, agrees that if he is made chairman of Iron Products Limited (a private company), he will speak against the import of foreign steel in a debate in the House of Commons.
(b) Bloggs, who is not an MP, goes to the House and, from the Stranger's Gallery, interrupts a debate by shouting defamatory statements concerning a local councillor.
(c) White, MP, makes a speech in the House in which he admits distaste

for religious fundamentalists, and for members of the '21st century Church of the Brotherhood of Men', in particular. He later makes a rather more moderate speech on television. The organisers of the Church wish to sue for libel, and want to use his parliamentary speech as evidence of malice. **(6–7)**

4. Discuss the position of reporters and broadcasters of parliamentary proceedings in terms of parliamentary privilege. **(9)**

5. Outline the penal jurisdiction of each of the two Houses of Parliament. How is this jurisdiction exercised in practice? **(12–14)**

6. What is the function of the courts of law when confronted with a claim of parliamentary privilege? **(15)**

Part three

The individual

9

Civil liberties

General

1. Rights and duties

According to some theories of jurisprudence (legal philosophy), rights and duties are related, so that for every right (or power) there is a correlative duty. In constitutional terms, what this means is that rights are relative: one person's rights are not unlimited, since if they were, their exercise would inevitably come into conflict with some other person's rights. Thus, in any civilised society, one of the functions of the constitution is to ensure a balance of rights, interests and powers, so that the rights of one individual are weighed against those of another, and against those of the society as a whole. In practice, then, rights will be limited by law, For example, an individual's freedom of speech is not unlimited, and in the UK a person cannot lawfully commit libel or blasphemy, nor betray official secrets in the exercise of freedom of speech.

On the other hand, in modern democracies, it is accepted that the rights (or freedoms) of the individual should also be upheld as far as possible and, to that end, protected by the law. (There are broadly two ways of achieving this: *see* 2, below.) Regarding duties, it is also accepted that the individual is under specific duties with regard to the State, in return for its protection. First and foremost, he is under a duty to obey the law. Depending on the requirements of the country he lives in, he will also be under many other duties. For example, a person may (subject to limited exemptions) be under a duty to serve in the armed forces or fight for his country in time of war; to serve on a jury; or to assist in keeping the peace if called upon to do so. (All of these duties exist, or have in the past existed in the UK.) In some countries, such as Australia, eligible individuals are under a legal duty to vote in elections.

2. Protection of rights

It is generally accepted that at least some rights, usually the most basic ones, should be protected in some way or another, by the law. Broadly speaking, there are two ways of doing this:

(a) *A Bill of Rights.* In many countries (such as the USA) a Bill of Rights has been included in the (written) Constitution. This gives to those rights the same status as the Constitution itself: such rights therefore become fundamental and entrenched in the sense that they cannot be changed or removed except by a change in the Constitution itself. Thus, an Act passed by a state legislature, or even an Act of Congress, cannot remove or alter any of the rights enshrined in the American Bill of Rights.

Most countries nowadays have written constitutions including a Bill of Rights (though it may have some other title, such as Charter of Rights, etc.).

(b) *Remedies.* Another means of protecting individuals' rights is to provide a comprehensive system of remedies, so that if one person tries to prevent another from exercising his rights, he can go to the courts to have that person restrained or prosecuted, or to obtain damages by way of compensation.

In essence, this is what occurs in the UK, partly, of course, because the UK has no written constitution. This does not mean, of course, that countries, such as the USA, whose constitutions include a Bill of Rights, do not provide a system of remedies which come into play when an individual's right are infringed. Nor does it mean that a Bill of Rights could not be enacted in Britain: indeed, there have been several attempts over the years to do just that. The main difference lies in the fact that, in the UK, the rights of the individual have no special status and, just like any other principles or rules of law, they can be changed or even removed by a simple change in the law, particularly by Act of Parliament, but also (to some extent) by judicial decisions.

For this reason, it cannot be said that, in the UK, the individual enjoys any fundamental rights at all, unlike the USA. Indeed, some writers go so far as to say that, in the UK, we do not have rights but remedies, such is the emphasis on the latter in judicial proceedings. Perhaps a better way of describing the situation, however, is to say that in the UK there are no fundamental rights, but there are freedoms, or civil liberties. These freedoms are residual in nature, that is, they are what remain, at any given time, when the limitations imposed by the law have been taken into consideration.

3. A Bill of Rights

From what has been said in 1 and 2, above, one should not conclude that there has been little concern for the liberty of the individual in the UK. On the contrary, many of the rights which have been included in the written constitutions of other countries, such as the USA, were rights which, at common law, existed in the UK (though in the form of freedoms). Such rights were the particular concern of British thinkers such as Locke, Hobbes, and J.S. Mill.

The reason why the UK has no Bill of Rights is essentially that it has no written constitution (*see* 1). It is commonly felt that a Bill of Rights would be ineffective in the UK since, like any other rule of constitutional law, it could be changed or abolished, in accordance with the doctrine of parliamentary sovereignty. Not everyone agrees with this, however, and two eminent peers, Lord Wade (in 1976) and Lord Scarman, the former Law Lord (in 1988), have attempted to introduce a Bill of Rights. In both cases, this has been based on the European Convention on Human Rights and Fundamental Freedoms 1950, an international agreement to which the UK is a member.

(a) *The European Convention on Human Rights.* This Convention, to which virtually all European nations are signatories, sets out a number of fundamental human rights and freedoms which signatory states have agreed should be protected. These include the rights to life, free expression and association, and freedom from torture, discrimination and other treatment considered incompatible with fundamental freedoms. As an international Convention, it is not enforceable in British courts: however, an enforcement machinery exists, whereby a country in breach of its obligations can be taken to a court of human rights by another country involved in the Convention, or by a commission on human rights. Many cases have been brought against the UK, with the result that UK law has sometimes been changed by Parliament so as to comply with our human rights obligations.

(b) *Incorporating the Convention into English law.* Obviously, those (like Lords Wade and Scarman) who have advocated the incorporation of the European Convention into English law are well aware that, due to the doctrine of parliamentary sovereignty, it could be repealed, and cannot really be entrenched. However, it could (they agree) be made difficult to repeal by including a provision rather like section 2(4) of the European Communities Act (*see* 5:15) to the effect that both past and future legislation should be interpreted and take effect in the light of the provision of the Convention.

Quite apart from such practicalities, however, its proponents argue that there would be distinct advantages in incorporating the Convention into English law: in particular, it would enable British judges in British courts to decide human rights issues, rather than the European judges sitting in the European Court in Strasbourg.

Specific freedoms

4. Sources

In practice, the individual enjoys many freedoms under English law, and in the British Constitution. These freedoms, being residual in nature, derive from a variety of sources, in much the same way as other constitutional principles. Important freedoms derive from statute (e.g. freedom from discrimination on racial grounds: Race Relations Act 19760; the common law (personal liberty: *see* 10); and nowadays, European Community Law (e.g. Article 119, requiring member states to uphold the principle of equal pay: *see* 5). Many of the common law freedoms may also be described as customary in origin (e.g. the presumption that a person should be permitted the freedom to enjoy his property, as expressed, somewhat whimsically, in the saying 'an Englishman's home is his castle').

In addition to these, individuals in the UK enjoy a large number of social and economic freedoms (e.g. the right to vote; the right to medical treatment; and the right to education, etc.). These social and economic rights vary greatly according to governmental policy and the economic prosperity of the nation; they are usually the first to be affected, for instance, in time of recession or emergency. Furthermore, unlike the fundamental freedoms (the right to life, etc.) an individual is not born with such freedoms.

5. Freedoms and status

In this context, status refers to the nationality of the individual. In general, most of the freedoms available to the individual in the UK are enjoyed by him irrespective of status (*see* 13). Thus, individuals other than British citizens enjoy freedom of expression, personal liberty and freedom of association. Furthermore, such individuals may own property, make contracts, work, and invest money in the UK. There are, however, certain important exceptions to this:

(a) *Enemy aliens.* An enemy alien is the citizen of a country which is at war with the UK. An enemy alien enjoys no rights or freedoms under English law, and both his person and property are unprotected, so that he may be interned (imprisoned without trial) for the duration of the war, and his property forfeited to the Crown.

(b) *Civic rights.* These include the right to vote in parliamentary and local elections. This right may only be exercised by Commonwealth citizens and citizens of the Republic of Ireland (subject to the qualifications, including the residence requirement, discussed at 6:12). Aliens do not enjoy such rights.

Commonwealth citizens are British citizens of British Dependent Territories, such as Bermuda; British overseas citizens; and citizens of independent Commonwealth countries: British Nationality Act 1981.

(c) *Deportation.* Whilst aliens (including the citizens of independent Commonwealth countries) enjoy most of the normal freedoms while they are within British territory, it should be remembered that they do not have any automatic right to enter and remain in the UK at all. Such a right (known as the 'right of abode') is enjoyed only by British citizens and (under EC Law) EC citizens. This does not mean, of course, that aliens are not permitted to enter and even take up residence in the UK; however, such entry and residence is conditional. Under the Immigration Act 1971, provision was made for aliens to be refused leave to enter the UK if they failed to meet the requirements set down in special rules.

It also provides (section 3) that an alien may be deported where he fails to meet any conditions, including time limits, on his stay here, or where the Home Secretary deems his presence in the UK 'not conducive to the public good'. He may also be deported if he commits a criminal offence whilst here, or if any member of his family is deported. Although the matter of deportation is regulated by the Immigration Act 1971 (so that statutory procedures must be complied with) it has been held that the question, whether a person's presence is 'not conducive to the public good' is one for the Home Secretary alone, in his capacity as minister responsible for that aspect of national security. As such, it is part of the royal prerogative, and its exercise cannot be challenged on the grounds that, for instance, the Home Secretary fails to give reasons for his decision: *R* v. *Home Secretary, ex p. Hosenball* (1977). The fact that the deportee has resided in the UK for many years, and raised a family here, is irrelevant: *R* v. *Home Secretary, ex p. Cheblak* (1991).

British citizens cannot be deported, since they enjoy the legal right to enter and reside permanently in the UK, free of immigration control. A British citizen may, however, be extradited (i.e. sent to a foreign country to stand trial for an offence committed there): Extradition Acts 1870–35. Extradition will only be made to a country with which the UK has an extradition treaty; it should not be ordered if the offence concerned is political in character.

In one instance, the freedom of British citizens to enter the country (or at least travel from one part of it to another) may be limited. Under the Prevention of Terrorism Act 1989, Part II, the Home Secretary is empowered to make an order excluding an individual from Great Britain, or from Northern Ireland. Passed to help prevent the spread of terrorism between Northern Ireland and the mainland, this is a serious infringement of civil liberties, since it may well restrict a British citizen's freedom of movement.

6. Specific civil liberties

It is not possible here to give a comprehensive list of all of the civil liberties (or freedoms) enjoyed by the individual under the British Constitution, nor to discuss them fully. Two of the most fundamental (and therefore more important) civil liberties, namely, personal liberty and freedom of assembly, are discussed in 10 and 11.

What follows is a series of brief notes on some of the most important civil liberties, other than those two, which may be said to exist in English law.

Since these are residual in nature particular attention must be paid to the restrictions on them; it is often the restrictions which define the scope of the civil liberty or freedom concerned.

7. Freedom of expression

Unlike its equivalent in the USA (which is protected by the First Amendment), freedom of expression in the UK is circumscribed by many laws. These include:

(a) *Libel and slander.* A statement which tends to 'lower the plaintiff in the estimation of right-thinking members of society' is defamatory (*Sim* v. *Stretch* (1936)). The plaintiff may sue for libel (if the statement is published in 'permanent form') or slander if temporary.

(b) *The Official Secrets Acts 1920 and 1989.* These prohibit the publication and dissemination of many kinds of information (relating to security and intelligence, defence, the detection of crime, and international relations) by Crown servants or contractors, or which was obtained from Crown servants or contractors. Disclosure of such information by members or ex-members of the security services is an offence of strict liability. It is no defence to a charge under these acts that publication was in the public interest.

(c) *Obscene publications.* The Obscene Publications Act 1959 makes it an offence to publish material which 'tends to corrupt and deprave' readers or viewers: section 1. However (somewhat paradoxically) it is a defence under section 4 to show that publication is 'for the public good, on the ground that it is in the interests of science, literature, art or learning'.

(d) *Blasphemy.* Publication of material which vilifies Christ or the Christian faith may constitute the common law offence of blasphemous libel. Such publications have been said to have 'a supposed tendency to shake the fabric of society', which is in turn, 'based in the Christian faith': *per* Lord Sumner, *Bowman* v. *The Secular Society* (1917).

It is not necessary for the defendant to intend to blaspheme: it is sufficient if he intends to publish the offensive matter: *R* v. *Lemon* (1979). Nor is it an offence to vilify any other religion: only Christianity is protected by the law of blasphemy: *R* v. *Bow Street Magistrates Court, ex p. Chowdbury* (1990).

In addition to the above, freedom of expression and speech are circumscribed by particular Acts, such as the Public Order Act 1986 (*see* 11).

8. Freedom from discrimination

This has been an area of considerable development since the 1960s, when the first Race Relations Act was passed in an attempt to curb discrimination on racial grounds and to promote racial harmony. There are two fields in respect of which the law seeks to prevent discrimination:

(a) *Discrimination on grounds of race.* Section 1 of the Race Relations Act 1976 provides that discrimination on grounds of race (defined as race, colour, nationality or national or ethnic origin), whether direct or indirect, in respect of the areas covered by the Act, is unlawful. The areas covered include such things as employment, educational and training opportunities, and housing. To monitor the Act's application, a body called the Commission for Racial Equality was established. As well as the Race Relations Act, the Public Order Act 1986, Part III provides for a number of offences involving conduct which is intended to, or tends to, incite racial hatred.

(b) *Discrimination on grounds of sex.* The Sex Discrimination Act 1975 (and with it the Equal Pay Act 1970) makes broadly similar provisions to those in the Race Relations Act 1976, except here, of course, it is discrimination on grounds of sex which is prohibited. The 1970 Act seeks to address the problem of women being paid less than men for doing the same (or 'like') work as men. This problem is also addressed by Article 119 of the Treaty of Rome and, nowadays, most cases involving alleged unequal treatment of women in connection with employment matters involve claims under EC law, as well as British law. (*See* 5 for a discussion on EC law in relation to sexual discrimination and equal pay.) As with the Race Relations Act, a supervisory body, the Equal Opportunities Commission, was established under the 1975 Act.

In recent years, there has been much discussion of extending the protection of the law to other minority groups, thus extending the concept of freedom from discrimination so as to include discrimination on grounds of religion, political belief, and sexual proclivity. So far, however, such developments are merely subjects for debate and proposal, and it is only the two areas (race and sex) discussed above which are specifically protected by English law, in the sense that discrimination on grounds of race or sex are unlawful.

9. Other residual freedoms

As Sir Robert Megarry VC put it, 'England is not a country where everything is prohibited except what is expressly permitted. It is a country where everything is permitted except what is expressly prohibited.' (*Malone* v. *Metropolitan Police Commissioner* 1979.) What this means, in effect, is that in the UK the individual is free to do what he wishes, provided that in so doing, he does not break any law. Accordingly, it is impossible to enumerate those freedoms which are enjoyed by the individual in the UK, since they are, in theory anyway, too numerous. The civil liberties discussed above and in chapters 10 and 11, were selected either because they are fundamental (e.g. perusal liberty) or because the law specifically protects them (e.g. freedom from discrimination on racial grounds) or simply because of the large amount of law they generate such as freedom of assembly and personal liberty, where there are major relevant pieces of legislation.

Many other residual freedoms exist. Like all civil liberties, they are limited by law, but they are not, for the most part, specifically protected, and such protection as there is relies on the normal remedies provided by the common law. Thus, one may be said to enjoy freedom of worship, in that the individual may attend any place of religious worship, or subscribe to any faith or system of belief he wishes. Such a freedom is clearly not easy to specifically protect. On the other hand, a person interfering with another's freedom to attend a church, for instance, may be guilty of assault, trespass etc. Similarly, we enjoy freedom of association, freedom of political affiliation and freedom of labour (i.e. freedom to work for whom one chooses).

10. Privacy

The desirability of enacting a statutory right to privacy is an issue which has exercised politicians, academics and others for some years now, and has been the subject of more than one Royal Commission (e.g. the Younger Report in 1972). Whilst no such development has yet occurred, the debate has recently been fuelled by a number of revelations concerning the private lives of leading politicians, and even members of the Royal Family, in the Press and other media. In some cases, intimate photographs taken by concealed cameramen, who are often trespassing on private property, have also appeared, Two proposals have recently been made to deal with such conduct.

(a) *The enactment of a statutory right of privacy.* This would principally address the means whereby personal information was obtained so that, for example, it could be an offence to publish, or otherwise use, material obtained by means of trespassing, or by an unlawful telephone 'tap'. Whether such a law would apply only to the Press or generally, is a matter for debate: in general, a law which applies only to a particular group, and is not universal in its application, is viewed with some distaste.

(b) *The provision of a statutory regulatory body for the Press.* This was the proposal of the Commission of Inquiry into the Press which reported in 1991 (the Calcutt Report) and has re-convened in 1992. Following the 1991 report, the Press agreed to introduce a new self-regulatory body, the 'Press Complaints Commission', to deal with allegations of invasion of privacy by journalists where these could not be justified in the public interest. As a 'voluntary' body, however, the Commission is felt by many to be inadequate and there is a real possibility that the original Calcutt proposals will, in due course, be implemented, and a statutory body with real powers to enforce its code of conduct will be created.

Progress test 9

1. Indicate the two best-known ways of protecting the rights of the individual in a Constitution, highlighting the difference between them. **(1–2)**

2. What impact upon his freedom in English law does the status (in terms of nationality etc.) of the individual have? **(5)**

3. Discuss, in outline, the more important civil liberties enjoyed by the individual in the UK, indicating the chief limitations on such liberties. **(6–9)**

4. What is meant by the statement that civil liberties in Britain are 'residual' in nature? **(2, 9)**

10

Freedom of the person and property: the Police and Criminal Evidence Act 1984

Introductory

1. General

Freedom of the person – personal liberty – is probably the most fundamental of all those freedoms enjoyed under English law. Regarding freedom of property, it is said that 'an Englishman's home is his castle'. As is usual with such freedoms, however, both are residual in nature, and whilst they are protected in various ways by the law, neither is absolute, since invasions of both freedoms are permitted in certain circumstances. Powers to enter premises and to deprive an individual of his personal liberty are enjoyed by those responsible for the criminal justice system, and by the police in particular.

(a) *Protection.* In the UK, most individual liberties are protected somewhat indirectly. It is said that English law provides not rights but remedies. Thus, if I allege that a person has unlawfully entered my premises, I may seek a remedy in the courts by means of a common law action in trespass. Similarly, if I maintain that the police have arrested and detained me without due cause, I can take proceedings against them for false imprisonment, another common law claim in tort. These, and many others, are the traditional means whereby our freedom is protected, and they remain very important. In recent years, however, they have been supplemented by what may be regarded as ancillary safeguards, many of which are contained in the Police and Criminal Evidence Act 1984. Thus, for example, if the police conduct their interrogation of a suspect improperly, any evidence thereby obtained (particularly any confession made by that person) may be inadmissible as evidence in subsequent criminal proceedings against that individual.

(b) *Lawful invasion of liberty.* One's personal liberty and/or property might be lawfully infringed in a number of ways, many of which are now the subject of the Police and Criminal Evidence Act (known as PACE). Thus, for instance, the police are empowered to stop and search an individual or vehicle, to enter premises for the purpose of making a search or an arrest, and to arrest a person whom they reasonably suspect of a crime. (All of these, as well as the powers enjoyed by private citizens are dealt with in detail below.)

The point to bear in mind here, however, is that these powers apply to a person who has not, at the revelant time, been convicted by a court of any criminal offence. Obviously, a person may be deprived of his freedom (in the form of a custodial sentence) or property (in the form of a fine or loss of a driving licence) on actually being convicted. Nevertheless, the powers of search, seizure, arrest and detention enjoyed by the police must also be seen in the context of the criminal justice system: it is in order to secure a person or evidence, with a view to eventual criminal proceedings, that they arise.

2. The Police and Criminal Evidence Act 1984 (PACE)

This important piece of legislation is probably the most radical and comprehensive attempt yet made to codify, clarify and, where necessary, reform the law relating to powers of arrest, search and seizure, and to a wide variety of related matters, such as the treatment of persons detained for questioning by the police, admissibility of evidence in criminal proceedings, and complaints against the police.

The Act itself is divided into eleven parts, each dealing with a major topic. The Act also provides for Codes of Practice to be issued by the Home Secretary; these supplement the provisions of the Act itself by laying down detailed procedures for such matters as the detention, treatment and questioning of suspects (Code C) and the tape recording of interviews (Code E). Several of these procedures are at least as important as the provisions of the Act itself. Accordingly, reference will be made to the Codes at appropriate points in the discussion.

3. The Act and the existing law

Whilst much of the law relating to police powers of search and arrest, etc. is now contained in PACE this does not mean that all of the existing law was repealed when the Act received the royal assent. In some instances, existing laws were expressly retained; in others, they were included, unchanged, in PACE. Thus certain provisions in PACE replace old statutory ones, and others enact principles of common law. In some instances, therefore, case law prior to 1984 may still be regarded as good law. In the discussion that follows, an attempt will be made to indicate clearly how much of the law which existed before PACE has been retained, and how much has been changed.

Part I: powers to stop and search

4. Existing powers of stop and search

For many years, the law has recognised the need for the police to enjoy the power to stop and search persons whom they reasonably suspect of possessing certain items, such as firearms and illegal drugs. Accordingly, various statutes have conferred powers of stop and search upon the police. These include the Firearms Act 1968 and the Misuse of Drugs Act 1971. Such statutes are limited in scope, in that the powers which arise are only to search for the specific items in question (e.g. firearms or drugs). Generally speaking, such powers have been preserved by PACE. In addition to these, however, certain statutes conferred rather more general powers upon the police. These included the Vagrancy Act 1824 and various local Acts, promoted by local authorities and applicable only in the areas concerned (e.g. the Metropolitan Police Act 1839). These have been repealed by PACE, and replaced by a new power contained in section 1.

5. The new power

Under PACE there is now a general power on the part of a police constable (PC) to stop and search any person, or vehicle, or anything which is in or on a vehicle, for stolen or prohibited articles. For the purposes of such a search, the constable may detain a person or vehicle: section 1(2).

(a) *Stolen articles.* The word 'stolen' is not defined in PACE. It is likely, however, that the power of stop and search will arise in relation to items which have been stolen in the sense used in the Theft Act 1968: accordingly stolen articles will include articles obtained by burglary, deception or blackmail as well as those which have been stolen in the strict sense of the word.

(b) *'Prohibited articles'.* These are defined in section 1 of PACE. They are any offensive weapon (i.e. an article made or adapted for use in injuring someone or intended for that purpose); and any article made or adapted for use or intended for use in connection with any of the following, namely: burglary, theft, taking a motor vehicle without consent and obtaining property by deception: section 1(8), PACE.

6.   Limitations on the power to stop and search

The new power, summarised above, is subject to a number of limitations, and can only be exercised in certain circumstances.

(a) A constable cannot stop and search a person or vehicle unless he has reasonable grounds for suspecting that he will find stolen or prohibited articles as a result of his search: section 1(3).

(b) The power may only be exercised in a public place: section 1(1). Furthermore, where the power to stop and search in a public place arises, it is limited in that a constable cannot require that a person removed in public any of his clothing other than an outer coat, jacket or gloves: section 2(9). A person is not, for instance, obliged to remove his headwear in public. (Intimate searches, however, can be made at a police station, following an arrest.)

(c) A constable has the power to stop and search a person or vehicle in a garden or yard: section 1(2)(a). This power is limited, however, to persons other than the occupier of the garden or yard or the owner of any such vehicle.

7.   Requirements involved in stop and search

As well as limiting the power to stop and search by imposing on it certain conditions, PACE lays down certain requirements which must be observed by the constable exercising the power.

(a) *Giving of information.* At common law, a constable seeking to search a person was obliged to inform him, so far as possible, of the reasons for the search: this obligation arose also, of course, in connection with arrest: *Christie* v. *Leachinsky* (1947). PACE has given statutory effect to this requirement but has tightened up the relevant procedures so that a constable exercising the power to stop and search is under a duty to take reasonable steps to bring certain information to the attention of the person involved (i.e. the person searched or person in charge of the vehicle searched). This information includes evidence (if he is not in uniform) that he is a constable; his name and that of his station; the object of the proposed search; his grounds for proposing to make it; and the fact that the person searched is entitled to a copy of the 'search record', if any: sections 1, 2(2) and (3).

This information must be communicated before the search commences: section 2(2). If it is not, the search is unlawful. It should be noted that these requirements apply not only to the general power of stop and search created by section 1 of the 1984 Act, but also to all powers of search where no arrest is made: section 2(1). Therefore, for example, a constable wishing to search a person for drugs under the Misuse of Drugs Act 1971 (whose provisions are retained) is obliged to comply with this requirement.

(b) *Reasonable time.* Whilst detention for the purpose of making a search is authorised by the Act, this must be 'of such time as is reasonably required to permit a search to be carried out either at the place where the person or vehicle was first detained or elsewhere': section 2(8).

(c) *Record of search.* Unless it is not practicable for him to do so, a constable shall make a written record of any search carried out by him: section 3(1). This record should contain certain information; in particular, the object and grounds for making the search, the date, time and place at which it was made, and whether or not anything was found, or any damage or injury caused as a result of the search: section 3(6). The record should also contain the name of the person searched, or, if unknown, his description: section 2(3) and (4). The person searched is entitled to a copy of this record if he asks for it within 12 months: section 2(9).

8. Stop and search of vehicles

(a) PACE provides for the power to stop and search vehicles as well as persons. Generally the same conditions and requirements apply. However, certain of these are obviously inappropriate so that, for example, a constable does not have any duty to provide information where he proposes to search an unattended vehicle.

(b) Nothing in PACE extends the police power actually to stop a vehicle. This power can only be exercised by a uniformed constable: failure to stop when required to do so by a uniformed constable remains an offence under section 159 of the Road Traffic Act 1972.

(c) PACE expressly provides for road checks. A road check is subject to certain conditions:

(*i*) It must be authorised in writing by a police officer of the rank of superintendent or higher;

(*ii*) It must be instituted only for the purpose of ascertaining whether a vehicle is carrying a person who has committed a serious offence; a witness to such an offence; a person intending to commit such an offence; or a person unlawfully at large: section 4(1). An officer may only authorise a road check if he has reasonable grounds for believing that the person sought is, or is about to be, in the locality in which vehicles would be stopped by the road check: section 4(5).

(*iii*) Authorisation may not be for an indefinite period, and must not exceed seven days: section 4(11). The period may be extended, however, by a superintendent (or higher) for further periods of up to seven days, by means of written notice: section 4(12); and

(*iv*) Where a person is stopped by means of a road check the person in charge of the vehicle is entitled to a written statement of the purpose of the check. (If a search is made the same requirements as to searches generally apply.)

9. Repeals

PACE repeals the stop and search provisions of various earlier enactments: these include section 8 of the Vagrancy Act 1824; section 11 of the Canals (Offences) Act 1840; and section 19 of the Pedlars Act 1871; as well as various local Acts. The important powers contained in section 47 of the Firearms Act 1968; section 23 of the Misuse of Drugs Act 1971; and the Prevention of Terrorism (Temporary Provisions) Act 1984 (now 1989), are preserved.

Part II: powers of entry, search and seizure

10. Common law

At common, law, the only general powers of entry, search and seizure which existed could be summarised as follows:

(a) A constable could enter and search premises in order to make an arrest where he had reasonable grounds for believing that the person he wished to arrest was to be found in those premises. If necessary he could use reasonable force to effect entry in these circumstances: *Swales* v. *Cox* (1981).

(b) A constable could enter premises for the purpose of preventing a breach of the peace: *Thomas* v. *Sawkins* (1935).

(c) A constable could enter premises for the purpose of searching them under a search warrant. If found, items referred to in the warrant could be seized.

(d) Where a constable entered premises lawfully (pursuant to a warrant, or any of the other powers mentioned above) he could seize goods which he reasonably believed to be evidence of an offence, including one other than the offence under investigation: *Ghani* v. *Jones* (1970). Other than these, no general powers of entry, search and seizure existed at common law.

11. Statutory powers

Various statutes conferred specific powers of entry, search and seizure, not only upon police constables, but upon other officials, such as customs officers.

12. The 1984 Act

The effects of PACE are to strengthen and clarify police powers of entry, search and seizure. The Act provides specific safeguards, and deals expressly with the question of retention of seized goods, previously something of a problem. The main effects are summarised below.

13. Search warrants

Section 8(1) of PACE provides that, on an application made by a constable, a magistrate may, if he is satisfied that there are reasonable grounds for believing that a serious arrestable offence has been committed, and that articles specified in the application which are likely to be of substantial evidential value are on the premises, issue a warrant authorising a constable to enter and search the premises. A constable may seize anything for which a warrant has been issued: section 8(2).

14. Conditions

The power to apply for and act on a search warrant is a general one, applicable to all serious arrestable offences. However, certain conditions attach to it. These are set out in section 8(3). A warrant should only be issued in the following circumstances:

(a) It is not practicable to communicate with any person entitled to grant entry to the premises; or
(b) If it is, it is not practicable to communicate with any person entitled to grant access to the evidence; or
(c) Entry will not otherwise be granted; or
(d) The purpose of a search may be frustrated or seriously prejudiced otherwise.

15. Purpose of warrant

Notwithstanding the above conditions the new power is wider than anything that existed before. Prior to 1984, there was no general power to grant search warrants. Such a power arose under a variety of statutes, e.g. section 26 of the Theft Act 1968; section 23 of the Misuse of Drugs Act 1971; and section 23 of the Obscene Publications Act 1959. Accordingly, such powers were highly specific so that, for instance, a warrant to search for drugs could only be issued under the Misuse of Drugs Act 1971. As Lord Denning put it in *Ghani* v. *Jones* (1970). 'No magistrate has the power to issue a search warrant for murder.' Under PACE, such a power now effectively exists. On the other hand, the existing powers are preserved so that, for example, a warrant to search for drugs must be made in accordance with the Misuse of Drugs Act 1971. The general power in PACE exists over and above these specific powers: section 8(5).

16. Limitations

A magistrate may not issue a warrant to search for material in any of the following categories:

(a) *Material subject to legal privilege,* i.e. confidential communications, such as those between solicitor and client: section 10.
(b) *Excluded material,* i.e. personal records held in a business capacity, human tissue or fluid taken for diagnostic purposes, and journalistic records (so long as these are held in confidence): section 11.
(c) Special procedure material, i.e. journalistic material which is not excluded and other confidential material which is not subject to legal privilege. A special procedure outlined in Schedule 1 of the Act applies to this. Access to such material may be granted by a circuit judge, by means of an order. If a person fails to comply with such an order, the judge may issue a warrant authorising search of that person's premises.

17. Safeguards

As with stop and search, PACE provides that a constable is under a legal duty to provide certain information. Here, however, the information is given to the magistrate in the original application for a warrant. It must be sworn by the constable and includes the grounds for the proposed search, the premises, and the items sought. A warrant may be used only once and accordingly, it is dated. The relevant Code of Practice (Code B) also requires that any information contained in or giving rise to a search warrant is checked, and any warrant should normally be authorised by an inspector, or higher ranking officer: section 15. Furthermore, an officer executing a warrant must identify himself and produce the warrant to the occupier of the premises being searched: section 16 and Code C. (These safeguards apply to all warrants executed by the police, including those authorised by earlier Acts like the Misuse of Drugs Act.) Failure to comply with any of the above will make a search unlawful.

In *R* v. *Longman* (1988), however, a search was lawful even though the police resorted to a trick to gain entry to premises they wished to search for drugs. A WPC posed as a delivery girl, and when the occupier opened the door, policemen burst in. Whilst they failed to identify themselves or produce their warrant, the search was nevertheless lawful since the occupier had, in any case, made it impossible for them to do so.

18. Entry and search without a warrant

PACE provides for two categories of such powers, namely entry and search for the purposes of arrest, and entry and search after arrest. (Entry for the sole purpose of searching for goods or other articles requires a warrant, as discussed above.)

19. Entry for the purpose of arrest

Under section 17, a constable now has the power to enter and search any premises on the following grounds:

(a) To execute a warrant of arrest (*see* 23);
(b) To arrest a person for any arrestable offence (*see* 23);
(c) To arrest a person for certain statutory offences which are arrestable (namely, use of police uniform, possession of offensive weapons in public, conduct likely to cause a breach of the peace (all in the Public Order Act 1936), or unlawfully entering and remaining on property under the Criminal Law Act 1977);
(d) To recapture a person unlawfully at large; and
(e) To save life or limb, or property.

As usual (except for (e)) a constable must have reasonable grounds for believing the person sought is on the premises. These powers replace all previous common law or statutory powers of entry and search without a warrant on the part of the police, e.g. section 2,

Criminal Law Act 1967. Ordinary citizens' powers, however, are unchanged.

20. Entry after arrest

Under section 18, a constable has the power to enter and search the premises of any person who is lawfully under arrest, so long as he has reasonable grounds for believing that there is evidence of any arrestable offence, whether or not it is the one for which the person was arrested, on the premises. He may seize and retain anything searched for. (These powers do not apply to 'privileged' material: *see* **16**, above.) This provision reverses the common law position stated in *McLorrie* v. *Oxford* (1982).

21. Seizure of property

So long as they are not subject to legal privilege, any items which a constable has reasonable grounds for believing have been obtained unlawfully, or are evidence of any offence, may be seized where such seizure is necessary to ensure their availability as evidence. A constable is empowered to exercise this power so long as he is lawfully on the premises: section 19.

(a) The Act applies to evidence in the form of computerised information, so that if this is in accessible form, it can be seized: section 19; and if it is not in accessible form the constable can require that it can be transcribed into visible, legible form, so that it can be removed: section 20.
(b) A constable must, however, if required by the occupier of premises searched, provide a record of anything seized: section 21. Code B also requires the police to provide a summary of the powers they have exercised, and the reasons.
(c) Anything lawfully seized by a constable may be retained so long as is necessary in all the circumstances: section 22. Where the item seized can be copied and this copy will suffice, the item should be returned. However, certain items should not be returned after their owner has been released, whether on bail or otherwise; these include weapons, or items used for the purpose of escaping from the country: sections 21 and 22.

Part III: arrest

22. Arrest generally

The law on arrest remains somewhat complex, since not all

powers of arrest are included in PACE. Certain powers of arrest (both statutory and common law) enjoyed by the police and other individuals are retained. Furthermore, the law relating to arrest with a warrant, contained in the Magistrates Courts Act 1980, has also been largely retained. It is important to note, however, that whilst specific powers of arrest might derive from the common law, or from some statute passed either before or after PACE, the provisions of the 1984 Act will nevertheless apply in connection with such things as the manner in which an arrest may be lawfully made, the information communicated to a person being arrested, and his subsequent treatment whilst in custody, irrespective of which specific power of arrest is being used.

23. Arrest with a warrant

Under section 1 of the Magistrates Courts Act 1980, a justice of the peace (JP) may, upon an information (a sworn statement giving the grounds for a person's arrest) being laid before him by a police constable, issue a warrant for the arrest of the relevant person. Warrants are normally only issued where the relevant person is suspected of an indictable offence, or one punishable by imprisonment: if not, a summons should be issued instead. If this is not possible (e.g. where the suspects' name and address are unknown) a warrant may be issued for his arrest.

(a) *General warrants.* It was held in *Entick* v. *Carrington* (1765) that a warrant for the search and seizure of a man's property was invalid when it did not state any offence for which the property was sought. Such general warrants (as they are known) are not lawfully valid: the same principle is true also of arrest warrants.

(b) *Execution of the warrant.* When a constable uses a warrant in making an arrest, he is said to execute it. At common law, there was an element of doubt as to whether, in order lawfully to execute a warrant, a constable had to actually have it in his possession. In *Purdy* (1975) it was held that, when a constable left a warrant in the police car parked close by the suspect's home, it was nevertheless a valid execution of the warrant when he arrested him.

The position was clarified by the Magistrates Courts Act 1980, section 125 of which provides that a warrant can be validly executed even if it is not in the possession of the arresting officer, but it must be shown to the person being arrested, at his demand, as soon as practicable. Section 33 of PACE amended the provision in the Magistrates Courts Act slightly, so that those provisions now apply not only to warrants issued for serious criminal offences, but also to those issued under the Army, Air Force and Naval Discipline Acts, the Reserve Force Act 1980, the General Rate Act 1967 (as amended), and the Domestic Proceedings and Magistrates Courts Act 1978.

24. Arrest without a warrant

Arrest without a warrant is also known as summary arrest. Powers of summary arrest arise in three ways:

(1) At common law;
(2) Under particular statutes; and
(3) By virtue of sections 24–25 of PACE. It should be noted that powers of summary arrest, unlike the power to arrest with a warrant, are enjoyed by private citizens as well as police constables. However, such powers as are enjoyed by private citizens are not always the same as those enjoyed by PCs.

25. Common law powers of arrest

At common law, any person has the power to arrest for a breach of the peace. Nothing in PACE affects this: furthermore section 40 of the Public Order Act 1986 expressly preserves it.

According to Watkins J in *R* v. *Howell* (1982) there is a power of arrest for breach of the peace in the following circumstances:

(*i*) Where a breach of the peace is committed in the presence of the person making the arrest; or
(*ii*) Where the arrestor reasonably believes that such a breach will be committed in the immediate future by the person being arrested; or
(*iii*) Where a breach of the peace has been committed and it is reasonably believed that a renewal of it has been threatened.

In addition, a police constable (but not a private citizen) may take reasonable steps to prevent an apprehended breach of the peace, including entering and remaining on premises: *Thomas* v. *Sawkins* (1935).

26. Statutory powers of arrest

Over the years, a wide variety of statutes have created powers of arrest, mainly on the part of police constables, but also on the part of particular officials (such as customs and excise officers) and even private individuals. Section 26 of PACE repeals all those statutory powers of summary arrest enjoyed by police constables which were conferred before 1984, with 10 exceptions which are preserved in Schedule 2. Statutory powers of summary arrest enjoyed by other officials, and by private individuals (which were far less numerous) were preserved. Certain Acts passed since PACE, such as the Public Order Act 1986, have conferred new powers of summary arrest on constables.

27. PACE, sections 24–25

One of the functions of PACE was to codify, so far as possible, the law on arrest. Hence the repeal of most of the statutory powers of summary arrest formerly enjoyed by PCs. The underlying principle of section 24 of PACE was to utilise the concept of general powers of arrest, first devised in the Criminal Law Act 1967 which, in conjunction with the new, extended powers of arrest created for the first time in section 25 of PACE, should be sufficient to deal with most situations.

28. General powers of arrest

The common law and statutory powers of arrest discussed in **25** and **26**, above, arose only in connection with specific offences, identified in the statute or rule of common law concerned. Thus, for instance, section 137 of the Highways Act 1980 provided the police with the power of summary arrest for wilful obstruction of the highway (this has been repealed by PACE), and, as mentioned at **25**, above, any person may make a summary arrest for breach of the peace.

Section 24 of PACE, however, provides for general powers of arrest; that is, the powers of summary arrest in connection with any offence, provided that the offence is one to which the section applies. Such offences are referred to as arrestable offences. According to section 24(1) these are as follows:

(a) Offences for which the penalty is fixed by law (such as murder and treason, which carry a mandatory life sentence);
(b) Offences for which a person may, on a first conviction, be sentenced to imprisonment for five years, or which are covered by section 33 of the Magistrates Courts Act 1980 (these offences are those involving criminal damage, other than arson); and
(c) Offences specifically listed in section 24(2), namely customs offences: offences under the Official Secrets Acts 1920 and 1989; certain offences related to prostitution; taking a motor vehicle; and

going equipped to steal. Attempting, conspiring at, aiding, abetting, counselling or procuring an arrestable offence are also arrestable for the purposes of PACE: section 24(3).

29. Powers enjoyed by 'any person'

According to section 24(4) any person may make an arrest without a warrant in the following circumstances:

(a) Anyone who is in the act of committing an arrestable offence; and

(b) Anyone whom he has reasonable grounds for suspecting to be committing an arrestable offence.

Under section 24(5) where an arrestable offence has been committed, any person may arrest without a warrant the following:

(a) Anyone who is guilty of the offence; and

(b) Anyone whom he has reasonable grounds for suspecting to be guilty of the offence.

30. Powers enjoyed by police constables

Since the powers referred to in 29, above, are enjoyed by 'any person', they are also enjoyed by police constables. However, PCs have further powers, not enjoyed by private individuals. Section 24(6) provides:

Where a constable has reasonable grounds for suspecting that an arrestable offence has been committed, he may arrest without warrant anyone whom he has reasonable grounds for suspecting to be guilty of the offence.

Further, section 24(7) provides:

A constable may arrest without warrant:

(a) Anyone who is about to commit an arrestable offence;

(b) Anyone whom he has reasonable grounds for suspecting to be about to commit an arrestable offence.

Accordingly, the powers of summary arrest enjoyed by PCs are wider than those enjoyed by others, in that a PC can make an arrest where an arrestable offence is merely suspected of having been committed or of being about to be committed. A private citizen's powers of arrest 'on suspicion' arise only in connection with an offence which has been committed or is being committed. This was, in fact, broadly the case at common law. In *Walters* v. *W.H. Smith* (1914) a private detective employed by the defendants arrested a person whom he suspected of having committed theft. The arrest was held to be unlawful, since no offence had, in fact, been committed.

31. 'Reasonable grounds for suspecting'

Many arrests are made on the basis of 'reasonable grounds for suspecting' that the person being arrested is guilty of an offence. This phrase is not elucidated in PACE itself. However, this (and very similar phrases in earlier legislation) have been discussed in the cases.

(a) *In Hussein* v. *Chong Fook Kam* (1970), the Privy Council considered the matter. According to Lord Devlin, '. . . suspicion is a state of conjecture or surmise where proof is lacking. It arises at or near the starting point of an investigation of which the obtaining of *prima facie* proof is the end.'

(b) More recently, in *Castorina* v. *Chief Constable of Surrey* (1988) the Court of Appeal held that three questions should be asked:

(*i*) Did the arresting officer suspect that the person being arrested was guilty of the offence?

(*ii*) If so, was there reasonable proof of that suspicion?

(*iii*) If the answers to both of the above questions is 'yes' then the officer had a discretion whether or not to arrest: the question then is whether he exercises this discretion reasonably.

The last of these questions (whether the discretion has been exercised reasonably) was considered by the House of Lords in *Holgate-Mohamed* v. *Duke* (1984). The appellant lodged in a home where a burglary had taken place. Some of the goods burgled were displayed in a jeweller's window: on being questioned, the jeweller explained that the goods had been sold to him by a person answering the appellant's description. A PC visited the appellant for questioning at home, and became suspicious of her. He decided to arrest her, thinking she would be more likely to answer questions if arrested and taken to a police station. She claimed her arrest was unlawful.

The House of Lords held that, provided the PC had reasonable grounds for suspecting that she was guilty of the offence, his arrest of the appellant was lawful, and the belief that she was more likely to answer questions if arrested was a proper consideration for him to take when exercising his discretion. Generally, the principle which applied was the same as that applicable to any statutory power involving discretion, namely the *Wednesbury* principle (*see* 15:5).

32. Extended powers of arrest

Section 25 of PACE provides for new extended powers of arrest. These are enjoyed only by police constables, not by private citizens.

(a) Subsection (1) states: 'Where a constable has reasonable grounds for suspecting that any offence which is not an arrestable offence has been committed or attempted or is being committed or attempted, he may arrest the relevant person if it appears to him that service of a summons is impracticable or inappropriate because one of the general arrest conditions is satisfied.'

(b) The general arrest conditions are set out in section 25(3):

(1) The name of the relevant person is unknown to, and cannot be readily ascertained by, the constable;

(2) The constable has reasonable grounds for doubting whether a name furnished by the relevant person as his name is his real name;

(3) (*i*) The relevant person has failed to furnish a satisfactory address for service; or

(*ii*) The constable has reasonable grounds for doubting whether an address furnished by the relevant person is a satisfactory address for service;

(4) The constable has reasonable grounds for believing that arrest is necessary to prevent the relevant person doing the following:

(*i*) Causing physical harm to himself or any other person; or

(*ii*) Suffering physical injury; or

(*iii*) Causing loss of or damage to property; or

(*iv*) Committing an offence against public decency; or

(*v*) Causing an unlawful obstruction of the highway.

(5) The constable has reasonable grounds for believing that arrest is necessary to protect a child or other vulnerable person from the relevant person.

The Section goes on:

ss.(4) For the purpose of subsection (3) above an address is a satisfactory address for service if it appears to the constable

(a) that the relevant person will be at it for a sufficiently long

period for it to be possible to serve him with a summons; or
(b) that some other person specified by the relevant person cannot be served at it.

ss.(5) Nothing in subsection (3)(4) above authorises the arrest of a person under sub-paragraph (iv) of that paragraph except where members of the public going about their normal business cannot reasonably be expected to avoid the person to be arrested.

ss.(6) This section shall not prejudice any power of arrest conferred apart from this section.

33. Requirements in making an arrest

At common law, a person being arrested was entitled to know that he was, in fact, under arrest, and the true grounds for his arrest.

(a) In *Christie* v. *Leachinsky* (1947) a man was arrested, purportedly under a local Act, on suspicion of theft. The Act in question, however, authorised the PCs concerned to arrest him (for unlawful possession) only if his name and address were unknown. The suspect's name and address were known; accordingly, the suspect had not been given the true grounds for his address. The House of Lords held that a person being arrested should normally be told that he was being arrested; he should also be told the true grounds for his arrest, though technical language need not be used. The only exception to this arose when the suspect's own behaviour made this impossible, as by using violence to resist or avoid arrest.

(b) These requirements are now contained in section 28 of PACE which provides that, when an arrest is made, if the person being arrested is not told of this at the time, then in any case he should be informed as soon as is practicable: section 28(1). Where the arrest is made by a PC, this applies even where the fact of the arrest is obvious: section 28(2). The person arrested must be informed of the grounds of the arrest at the time, or as soon as is practicable thereafter: section 28(3). No arrest is lawful unless these requirements are complied with, subject to the provisions of section 28(5). This states that a person need not be informed that he is under arrest, or the grounds for his arrest, if it is not reasonably practicable for him to be so informed by reason of his having escaped from arrest before the information could be given. It has been held that the precise words, 'You are under arrest' do not have to be used: *R* v. *Brosch* (1988).

(c) The decision in *Christie* v. *Leachinsky* (1947) has recently been approved, insofar as the grounds for arrest are concerned. In *Abassy* v. *Metropolitan Police Commissioner* (1990), a PC observed a car being driven erratically, and stopped it. He became suspicious as to whether the car's driver was its owner, or authorised to drive it, and arrested him for 'unlawful possession'. The Court of Appeal held that this was sufficient. The fact that it was unlawful possession of a motor vehicle for which the PC was arresting him must have been obvious to the suspect from the PC's questioning. The fact that he did not mention a vehicle when giving grounds did not make the arrest unlawful.

34. Voluntary attendance at a police station

In *R* v. *Inwood* (1975) the defendant went to a police station to 'help police with their inquiries' (i.e. to voluntarily answer questions). He had not been arrested. In the course of the interview, the PC concerned became suspicious of the defendant, and when he attempted to leave, sought to prevent him. The defendant assaulted the PC. The Court of Appeal quashed his conviction for assaulting a PC in the execution of his duty. At he time of the assault, he had not been arrested, and was therefore free to leave. The PC had no power to prevent him, and was therefore not in the execution of his duty in attempting to prevent him.

Section 29 of PACE enacts this principle. It states:

Where for the purpose of assisting with the investigation a person attends voluntarily at a police station or at any other place . . . without having been arrested:

(a) he shall be entitled to leave at will unless he is placed under arrest;

(b) he shall be informed at once that he is under arrest if a decision is taken by a constable to prevent him leaving at will.

35. Ancillary powers

(a) *Re-arrest*. Where a person has been arrested for an offence and is taken to a police station, and it appears to a PC that, if he were released, he would be liable for arrest for some other offence, he shall be arrested for that offence: section 31.

(b) *Search*. A constable may search an arrested person in any case where the arrest takes place other than at a police station, where this seems necessary to protect the arrested person, or another, or where the constable suspects him of possessing anything he may use to assist in an escape, or which may be evidence of an offence. A PC may also enter premises in which the arrest has taken place to search for evidence: Section 32.

Part IV: detention

36 Detention

The detention of a person starts with his arrest. Section 30 of PACE provides that a person who is arrested by a constable, or taken into custody by a constable having been arrested by someone else, should be taken to a police station as soon as practicable. If possible, this should be one designated for the purpose of keeping arrested persons in detention; if not, then the arrested person must be transferred to such a station within six hours. Part IV of PACE provides for a new procedure, with built-in safeguards, applicable to detention at a police station. In addition, one of the Codes of Practice (*see* 44, below), namely Code C, lays down certain detailed procedures which must be followed by the police when detaining an arrested person.

37. The custody officer

PACE provides that one or more police officers holding the rank of sergeant or above should be allocated to each designated station as custody officer: section 36. It is the function of the custody officer, who must be unconnected with the investigation itself, to keep an arrested person's detention under review at regular intervals so as to ensure that continued detention is both necessary and properly conducted, or that the person is duly released, with or without being charged, and with or without bail: section 34.

Where a person is detained without having been charged, review of his detention must be made by an inspector (or higher-ranking officer); review of detention after charges have been made is done by the custody officer himself. In either case, the custody officer must make an initial decision as to whether, on an arrest being made and a person's being brought in to the station, sufficient evidence exists for charges to be brought. If not, the arrested person should be released, with or without bail, unless the custody officer believes there are reasonable grounds for believing that detention without charge is necessary in order to secure or preserve evidence: section 37.

38. Detention without charge

An arrested person should not normally be detained without being charged for longer than 24 hours: section 41(1).

(a) However, an office of at least the rank of superintendent may authorise an extension of this period for up to 36 hours, where he has reasonable grounds for believing:

(*i*) Detention without charge is necessary to secure or preserve evidence; *and*

(*ii*) The offence is a serious arrestable one (defined in section 115 and Schedule 5, and including treason, murder, rape and drug trafficking); *and*

(*iii*) The investigation is being conducted diligently and expeditiously: section 42.

(All *three* of these requirements must be satisfied.)

(b) Any further detention without charge can only be authorised by a magistrate's warrant: section 43. This must be applied for under oath (raher like an arrest warrant), and is subject to similar conditions as those in (b), above. Such detention should not be for longer than 36 hours, nor end later than 96 hours after the arrest.

Whatever the period of detention is, it is subject to the review procedure, mentioned in **23**, above.

39. Detention after charge

Sooner of later, a person who has been arrested and taken into police custody must either be charged with an offence, or released. Thus must occur, at the latest, within 96 hours, as discussed above. Once charges have been preferred, it is the duty of the custody officer to order that person's release, either on bail or without bail, unless:

(a) his name and address cannot be ascertained, or the name and address appear to be untrue; or

(b) the custody officer has reasonable grounds for believing that continued retention is necessary for his own protection or for preventing harm to other persons or to property; or

(c) the custody officer reasonably believes he will jump bail (i.e., fail to attend court to answer the charges): section 38.

In such a case, the person concerned must be brought before a magistrate who decides whether the person concerned should be released on bail or remanded in police custody: section 5(46)–(48).

This must be done as soon as practicable. A person has a 'general right to bail' (Bail Act 1976), and this should be denied only if the magistrate is satisfied that continued detention (remand) is necessary for the reasons given above, or where there are grounds for believing that the person concerned would abscond, and/or interfere with the course of justice, and/or commit further offences while on bail. Where a person is remanded in custody, his continued detention is subject to the review procedure discussed above. The period of detention also counts towards any custodial sentence he may eventually receive: section 49.

A record should be kept of a person's detention, both before and after charge: section 51.

Part V: questioning and treatment of persons by police

40 General

This part of the Act, along with Code C (the Detention Code: *see* 45, below) replaces a variety of common law and statutory rules and guidelines, including the famous 'Judges' Rules' which used to govern most aspects of police questioning and treatment of suspects.

41. Search

The custody officer may authorise the search of an arrested person, where he considers this necessary. Searches may be authorised, however, in other ways.

(a) Section 53 of PACE abolishes all common law powers of search and all but one statutory power of search by a police constable. (The exception is the search of suspected terrorists: Prevention of Terrorism Act 1989.)
(b) As well as a general search, authorised by the custody officer, an officer of the rank of superintendent or above may authorise an intimate search (that is, one for certain concealed items) where he has reasonable grounds for believing that such items are concealed on the arrested person. These items include proscribed drugs, as well as items which he could use to cause injury to himself or others. Such searches must be conducted by a medical practitioner, unless this is not practicable.

A record must be kept of any search, whether general or intimate, and the person being searched must be told of the reasons for it.

42. Rights of arrested persons

Arrested persons now have certain statutory rights.

(a) Section 56 provides that a person is entitled, if he requests, to have one person known to him notified that he has been arrested and is being detained, as soon as practicable.

(b) He is also entitled, if he so requests, to consult a solicitor, privately and at any time (which means in effect that he may have a solicitor present during questioning): section 58. A system of duty solicitors has been introduced to cater for this right.

There are exceptions to (a) and (b), above, so that an officer of the rank of superintendent or above may authorise a delay in the granting of these rights where the offence in question is a serious arrestable one and there are reasonable grounds for believing that if the request is granted one of the following may occur:

(*i*) It will lead to interference with evidence; or

(*ii* It will lead to the alerting of other suspects; or

(*iii*) It will hinder the recovery of any property obtained by means of an offence; or (in the case of consultation with a solicitor)

(*iv*) The offence is one involving drug trafficking, and the recovery of any proceeds may be hindered.

('Serious arrestable offences' are defined in section 115 and in Schedule 5 of the Act: *see* **38**, above.)

The above rights are very important; the effects of a breach of these, particularly section 58, are discussed below.

43. Other rights and safeguards

As well as sections 56 and 58, PACE contains a number of rights and safeguards: These are mainly contained in the Codes of Practice, and (regarding detention and questioning and treatment of suspects,) Code C in particular.

Further, section 60 provides for the tape-recording of all interviews which take place in police detention.

44. The Codes of Practice

These are provided for in sections 66–67, which authorise the Home Secretary to issue Codes of Practice in the form of delegated legislation. As usual with delegated legislation, they must be approved by Parliament before taking effect. There are five of these: Code A deals with Stop and Search; Code B with Search of Premises; Code C with Detention and Questioning; Code D with Identification, and Code E with tape-recording. For present purposes, Code C is the most important: it is Code C which has replaced the old Judges' Rules.

45. Code C: the Detention Code

This imposes certain requirements on the police.

(a) A custody record must be kept of every aspect of a person's detention by the police.

(b) Certain minimum standards of treatment must be met.

These include the requirements that a person should not be held incommunicado, that he should have adequate meals and exercise, and should be allowed a period of eight hours sleep in every 24, so far as practicable (paragraphs 5 and 8).

(c) Over and above these, Code C requires that a person who has been detained should be informed of his right to have someone informed of his arrest, and to consult with a solicitor (paragraph 3).

In *Beycan* (1990), an arrested person was asked if he was happy to be interviewed without a solicitor or other person being informed. He agreed, and the police claimed he had waived his rights. The court held that such an invitation did not amount to informing him of his rights, and was therefore in breach of the Code: accordingly his 'confession' (on which the prosecution relied) was inadmissible in accordance with section 76 (*see* 46 and 47, below).

(d) A person suspected of an offence must be cautioned before being questioned in connection with an offence or before questioning is resumed after a break. The caution must be in the (now familiar) terms; 'You do not have to say anything unless you wish to do so, but what you say may be given in evidence.' A person should also be cautioned when arrested and/or charged.

(e) Of the other Codes, Code D (on identification) is also important. It provides that an identification parade be held at the request either of the police or of the suspect. In either case, the suspect must consent to such a procedure, though his refusal can

be referred to in evidence in court, where a witness may be invited
to identify him in the dock, in any case. The Code also lays down
guidelines for identification by photographs ('mug shots').

Parts VII and VIII: evidence in criminal proceedings

46   Admissibility of confessions and other evidence

The most important provisions in these two parts of the Act are
those dealing with the admissibility of confessions and other
evidence and, in particular, the circumstances in which they should
be excluded as evidence altogether.

47.   Confessions

Section 76 provides that if in any criminal proceedings it is
represented by the defence that a confession has or may have been
obtained

(a) by oppression of the person making it; or
(b) in consequence of anything said or done which, in the
circumstances, is likely to make it unreliable

the court shall not allow the confession as evidence, unless the
prosecution can prove beyond all reasonable doubt that it was not
so obtained. (Section 76(3) provides that the court may itself
require such proof from the prosecution.)

(a) *Oppression.* In *Miller* (1986) a schizophrenic was subjected to
lengthy interrogation, before confessing to a crime. It was argued
that merely interrogating such a person for a prolonged period
amounted to oppression. The court held that, provided this
involved only normal questioning, it did not. Had the police
intended, by their questioning, to induce a state of mental disorder,
that would have been different, and may well have amounted to
oppression.

In *Fulling* (1987) it was held that the normal dictionary
meaning should be applied to the term, so that oppression involves
'The exercise of authority in a burdensome, harsh or wrongful
manner; cruel or unjust treatment'. Obviously, physical violence
would be included.

(b) *Reliability.* In *Trussler* (1988), a drug addict was kept in custody
for 18 hours without rest (and therefore in breach of Code C),

before 'confessing'. It was held that this confession was unreliable, and therefore should be excluded.

In *Moss* (1990) a person of very low intelligence was quetioned on nine separate occasions; he was denied a solicitor until after the fifth interview, at which he 'confessed'. It was held that his confession should have been excluded, since the failure to permit him access to a solicitor was something done which, in the circumstances, rendered his confession unreliable.

48. Other evidence

Section 78 provides that a court may refuse to allow any evidence brought by the prosecution if it appears that, having regard to all the circumstances, admission of the evidence would have such an adverse effect on the fairness of the proceedings that the court ought not to admit it. This provision modifies the old common law rule, which seemed to give the court a complete discretion over the admissibility of evidence other than confessions. Thus, in *Absolam* (1989), a conviction was quashed when the accused had not been informed of his rights (though a conviction for another, lesser, offence was upheld).

In *Mason* (1988) a man's conviction was quashed when the police had deceived him by claiming to have evidence they did not, in fact, have. However, fairness to the accused is not the only factor. In *Walsh* (1989) it was felt that section 78 entitled a court to exclude evidence only if the unfairness caused would have such an adverse effect on the proceedings that the fair and proper administration of justice demanded its exclusion.

Parts IX–XI

49 General

Parts IX, X and XI of PACE deal with police complaints and discipline, obtaining the views of the community, and miscellaneous matters. These are summarised very briefly in the following paragraphs.

50. Police complaints and discipline

Part IX of PACE provides for a Police Complaints Authority (PCA) replacing the Police Complaints Board: section 83. Sections 84–105 provide for an elaborate system of complaints and discipline partly based on existing regulations made under the Police Act

1964 (and subsequent legislation) and partly new. The essence of complaints against the police remains the same, however, in that, in the first instance at least, they are normally dealt with internally by the police themselves. Certain complaints are made or referred to the PCA: these are those where death or serious injury is involved. As well as these, any complaint which after investigation reveals that a constable should be charged with a criminal offence must be reported to the PCA and to the Director of Public Prosecutions whose job it is to decide whether or not to initiate criminal proceedings. In such cases, disciplinary proceedings, if any, will be taken by the PCA; otherwise the chief officer of police investigating the complaint decides on appropriate action.

51. Other matters

PACE provides that every police authority should, after consulting with the Chief Constable in its area, make arrangements for obtaining the view of the community concerning the policing of the area, and for the prevention of crime. (In the case of London, this is done by the Metropolitan Police Commissioner, under the guidance of the Home Secretary, in consultation with the London borough and district councils.) An important provision in this part of the Act is section 117. This provides that where any provision of the Act confers a power upon a constable, the constable may use reasonable force, if necessary, in the exercise of that power. This is a comprehensive provision and applies to all powers in the Act, including arrest, search, stop and search, seizure, etc.

Progress test 10

1. To what extent is there a 'right of personal liberty' in the UK. To what extent, and in what circumstances (generally) can this 'right' be lawfully infringed? (1)

2. Outline the main powers of stop and search now available to the police. What are the lawful requirements involved in the exercise of these powers? (4–7)

3. In what circumstances (either under the common law or statute) may a police constable lawfully enter premises, search them and seize property found in the course of his search? What safeguards exist to ensure that such searches are justified and properly conducted? (10–21)

4. Discuss the lawfulness of the police's conduct in the following situations:

(a) A PC obtains a magistrate's warrant for Sneaky's arrest. No offence is specified in the warrant.

(b) A PC goes to arrest Sneaky at his home, but forgets the warrant, which he leaves in his desk at the police station. **(23)**

5. Outline the powers of summary arrest available to a PC under the Police and Criminal Evidence Act 1984. **(24, 27–28, 30, 32)**

6. What information must a PC give to a person: **(a)** when arresting him in a place other than a police station; and **(b)** who has attended voluntarily at a police station, but whom the PC now suspects of an offence and wishes to detain? **(33–45)**

7. Outline the main provisions in PACE for the protections of persons who have been arrested and placed in police custody. **(36–45)**

8. In what circumstances might: **(a)** confessions; and **(b)** other evidence be inadmissible as evidence in court as a result of the conduct of the police in relation to a person's detention? **(46–48)**

11

Freedom of assembly: the Public Order Acts 1936 and 1986

Introductory

1. Freedom of assembly

It has been said that 'amongst our fundamental human rights there are, without doubt, the rights of peaceful assembly and public protest, and the right to public order and tranquility' (*Per* Lord Scarman, Report on the Red Lion Square Disorders, 1975). What is obvious about the rights referred to above is that they are fundamentally conflicting ones, or at least potentially so. The exercise of their right to public protest by some individuals is bound to pose a possible threat to public order and tranquility. Thus, finding the correct balance between these competing claims is the problem faced by the law.

2. Is there a right of assembly?

It should be made clear at the outset that if there is such a thing as a right of assembly at all, then it is no more or less than the result of each individual concerned asserting his or her rights. An assembly, in this context, is merely a group of individuals gathering together, and therefore has no rights of its own (unlike corporations or certain associations, such as trades unions). Even those rights enjoyed by individuals are restricted in scope; as mentioned earlier, in England, one has 'liberties' (and, to a certain extent, remedies), rather than rights, for the most part. Thus, individuals may gather together in public or private places freely, and for whatever purpose they wish, provided that in so doing, they do not break any of the many laws which have a bearing on public order and related matters. Accordingly, a discussion on freedom of assembly really amounts to a study of those laws, which are quite numerous, and which restrict the freedom. As far as assemblies, or other uses of public highways are concerned, it can be said that every member of the public enjoys the right to use the highway reasonably. This is a common law right. In *Hickman* v. *Maisey* (1900) it was said to amount to the right to pass and re-pass along the highway. Anything beyond that might amount to an unlawful obstruction of this highway: section 137, Highways Act 1980. Thus, the right of assembly is a somewhat limited one. The restrictions which apply are both common law and statutory ones.

Common law

3. Common law restrictions

At common law, the most significant area touching on assemblies and public order arises from the general duty of the police to keep the peace, and from the power to arrest for the offence of breach of the peace. The following are examples of how these have applied to assemblies, and to situations involving public order as such.

(a) In *O'Kelly* v. *Harvey* (1883) it was held that a police constable (PC) could lawfully disperse an assembly if he had reasonable grounds for believing that was the only way of preventing a breach of the peace.

In *Humphries* v. *Connor* (1864) a PC removed an orange lily which was being worn by a Protestant marcher, on the grounds that it might be offensive to Catholics, and thereby cause a breach of the peace. In an action against the officer for assault, it was held that he acted lawfully in doing so, since it was his duty to prevent breaches of the peace.

(b) In *Duncan* v. *Jones* 1931 a police officer asked a woman who was about to address a public assembly to move on, on the grounds that disorder had occurred in that location at a previous assembly addressed by her. She refused and was arrested and charged with obstructing a constable in the execution of his duty. It was held that, despite the fact that obstruction of a PC is not an arrestable offence, the PC had acted within his powers, and that her conviction should stand, since he had arrested her to prevent a likely breach of the peace. (*See* also 10: **25**.)

(c) In *Moss* v. *McLachlin* (1985), the police set up a road block to prevent 'flying pickets' from joining their colleagues on the picket lines during the miners' strike in 1984. This took place several miles from the mine where the picket line was situated. When the flying pickets forced their way through the road block, they were convicted for obstructing the police in the execution of their duty, contrary to Section 51 of the Police Act 1964, since there was sufficient evidence of a likely breach of the peace, had they reached their destination, to justify the road block, thus bringing the police within the scope of their duty.

Statutory offences

4. Statutes

Apart from the Public Order Acts 1936 and 1986 (which are discussed in detail below) there are a number of statutes which relate to public order and to freedom of assembly, normally by creating specific offences which might be committed by those organising or participating in processions, assemblies and meetings, and which may therefore be said to limit the right of assembly. Some of these carry powers of arrest, or powers which regulate assemblies.

(a) Section 52 of the Metropolitan Police Act and section 22 of the City of London Police Act 1839 empower the Commissioner of Police to issue directions for the purpose of ensuring streets in London are not obstructed by such things as assemblies and processions. In London, as elsewhere, local by-laws may also operate to similar effect (e.g. the Trafalgar Square Regulations: contrary to common belief, there is no public right to hold open-air meetings in Trafalgar Square).

(b) *Section 137, the Highways Act 1980.* As mentioned earlier, it is an offence wilfully to obstruct the highway. According to *Arrowsmith* v. *Jenkins* (1963) (concerning an earlier, similar Act) an obstruction is wilful even though the obstruction is not actually intended: it is enough if the assembly which brings about the obstruction is intended to take place, and an obstruction is thereby caused. This was followed in *Hirst* v. *Chief Constable of West Yorkshire* (1986).

Whilst it is no longer an arrestable offence, a person guilty of obstruction may satisfy one of the general arrest conditions laid down in section 25 of the Police and Criminal Evidence Act 1984 (*see* 10: **32**), and thereby be liable to arrest.

(c) *Section 1 of the Public Meetings Act 1908* as amended by section 6 of the Public Order Act 1956 makes it an offence to disrupt a public meeting: an offender can, at the request of the chairman of the meeting, be removed by a constable, and arrested if he refuses to give his name and address (which could, in any case, satisfy a general arrest condition under section 25, PACE).

(d) It is an offence for a person to have in his possession an offensive weapon in any public place or at any public meeting: Prevention of Crime Act 1953, as amended.

Until the Public Order Act 1986, repealed them, there were also a number of ancient statutes, largely fallen into disuse, which regulated assemblies (e.g. the Tumultuous Petitioning Act 1661 and Seditious Meetings Act 1817).

The Public Order Act 1936

5. Background

The 1930s in Britain were attended by the rise in rival political factions, distinct from the mainstream political parties. The policies and public activities of these parties were often extreme in nature, and on some occasions, meetings, demonstrations and processions were the occasion of serious public disorder, and sometimes violence between rival factions. These factions included the British Union of Fascists, known as 'blackshirts' because of the 'uniforms' they wore on public occasions. The Public Order Act 1936 was therefore designed to address the problems posed by such organisations, as well as the regulation of processions and assemblies generally.

6. The Public Order Act 1936

The background and intention behind the Act is discussed at 5, above. In general, it is those parts of the Act (sections 1 and 2) dealing with political factions which have been retained, and are therefore still good law. Those parts dealing with the regulations of assemblies and procession and related matters have been mostly repealed, and replaced by new provisions in the Public Order Act 1986. Accordingly these (repealed) sections will be mentioned for purposes of comparison only, in the paragraphs dealing with the 1986 Act (below).

7. Political uniforms

The Public Order Act (POA) 1936 makes it an offence for any person, in any public place or at any public meeting, to wear a uniform signifying his association with any political organisation, or with the promotion of any political object. An exception is made concerning the wearing of a uniform on any ceremonial anniversary or other special occasion; in such a case, provided no risk of public disorder arises, the chief officer of police may, with the consent of the Home Secretary, permit the wearing of such uniforms.

(a) The phrases 'public meeting' and 'public place' are defined in section 9. Public meeting includes any meeting in a public place and any meeting where the public, or any section thereof, are permitted to attend. Public place has been slightly re-defined by the 1986 Act so as to mean 'any highway or any place to which at the material time the public or any section of the public has access, on payment or otherwise, as of right or by virtue of express or implied permission': section 16.

(b) Uniform, on the other hand, is not defined. Whether commonly available garments, when worn together by members of a political organisation, constitute a uniform was considered by the Court of Appeal in *O'Moran* v. *DPP* (1975). Some men attended the funeral of a supporter of the Irish Republican Army (an illegal organisation) wearing sunglasses, dark berets and dark clothing. It was held that such garments could constitute a political uniform where:

(*i*) They had previously been worn in circumstances where a political association could be established; or

(*ii*) Where the intention of the wearer, according to the evidence, was to indicate his association with or support for a political organisation.

The Prevention of Terrorism (Temporary Provisions) Act 1976 in fact resolved the problem by making it an offence for a person to wear or carry, in any public place, an item of dress or other item signifying membership of or support for a proscribed organisation, of which the IRA is one. This Act was re-enacted in 1989.

(c) Prosecutions under section 1 of the POA 1936 can only be brought by or with the consent of the Attorney-General: section 1(2).

8. Private armies

The POA 1936 prohibits the organising or training of an association for the purpose of usurping the functions of the armed forces, or the police, or for the purpose of enabling that association's members to be employed for the use or display of physical force in promoting any political object, or in such manner as would arouse reasonable apprehension that any of these purposes is intended.

Once again, the consent of the Attorney-General is necessary for any prosecution under this section. The first successful prosecution occurred in *R* v. *Jordan and Tyndall* (1965) when two well-known leaders of extreme right-wing organisations were convicted of organising and equipping an association called Spearhead in circumstances raising a reasonable apprehension that it would be employed for the use or display of force to promote a political object. It was not necessary to establish actual 'battle plans'.

The Public Order Act 1986

9. Scope of the Act

The POA 1986 is rather wider in scope than its 1936 counterpart, much of which it replaces. It is arranged in five parts, as follows:

(a) *Part I: new offences.* This part abolishes certain common law and statutory offences concerned with public order, and replaced them with new statutory ones.

(b) *Part II: processions and assemblies.* This part contains the regulatory powers available to the police and other authorities for the prevention of disorder.

(c) *Part III: racial hatred.* This part deals comprehensively with all kinds of conduct, publication etc. which tend to incite racial hatred.

(d) *Part IV: exclusion orders.* This part deals with certain offences connected with football, and provides the police and other authorities with powers to deal with disorder at footall matches.

(e) *Part V: miscellaneous and general.* As well as the usual provisions falling under this heading (repeals, commencement dates, etc.), this part creates new offences and powers, namely:

  (*i*) Contamination of goods; and
  (*ii*) Mass trespass.

Part I: new offences

10. New offences

The new offences created in Part I of the POA 1986 are riot (section 1); violent disorder (section 2); affray (section 3); causing fear or provocation of violence (section 4) and harassment, alarm or distress (section 5). These replace the old common law offences of riot, rout, unlawful assembly and affray (section 1–3), and the statutory offence of using words or behaviour in a public place likely to cause a breach of the peace (section 5, Public Order Act 1936), all of which are abolished (section 9).

The most significant change, which is common to all of these new offences, is that the requirement of a breach of the peace, actual or likely, is absent. This requirement formed a part of the common law offences which have been replaced in Part I, as well as section 5 of the Public Order Act 1936. Instead, each of the new offences has its own requirements, which are discussed below.

11. Riot, violent disorder and affray

These three new offences have certain features in common. In particular, all involve the use or threat of unlawful violence. Violence is defined in section 8 thus:

. . . any violent conduct, so that:

(a) except in the context of affray, it includes violent conduct towards property as well as violent conduct towards persons, and
(b) it is not restricted to conduct causing or intended to cause injury or damage but includes any other violent conduct (for example, throwing at or towards a person a missile or a kind capable of causing injury which does not hit or falls short).

(a) *Riot.* Section 1(1) provides:

Where 12 or more persons who are present together use or threaten unlawful violence for a common purpose and the conduct of them (taken together) is such as would cause a person of reasonable firmness present at the scene to fear for his personal safety, each of the persons using unlawful violence for the common purpose is guilty of riot. Sections 1(2)–(6) qualifies this.

It is not necessary for violence to be used or threatened by all 12 persons simultaneously; it is not necessary for a 'firm' person to be actually present; the common purpose can be inferred by conduct. Above all, riot can be committed in private, as well as public, places.

It should be noted that only those persons who actually use unlawful violence are guilty of riot: those who merely threaten it, however, could be convicted of aiding and abetting riot, or of an offence under section 2. The maximum penalty for riot is 10 years imprisonment. Prosecution for riot or incitement to riot can only be brought by or with the consent of the DPP: section 7(1).

(b) *Violent disorder.* Section 2 provides:

> Where three or more persons who are present together use or threaten unlawful violence and the conduct of them (taken together) is such as would cause a person of reasonable firmness present at the scene to fear for his personal safety, each of the persons using or threatening unlawful violence is guilty of violent disorder.

As with riot, this offence can be committed in public or private places, violence need not be used or threatened by all simultaneously, and no 'firm' person need actually be present. The offence carries a maximum penalty of six months imprisonment.

(c) *Affray.* Section 3 provides:

> A person is guilty of affray if he uses or threatens unlawful violence towards another and his conduct is such as would cause a person of reasonable firmness present at the scene to fear for his personal safety.

Subsection (3) makes it clear that a threat cannot be made by the use of words alone. Furthermore, it will be noted that, unlike riot and violent disorder, the affray is committed only if the violence is used or threatened towards another. Like those offences, however, riot can be committed in public and private places, and no 'firm' person need actually be present. Affray is an arrestable offence by virtue of section 3(6): it carries a maximum of three years imprisonment.

12. Fear of provocation of violence

This offence, along with the offence of harassment, alarm or distress (section 5), replaces the old offence contained in section 5 of the Public Order Act 1936. Section 4 of the POA 1986 provides:

> A person is guilty of an offence if he:
>
> **(a)** uses towards another person threatening, abusive or insulting words or behaviour; or
>
> **(b)** distributes or displays to another person any writing sign,

or other visible representation which is threatening abusive or insulting, with intent to cause that person to believe that unlawful violence will be used against him or another by any person, or to provoke the immediate use of unlawful violence by that person or another, or whereby that person is likely to believe that such violence will be used or it is likely that such violence will be provoked.

The offence may be committed in private, as well as public places (section 4(2)) but a special defence exists whereby a person is not guilty if his conduct occurs in a dwelling and the other person is also inside a dwelling. The offence is arrestable (section 4(3)), and carries a maximum penalty of six months imprisonment.

13. The elements of the section 4 offence

There have been few reported cases on section 4 since the POA came into force. Fortunately, however, some of the key elements arose in the old offence, in section 5 of the Public Order Act 1936 and elesewhere.

Decisions on these, which frequently involve the meanings of the terms used (which are not actually defined in the POA 1986 itself) are therefore likely to remain good law.

(a) *Threatening, abusive or insulting*. The leading authority on this is *Brutus* v. *Cozens* (1973). A political demonstrator ran on to the court during play at a tennis championship, causing the match to be disrupted. The House of Lords had to consider whether his conduct was 'threatening, abusive or insulting'. They held that since no definition was actually given in the Act, then the terms should be given their normal, every day meaning.

Accordingly, whilst the defendant's conduct might have been irritating, disrespectful or even contemptuous of the rights of others, it was not threatening, abusive or insulting, and he was therefore not guilty of the offence.

On the other hand, in *Masterson* v. *Holden* (1986), it was held that homosexual embracing in a London street at 1.55 a.m. could be 'insulting'.

(b) *Provocation of violence*. Whilst it is an offence to intend that the person to whom the threatening, abusive or insulting words or behaviour is used is caused to believe that such violence will be used or provoked, it is also sufficient if that person is likely to believe that such violence will be used or provoked.

In *Jordan* v. *Burgoyne* (1963), a similar point was discussed. When charged with using threatening abusive or insulting words which were likely to cause a breach of the peace, Jordan claimed that because a sector of the audience involved were particularly sensitive to his words, he should not be convicted. It was only if his words were likely to provoke a 'reasonable' man (he argued) that the offence was committed. The court rejected this argument. A person must 'take his audience as he finds it', so that if persons actually present are provoked or likely to be provoked, the defendant is guilty.

The same is almost certainly true of section 4 of the POA 1986 so that if the person to whom the threatening, abusive or insulting words are used is likely to believe that violence will be used or provoked, it is irrelevant if he happens to be sensitive to the words in question.

14. Harassment, alarm or distress

Section 5(1) A person is guilty of an offence if he:

(a) uses threatening, abusive or insulting words or behaviour, or disorderly behaviour; or
(b) displays any writing, sign or other visible representation which is threatening, abusive or insulting

within the hearing or sight of a person likely to be caused harassment, alarm or distress.

Like section 4, an offence under this section can be committed in a private, as well as a public place (subject to the same exception as in section 4, regarding 'dwellings').

However, specific defences are created in section 5(3), so that a person is not guilty if he had no reason to believe that there was any person within hearing or sight who was likely to be harassed, alarmed or distressed; or where he was inside a dwelling and had no reason to believe that he could be heard or seen from outside; or where his conduct was reasonable.

The offence is not, in itself, arrestable; however, if an offender is asked to desist by a constable, but does not, and engages in further offensive conduct, the constable may arrest him: section 5(4). The maximum penalty is a fine not exceeding level three on the national scale.

15. Elements of the offence

(a) Unlike section 4, section 5 does not require that threatening, abusive or insulting words or behaviour are used towards another. It is sufficient, for the purposes of section 5, that the conduct occurs 'within the hearing or sight' of someone.

(b) 'Disorderly behaviour'. As well as threatening, abusive or insulting words or behaviour, 'disorderly behaviour' may also constitute an offence. The same principle as used in *Brutus* v. *Cozens* (1973) applies, so that the term disorderly is used in its ordinary meaning (as are 'harassment, alarm, and distress').

16. Mental element

Unusually, the POA dedicates a complete section to the mental element (*mens rea*) required in the various offences discussed so far.

Section 6(1) A person is guilty of riot only if he intends to use violence or is aware that his conduct may be violent.

(2) A person is guilty of violent disorder or affray only if he intends to use or threaten violence or is aware that his conduct may be violent or threaten violence.

(3) A person is guilty of an offence under section 4 only if he intends his words or behaviour, or the writing, sign or other visible representation, to be threatening, abusive or insulting, or is aware that it may be threatening, abusive or insulting.

(4) A person is guilty of an offence under section 5 only if he intends his words or behaviour, or the writing sign or other visible representation, to be threatening, abusive or insulting, or is aware that it may be threatening, abusive or insulting or (as the case may be) he intends his behaviour to be or is aware that it may be disorderly.

(5) For the purpose of this section a person whose awareness is impaired by intoxication shall be taken to be aware of that of which he would be aware if not intoxicated, unless he shows either that his intoxication was not self-induced or that it was caused solely by taking or administration of a substance in the course of medical treatment.

(6) In subsection (5) 'intoxication' means any intoxication whether caused by drink, drugs or other means, or by a combination of means.

(7) Subsections (1) and (2) do not affect the determination for the purposes of riot or violent disorder of the number of persons who use or threaten violence.

Part II: processions and assemblies

17. General

The POA 1986 confers upon the police and other authorities certain powers for the regulation of processions and assemblies. Whilst the old 1936 Act contained certain regulatory powers, the 1986 Act goes much further. In particular, for the first time, the police are empowered by the 1986 Act to regulate static assemblies, as well as processions.

18. Advance notice of public processions

Section 11(1) Written notice shall be given . . . of any proposal to hold a public procession intended –

(a) to demonstrate support for or opposition to the views or actions of any person or body;
(b) to publicise a cause or campaign; or
(c) to mark or commemorate an event unless it is not reasonably practicable to give any advance notice of the procession.

(It would not, for example, be reasonably practicable to give advance notice where, responding spontaneously to an accident outside a school, a group of parents marched to the town hall to protest the lack of road safety measures.)

The written-notice requirement does not apply where the procession is commonly or customarily held in the area, or where it is a funeral procession organised by a funeral director: section 11(2). Where applicable, notice must be delivered to a police station in the area at least six days before the procession occurs (section 11(3)) or, failing that, as soon as reasonably practicable (section 11(6)). It must specify the date and time of the intended procession, the proposed route, and the name and address of the organiser: section 11(3). Failure to comply with these requirements is an offence.

The organiser of a procession is also guilty of an offence if the date, time or route taken differ from those given in the notice: section 11(7). However, it is a defence for the organiser to prove that he did not know of, and neither suspected nor had reason to suspect, the failure to satisfy the requirements or (as the case may be) the difference of date, time or route: section 11(6). It is also a defence to a charge of deviating from the stated date, time or route, for him to prove that this was due to circumstances beyond his control, or from something done on the agreement or direction of a police officer: section 11(9).

19. Imposing conditions on public processions

Powers to impose conditions on public processions are conferred upon the senior officer of police by section 12.

If, having regard to the time and place and circumstances in which a public procession is being held or is intended, the chief officer of police reasonably believes that –

(a) it may result in serious public disorder, serious damage to property, or serious disruption to the life of the community; or
(b) the purpose of the organisers is the intimidation of others with a view to compelling them not to do an act they have a right to do or to do an act they have a right not to do, he may give directions imposing, on those organising or taking part in the procession, such conditions as appear to him necessary to prevent such disorder, damage, disruption or intimidation, including conditions as to the route of the procession or prohibiting it from entering any public place specified in the directions.

This provision (along with further ones in section 13) replaces broadly similar powers in section 3 of the POA 1936. However, certain doubts and ambiguities contained in the 1936 Act are resolved:

(a) Chief officer of police is defined, in relation to a procession being held, or where persons have already assembled for that purpose, as the most senior officer present. In relation to a procession planned in the future, he is the chief officer of police in the area: section 12(2).
(b) Directions given by the chief officer of police in relation to a procession planned for the future should be in writing; this does not apply to a procession in progress: section 12(3). Anyone organising or taking part in a procession who knowingly fails to comply with any direction duly given is guilty of an offence, and a constable in uniform may arrest without warrant anyone whom he reasonably suspects of committing such an offence: sub-sections 4–7.

20. Prohibiting public processions

Like its 1936 predecessor, the POA 1986 contains powers to prohibit public processions. Section 13 provides that if at any time the chief officer of police reasonably believes that, due to local circumstances, the powers under section 12 are insufficient to prevent a public procession in that area resulting in serious public disorder he may apply to the district council for an order prohibiting, for up to three months, the holding of all public processions, or any class of public processions in the area. On receiving such an application, the council may, with the consent of the Home Secretary, make the appropriate order: section 13(1) and (2). (These provisions do not apply in London, where the Metropolitan Police Commissioner may apply directly to the Home Secretary for such an order: section 13(4).)

Organising or participating in a procession contrary to such an order is an offence and a uniformed constable may arrest anyone he suspects of so doing: section 7–10.

It will be noted that an order applies to all processions, or all processions in a particular class (e.g. political ones), and not to a single procession alone. Furthermore, a prohibition order can only be made if serious public disorder is threatened; damage to property and disruption of the life of the community are insufficient grounds for prohibiting processions (though under section 12 they are sufficient for the imposition of conditions).

21. Imposing conditions on public assemblies

For the first time, POA 1986, in section 14, confers powers on the police to impose conditions upon public assemblies, as opposed to processions.

Again, it is the senior officer of police who is empowered under this section. If he reasonably believes:

(a) An assembly may result in serious public disorder, serious damage to property, or serious disruption to the life of the community: or

(b) The purpose of the organiser is intimidation (as defined in **19**, above).

He may give directions imposing such conditions as to the place where the assembly may be (or may continue to be) held; the maximum duration of the assembly or the maximum number of persons who may constitute it, as appear to him necessary for the prevention of such disorder, damage or disruption.

'Senior police officer' is defined in the same way here as in section 12, and once more, knowingly organising or participating in an assembly in breach of any such direction is an offence arrestable by a uniformed constable.

'Public assembly' is defined in section 16 as an assembly of 20 or more persons in a public place which is wholly or partly open to the air.

Part III: racial hatred

22. General

Part III of the POA 1986 deals with conduct intended or likely to stir up racial hatred, which is defined as hatred against a group of persons in Great Britain defined by reference to colour, race, nationality (including citizenship) or ethnic or national origin.

Until 1986, such conduct might be criminal under an amended section 5 of the POA 1936. The 1986 act, however, devotes a complete part, involving 13 sections, to the subject. It also separates offences relating to racial hatred from other public-order offences, something the 1936 Act (as amended by the Race Relations Act 1976) did not do.

23. Conduct intended or likely to incite racial hatred

Sections 18–22 make certain kinds of conduct which are (a) intended to incite racial hatred or (b) likely to incite racial hatred, criminal, provided that the conduct concerned is threatening, abusive or insulting (rather like sections 4 and 5).

Thus, section 18 makes it an offence to use threatening, abusive or insulting words or behaviour, or to display any written material which is threatening abusive or insulting, with intention to incite racial hatred, or whereby racial hatred is likely to be stirred up.

Sections 19–22 make similar provisions for the publication or distribution of written material (section 19); the production of a play performed in public (section 20); the distribution showing or playing of a recording, whether sound or visual (section 21); and the broadcasting of a programme, whether in sound or visual image (section 22). Section 23 makes it an offence, also, to possess such written material or recordings with a view to publishing, distributing or playing or broadcasting it.

Of the above offences, only that created by section 18 is an arrestable one.

A person who is not shown to have intended to stir up racial hatred is not guilty of any of the above offences if he did not know and had no reason to suspect that his words or behaviour, or the material (in whatever form) in question was threatening, abusive or insulting.

Section 24 provides that a magistrate may issue a search warrant, whereby a constable may be empowered to enter and search premises where it is suspected offending material is situated. Section 26 provides, however, that no offence is committed in relation to fair and accurate reports of proceedings in Parliament, or of judicial proceedings, provided these are held in open court. No criminal proceedings can, in any case, be initiated except with the consent of the Attorney-General.

Parts IV and V

24. Part IV: exclusion orders

Section 30 provides for exclusion orders, that is, an order prohibiting a person convicted of an offence under section 31 (below) from entering any premises for the purpose of attending a football match.

(a) Such an order must be made by a court, and then only if it is satisfied that it would help to prevent violence or disorder at or in connection with football matches which have been prescribed by the Home Secretary (*see* below). An exclusion order may only be made in addition to some other penalty (such as a fine).

(b) The relevant offences under section 31 are those which fulfil one of the three conditions set out below:

(*i*) The offence must have been committed during any period relevant to the prescribed match, while the accused was at, or entering or leaving the ground. (The relevant period starts two hours before the match commences, and ends one hour after the close of play.)

(*ii*) The offence must have involved either the use or threat of violence towards a person or property, or be an offence under section 5 of this Act (*see* above) *and* must have been committed during a journey to or from a match.

(*iii*) The offence must have been one under sections 1 or 1A of the Sporting Events (Control of Alcohol) Act 1985, which involves possession or consumption of alcohol on journeys to or from prescribed matches.

(c) A 'prescribed' match is any association football match prescribed by an order made by the Secretary of State: section 36. However, under section 37 the Secretary may extend the power to other sporting events. Under section 32, a constable who reasonably suspects that a person has entered premises in breach of an exclusion order may arrest him without a warrant.

25. Part V: miscellaneous and general

Despite the throwaway title, this part of the Act includes, as well as the usual list of repealed statutes etc., provision for certain new offences and powers of arrest which may be said to relate to public order generally.

(a) Section 38 makes it an offence for a person, with the intention of causing public alarm or anxiety, or injury to anyone consuming or using the goods, or economic loss to any person by reason of goods being shunned or steps taken to relieve public alarm or anxiety, to contaminate or interfere with goods, or make it appear that goods have been contaminated or interfered with, or to place such goods in a place where other similar goods are used, sold or supplied. It is also an offence to threaten the above (section 38(2)) or to possess such goods with a view to committing such an offence (section 38(3)).

(b) *Mass trespass.* Section 39 provides that, if the senior officer of police reasonably believes that two or more persons have entered land as trespassers and are present there with the common purpose of residing there for any period, that reasonable steps have been taken by or on behalf of the occupier to ask them to leave and

(1) that any of those persons has caused damage to property on the land or used threatening, abusive or insulting words or behaviour towards the occupier or any member of his family or staff or his agent; or

(2) that those persons have between them brought 12 or more vehicles on to the land

he may direct those persons or any of them to leave the land. Failure to obey such an order knowingly and within a reasonable time is an offence, as is re-entering such land as a trespasser within three months. A uniformed constable may summarily arrest anyone whom he reasonably suspects of either offence.

Progress test 11

1. To what extent is it correct to speak of a 'right' of assembly in the UK? To what extent is such a right restricted by the common law? **(1–3)**

2. Outline the provisions of the Public Order Act 1936 which still apply. **(6–8)**

3. What new offences were created by Part 1 of the Public Order Act 1986? Are there any common 'threads' running through these offences, and how do they differ in general from the common law offences they replaced? **(10–16)**

4. Discuss the legal issues in the following situations:
(a) Fred organises a massive procession to demonstrate against government policies. He does not inform the police. **(18)**
(b) A previous procession organised by Fred has led to violence. When he hears of the planned procession, Chief Constable Adams tells Fred that he must not take the procession along First Avenue. **(19)**
(c) On hearing that a political group opposed to Fred has arranged to violently attack Fred's group, Chief Constable Adams wishes to prohibit all processions in the area. Can he do this? He also decides that public meetings should not continue after nightfall. **(20–21)**

5. What powers are available to the police to deal with 'mass-trespass'? **(26)**

Part four

Executive authority and its control: administrative law

Executive authority and central government

General

1. The executive

According to Hood Phillips in his book *Constitutional and Administrative Law*, the executive is that organ of government which is concerned with the 'general and detailed carrying out of government according to law, including the framing of policy and the choice of the manner in which the law may be made to render that policy possible'.

It must be remembered, however, that there is no separation of powers in the UK, and that it is not, therefore, always possible to identify the executive as a discrete body. Furthermore, as Hood Phillips goes on to point out, the scope of executive functions is extremely wide. Unsurprisingly then, a large number of persons and bodies are involved in executive functions, and may therefore be said, broadly speaking, to be a part of the executive. The best that we can do, therefore, is to identify the scope of executive functions, and then to identify those persons and bodies who discharge such functions.

2. Executive functions and the State

In chapter 1, we referred to the concept of statehood. A State is a territory having its own people and organised system of government. However, it is not uncommon to identify executive functions with the State, since many of these functions spring directly and inevitably from statehood. For example, a State must be able to withstand threats from other countries, or from within. Accordingly, executive functions include (and arguably start with) defence of the realm and the keeping of the peace. In a modern and complex society like the UK, however, the State is involved in a far greater variety of matters than merely defence and keeping the peace. Not uncommonly, the State will also be the chief provider of certain services (such as education and health), and where it is not the provider, it may be concerned with managing and regulating many services and facilities (such as transport and broadcasting). The State will also have an interest in industry (possibly owning the nation's natural resources to prevent over-exploitation). It is the provision, management and regulation of these (and many more) which make up executive functions.

3. Executive bodies

As we saw, it is convenient to identify many executive functions with the State. In this context, however, the term the State is used in a very broad sense indeed, since some of the functions described in 2 above, involve various persons and bodies.

Historically, all such functions were exercised by the king (the Head of State) or in his name. The days of personal government by the king are, of course, long since gone, and executive functions have been largely delegated to others. It is still possible, however, to arrange the various bodies concerned in a kind of hierarchy.

Thus, the persons and bodies chiefly concerned with executive functions in the UK are as follows:

(a) *The Head of State* (the monarch);
(b) *Central government* (the prime minister, Cabinet and other government ministers);
(c) *The Civil Service* (consisting of the permanent advisers to the central government, and other officials);
(d) *The Privy Council*; and
(e) *The armed forces.*

What marks out the above bodies is that they all comprise, or are under the control of, central government. That is, they derive from that circle of advisers which, historically, made up the King's Council, or which (like the armed forces) are under its command.

However, there is another tier of bodies exercising executive functions of more recent provenance, and which came into being in their modern form as a result of the massive expansion of public services and amenities which have occurred since the nineteenth century.

(f) *The police service;*
(g) *Public corporations; and*
(h) *Local councils.*

4. The nature of executive power

Since all of the bodies identified in **3**, above, have some executive functions to discharge, it is inevitable that they will have some authority or powers to enable them to do so.

There are two main aspects to executive authority which must be understood: its nature and its origin.

(a) *Nature.* One of the chief features of executive authority is that it invariably involves some element of discretionary power, that is, the authority to take decisions as to what is to be done. The degree of discretion, however, varies according to the level of the person or body concerned. Thus, for example, a government minister has virtually unlimited discretion in the formulation of policy; in some matters of great practical importance (such as whether or not to go to war), the prime minister (PM) has a great deal of discretion. At this level, discretion is restrained principally by conventions (*see* 3).

On the other hand, a junior clerk in one of the various government departments (a civil servant) will have very little discretion, and what discretion he does have may well be interpretive in nature, rather than creative – for instance, whether an applicant is entitled to some benefit or another. At this level, it is usual for legal restraints to limit the discretion available; this is partly due to reasons given in 5, below.

(b) *Origin.* There are two sources of executive powers in the UK: the royal prerogative and statute.

(*i*) *The royal prerogative.* This is discussed in detail in chapter 13. Broadly, it refers to the authority once enjoyed by the king when he ruled absolutely, before Parliament began to assert itself and an independent judiciary existed. Some important executive functions have their origin in the royal prerogative. (However, as the discussion in chapter 13 shows, these have been much reduced in recent times, and of those that remain, many are now subject to regulation.)

Many of the functions of those bodies which comprise or are directly controlled by central government (*see* 3(a)-(e), above) fall into this category.

(*ii*) *Statute.* Since the seventeenth century, Parliament has enjoyed sovereignty. This has meant that as well as being the supreme law-maker, Parliament has been enabled to create new executive bodies, and confer executive powers on these or existing bodies. Thus, those bodies (*see* 3(f)-(h) above) which do not comprise central government, and which were either created or extended relatively recently fall into this category.

The distinction between the prerogative and statute as sources of executive authority is significant since the system of controls is largely different in each case.

5. Control of executive authority

For historical reasons, there are two broad systems of control which operate so as to restrain executive authority, depending on the origin of that authority.

(a) *The prerogative.* For historical reasons (*see* 13) the royal prerogative has been subject to few legal restraints. In other words, the exercise of powers deriving from the prerogative was not, until recently, subject to real control by the courts. As noted above, most of the functions of central government derive from the prerogative; these are, therefore, largely immune from control in the courts and in particular from judicial review (*see* 15). However, the exercise of prerogative powers (and therefore the functions of central government) are subject to control by means of the system of constitutional conventions which has developed over the years (*see* 3).

(b) *Statute.* Unlike the prerogative, statutory powers have always been subject to control in the courts. Indeed, the application and interpretation of statutes is one of the primary functions of the courts of law. Thus, the important process of judicial review has developed mostly in relation to statutory powers and functions. It is only relatively recently that the courts have begun to apply the principles of judicial review to the prerogative, and then only to a limited extent (*see* 13 and 15). The control of statutory powers is the central topic of the important field of administrative law (*see* 14).

6. The disposition of executive authority

It was established (above) that there are two tiers of executive bodies, based largely on the nature and source of executive power discharged by the body concerned. Thus, historically, those bodies comprising the central government exercise power deriving from the prerogative. The other bodies (police, public corporations and local councils) tend to exercise powers which have been conferred upon them more recently by statute (though some of these, particularly local councils, are actually very ancient in origin). Unfortunately, the picture is not quite as clear-cut as that. In practice, central government also exercises many statutory powers, along with its prerogative ones. Being statutory, these are subject to control by the courts, in the form of judicial review. Thus, to speak of the work of central government as based on the prerogative in its entirety would be false; just as it would be false to suggest that the activities of central government are never subject to judicial control, only conventional control (*see* 3). This is where the important field of administrative law comes in. Administrative law is concerned with the disposition of executive power and its control by the courts. However, the principles of administrative law have developed in relation to the use of statutory powers, whoever they are exercised by. Thus, the system of conventions, whereby prerogative powers (and therefore much of the work of central government) are controlled falls within the field of constitutional law, whereas the principles of judicial review, as well as the relevant procedures and other matters which developed in connection with statutory power comprise administrative law.

Central government

7. Central government

The Head of State in the UK is the Queen. Accordingly, the sovereign is, constitutionally, the head of the executive. However, as previously noted, the Queen enjoys only limited constitutional power, and since most executive functions involve some actual use of power and authority, the government of the country (i.e. the executive functions) is carried out largely in the name of the Crown (*see* 13). The persons or bodies who are chiefly concerned with these functions and which, along with the sovereign may be said to make up the central government, are as follows:

(a) The Prime Minister and other ministers of the Crown;
(b) The Privy Council;
(c) The civil service; and
(d) The armed forces.

The role of the monarchy (the sovereign and Royal Family) is discussed in chapter 13. In this chapter, we will be looking at those persons and bodies named above, and at the prime minister and other ministers of the Crown in particular.

8. Ministers of the Crown

The word minister means an adviser: a minister of the church, for example, is a spiritual adviser and guide. Ministers of the Crown are, therefore, advisers to the sovereign. However, in practice, it is nowadays the ministers themselves who actually take important constitutional decisions. By convention, the Queen must act on the advice given to her by her ministers, and by the prime minister in particular. (The word advice is used in a somewhat notional sense, since the Queen has no choice in the matter.)

The consequence of this convention is that, in practice, it is the ministers of the Crown who wield real political authority. Accordingly, the body of ministers has come to be identified with the government of the country as a whole, so that they are often referred to as 'the government'.

The prime minister and Cabinet

9. The prime minister (PM)

The term prime minister means first minister. It is a relatively recent term, however. The official title of the PM is First Lord of the Treasury, and the title prime minister has only been used in official documents since 1905. (Indeed, until the Ministers of the Crown Act 1937 was passed, it remained formally necessary for the PM to hold the official title of First Lord of the Treasury in order to entitle him to a salary!). The PM is first minister in both the literal and figurative senses.

(a) *Literally.* The PM is the first minister to be appointed when a new government is formed, following a general election (*see* 6). The procedure is governed by constitutional conventions. The leader of the political party which wins the election (and which can therefore command the support of the House of Commons) is summoned by the Queen and invited to form a government. On accepting this invitation, he becomes prime minister, and is officially appointed First Lord of the Treasury.

(b) *Figuratively.* The PM is the most important of the ministers of the Crown. It is the PM who decides who the other ministers will be (by convention, the sovereign must appoint his nominees), and it is the PM who actually tenders the advice of the government to the Queen, during weekly audiences designed for the purpose.

10. The functions of the PM

(a) *Forming a government.* Mention has been made of this function at 9, above. It is the PM who nominates persons for ministerial appointments. The most important of these appointments are of those ministers who will take responsibility for the important departments of State (e.g. the Department of Home Affairs, the

Foreign Office, etc.). Of these, a certain number (usually around 20 or so) will form a kind of inner circle of ministers around the PM: this is known as the Cabinet (*see* 11, below).

(b) *Day-to-day functions.* These include presiding over Cabinet meetings; attending audiences with and advising the Queen; making judicial and ecclesiastical appointments; and speaking and answering questions in the House of Commons, of which the PM, by convention, must be a member. (Parliamentary time is set aside on Tuesday and Thursday afternoons for prime minister's questions.) In addition, the PM takes decisions on the award of honours and represents Her Majesty's government in conferences and meetings with overseas political leaders and even Heads of State. He also attends ceremonial (but official) functions, like the annual dinner given by the Lord Mayor of London.

11. The Cabinet

The origins of the Cabinet are the same as those of the Privy Council (PC), in that both developed from that circle of advisers closest to the king, known as the King's council in medieval times. However, whilst Cabinet members are also members of the PC, that body has a wider membership, including judges, ex-politicians, etc. (*see* **22** and **23**, below). Basically, the Cabinet consists of those ministers whose advice the PM most values. These will invariably include the political heads of the most important departments of state, e.g. the Chancellor of the Exchequer, Home Secretary and Foreign Secretary, but it will also include some ministers without any clearly defined area of responsibility, e.g. the Chancellor of the Duchy of Lancaster. Subject to accepted practices (such as the above) the exact composition of the Cabinet is a matter for the PM; accordingly, Cabinets vary in size.

12. Functions of the Cabinet and Cabinet committees

The main functions of the Cabinet are two-fold.

(a) *The formation of government policy.* It is the chief function of the Cabinet to formulate official government policy, and to carry that into effect by means of legislation.

(b) *Responsibility for the central government department of State.* As mentioned above, the Cabinet consists of those ministers who are responsible for the major Departments of State. By convention, these ministers are individually responsible for the running of these departments (other, non-Cabinet ministers are responsible for their own ministries). The Cabinet as a whole is also subject to collective responsibility. (These two forms of ministerial responsibility are discussed further below.)

(c) *Cabinet committees.* Since the nineteenth century, a system of Cabinet committees has existed for the purpose of expediting government business, on the assumption that certain decisions are taken more effectively by a small group of people, rather than the full Cabinet. A typical example in the nineteenth century was the War Committee: in recent years, a War Cabinet has been used to formulate policy in time of war. Like the Cabinet itself, the composition of such committees is a matter for the PM (who may or may not chair a committee). Until recently, the identity of Cabinet committee members was normally kept secret: there are signs of this changing at the present times.

A particular instance of such a Committee is the inner Cabinet (or 'kitchen' Cabinet, as it is sometimes known) which many PMs have used. This is simply a small group of Cabinet members whose opinions the PM values.

13. Composition of the Cabinet

The basis of the Cabinet has been discussed at **11**, above. Whilst the exact membership is a matter for the PM, Cabinet ministers generally fall into two categories:

(a) Those ministers responsible for the major departments of State, which are considered vital for the work of government. These include (as well as the PM himself). the Home Secretary, the Foreign Secretary, the Chancellor of the Exchequer, and the Lord Chancellor (*see* **17**, below).

(b) Those ministers with relatively light departmental responsibilities. Such ministers are usually appointed by the PM for general reasons, such as their overall usefulness in policy-making, or for some occasional short-term scheme (such as promoting the so-called Citizens Charter introduced by the Major government in 1992), or they may have other non-Cabinet duties. These ministers include Lord President of the Council (who is Chairman of the Privy Council), the Chancellor of the Duchy of Lancaster, and the Lord Privy Seal.

It should also be noted that not all Cabinet ministers are necessarily members of the House of Commons. It is quite normal for the Cabinet to include lords, and for lords to hold other ministerial offices. In fact, under section 2(1) of the House of Commons

Disqualification Act 1975, the number of ministers who may sit in the Commons is limited to 95. Any further ministers (and there are normally around 120 in a government) must sit in the Lords.

14. Non-Cabinet ministers

A typical Cabinet will number some 20 members. However, there are normally around 120 ministers in the government at any given time. Clearly only a small proportion of these ministers will also be members of the Cabinet. Indeed, the ranks of non-Cabinet ministers may well include some departmental heads as well as other ministers. The hierarchy of ministers is as follows:

(a) *Departmental heads.* A minister with overall responsibility for one of the Departments of State is a departmental head. Such ministers are usually referred to as Secretaries of State, e.g. Secretary of State for the Environment; Secretary of State for Home Affairs. Whilst many departmental heads are also Cabinet members, not all are. A few departmental heads are not referred to as Secretary of State but retain ancient titles, e.g. the Chancellor of the Exchequer.

(b) *Ministers with responsibilities for individual ministries.* Most of the departments of State have within them several ministries. For example, the Department of the Environment contains the Ministry for Transport, the Ministry for Local Government, etc. A minister (sometimes referred to as Minister of State) will be responsible for each of these ministries. Such ministers are seldom, if ever, Cabinet members.

(c) *Junior ministers.* Under the authority of a Secretary of State or Minister of State will be a number of junior ministers, whose official title is Parliamentary Under-Secretary of State or Parliamentary Secretary. Whilst these ministers will be associated with a particular department of ministry (and may therefore be referred to as minister in the Home Office or minister in the Foreign Office, as the case may be) they do not have overall responsibility for a department or ministry. A junior minister may, however, have a de-limited area of responsibility within a department or ministry.

Ministerial responsibility

15. Ministerial responsibility

It is an aspect of the system of parliamentary democracy which characterises the British Constitution that, by convention, the government is accountable. However, this accountability is only indirect: government ministers are not, in the UK, elected to office, but appointed. This accountability of ministers is in the form of the conventions of ministerial responsibility. There are two varieties of this: collective and individual responsibility.

(a) *Collective responsibility.* This is quite a complex convention and involves two broad aspects.

(*i*) It is a convention that, once the Cabinet arrives at a decision, then every member of the Cabinet must support that decision. Thus, whatever disagreements may have arisen during discussion in a Cabinet meeting, the Cabinet must present a united front in public. If a Cabinet member feels unable to agree, he should resign.

The basis for this convention is the need for any advice tendered to the Queen to be unanimous. To ensure that it can work, it is also an aspect of the convention that secrecy surrounds Cabinet meetings, so that there is no risk of any dissent which may have occurred being made known and possibly undermining the solidarity of the decision.

(*ii*) Another aspect of collective responsibility is the convention that the government of the day must enjoy the continued support of the House of Commons. (As was noted at 9, above, the government is, in any case, drawn from the political party which succeeds in winning a majority of seats in the House of Commons at a general election: that is really another feature of the convention.) It applies to the government as a whole, and not only to the Cabinet (unlike the other aspects of collective responsibility, noted at (*i*) above). If the government ceases to enjoy the support of the Commons (e.g. on a vote of confidence), the PM should request the sovereign to dissolve Parliament, so that a general election can be held, after which one of the political parties may have the necessary support, and so be enabled to form a government.

(b) *Individual responsibility.* It is also a convention that a minister is responsible for what goes on in his department, ministry or other area of responsibility. Thus, this convention applies to all government ministers, whether Cabinet members or not. Ministers are responsible, both legally and politically, for everything which occurs in their areas of responsibility, including decisions and actions taken by civil servants, for (as Lord Greene put it) ' . . . the decision of the official is, of course, the decision of the

Minister': *Carltona* v. *Commissioners of Works* (1943). This political responsibility may necessitate the minister's resignation (e.g. Sir Thomas Dugdale in 1954, and that of Lord Carrington in 1981) if Parliament requires it, or to avoid embarrassment to the government as a whole which may, if a minister does not assume individual responsibility, have to assume it collectively. (These important conventions are also discussed in 3.)

16. The Shadow Cabinet
Another feature of the British system of parliamentary democracy is the official existence of a parliamentary opposition. Thus, the second largest party in the House of Commons leads Her Majesty's opposition, and it is, by convention, one of the duties of the opposition to call the government to account. To expedite this, the opposition appoints from amongst its own members a spokesperson for each of the various departments, ministries and other major areas of responsibilities. It is the job of an opposition spokesperson to shadow his ministerial counterpart: this involves two aspects:

(1) He is the person most immediately concerned with calling his ministerial counterpart to account, so that, for instance, the opposition spokesman on home affairs will ask questions on matters arising within the responsibility of the Home Secretary.
(2) He is the person who, in the event of the downfall of the government, is most likely to replace his counterpart in the new government. Thus, the Shadow Cabinet must be ready to assume the mantle of government at any time.

The departments of State

17. Departments of State
The origin of the central government departments of State lies in the medieval offices of State, which included the Lord Chamberlain, Lord Chancellor, and Chancellor of the Exchequer, which still exist. It was the responsibility of these office-holders to assist and advise the king in all kinds of matters. As well as these offices, the Privy Council (*see* 22, below) had an advisory role, and some of the modern departments of State originated in the Privy Council, where they were originally committees.

The modern system is largely post-war, since when many of the old ministries and boards, whose origins were as described above, were rationalised into the large departments of State (though some of the ancient titles of the various offices, such as the Chancellor of the Exchequer, were retained). Traditionally, ministries were created by the king, in the exercise of this prerogative. Nowadays, statutory approval is necessary for the creating of a new department or ministry, so as to authorise the salaries of the ministers concerned, and any other funds which may have to be granted anew. However, under the Ministers of the Crown Act 1975, it is possible for the functions of one department of State to be transferred to another by an order in Council (a form of delegated legislation: *see* 14:7-11) without the need for statutory approval.

The following are some of the most important departments of State, and the Ministries they include: unless otherwise stated, the head (minister responsible) of each department is known as Secretary of State.

(*i*) *The Home Office.* In some countries, this would be known as the Ministry for Internal Affairs. It is concerned with domestic, as opposed to foreign, affairs. Responsibilities include the police (indirectly) and law and order (but not the administration of justice, which is the responsibility of the Lord Chancellor's Department); prisons, immigration, deportation and extradition. The Home Secretary also has a role in such matters as licensing, drug enforcement and gambling, and the law relating to elections.

(*ii*) *The Foreign and Commonwealth Office.* As its title suggests, this is the department concerned with foreign policy and the Foreign Service.

(*iii*) *The Treasury.* An ancient department, its head is the Chancellor of the Exchequer. It is concerned with the supervision of national finance, and is therefore arguably the most important department of all. As well as the Chancellor of the Exchequer, its ministers include the Chief Secretary to the Treasury and the Economic Secretary. A junior Treasury minister (the Parliamentary Secretary) customarily acts as government Chief Whip in the Commons.

(*iv*) *The Lord Chancellor's Department.* This is the Ministry of Justice.

(*v*) *The Scottish Office and Welsh Office.* These are situated in Edinburgh and Cardiff, respectively, as well as in London. Scottish affairs and Welsh affairs generally fall within their responsibility. For example, policy decisions on education generally may be taken by the Education Secretary, whose Department will administer them for England. In Scotland and Wales, however, the actual administration of such policies will be the responsibility of the Scottish and Welsh Offices.

(*vi*) *Other departments.* These include the Ministry of Defence, Department of Education and Science, Department of Trade, Department of Health and Social Security, Department of the Environment (which includes Ministries of Housing, Transport and Local Government), and Ministry of Agriculture, Fisheries and Food.

The Civil Service

18. The Civil Service

The Civil Service consists of those servants of the Crown who are employed in a civil, as opposed to military, capacity, other than members of the judiciary. Unlike ministers of the Crown (who may lose office as the result of a general election), civil servants are permanent servants of the Crown. Accordingly, the most senior civil servants include a number of Permanent Secretaries, who are attached to the various Departments of State and ministries. At this level, the task of civil servants is advisory: they are the permanent advisors to the ministers concerned, and it is important, therefore, that they be politically neutral (*see* **21**, below) since that minister will change with a change of government. At the lower levels, however, the work of civil servants is basically administrative (i.e. the putting into effect of policy, rather than formulating it).

There are two branches of the Civil Service: the Home Civil Service, and the Diplomatic Service (whose members are employed by the Foreign Office).

19. Appointments and membership

Appointments to the Civil Service are made by the Civil Service Commission, established in 1855 for that purpose. The main entry requirements are also determined by the Commission, though the detailed conditions of membership of the Civil Service arise from various statutory, common law and prerogative sources, as well as delegated legislation. At common law, civil servants hold office at Her Majesty's pleasure (i.e. they are subject to dismissal at any time, without cause). However, certain provisions of the various Employment Protection and other, similar Acts passed from time to time apply today. Thus, a civil servant is now able to bring an action for unfair dismissal and, as a general rule, may belong to a trade union (but *see* **20**, below).

20. Security in the Civil Service

For obvious reasons, the question of security, and the attendant one of confidentiality, is vital where civil servants are concerned: many civil servants (and not only the highest ranking ones) are privy to confidential information relating to all kinds of topics, including defence matters, national security and ministerial and Cabinet information generally.

Accordingly, certain principles have been established:

(a) All civil servants 'sign' the Official Secrets Act 1989. (This means that the contents of this Act have been brought to the civil servant's attention, and he agrees to be bound by them.)

(b) Special arrangements exist with regard to those civil servants engaged in sensitive work (i.e. work with security implications). These arrangements were introduced in 1948; they are known as 'purging' and 'positive vetting'. Basically, these procedures are designed to ensure that persons with communist or fascist sympathies or affiliation are not permitted to be engaged in work of a sensitive nature.

(c) As noted above, civil servants are nowadays permitted to belong to trade unions, as a general rule. However, this was questioned in *Council of Civil Service Unions* v. *Minister for the Civil Service* (1984) (the GCHQ case). Civil servants employed in GCHQ (a government spying installation) were told that they would no longer be permitted to belong to trade unions, so as to eliminate the risk of industrial action disrupting activities there. The House of Lords held that, in normal circumstances, the employees would have been entitled to belong to a union, or at least to be consulted prior to any such decision. In this case, however, the Minister had satisfied the court that national security was at stake, and therefore, the House would not intervene. (This case is discussed in more detail at 13:9.) It should be noted that, like purging and positive vetting, this principle will apply only to work of a sensitive nature (i.e. with security implications), as at GCHQ. Civil servants whose work is not sensitive are not affected, and they may belong to trade unions.

21. Political activities

Quite apart from the restrictions imposed on civil servants engaged in work of a sensitive nature (**20**, above), civil servants may not engage in certain political activities.

(**a**) No civil servant may become a member of the House of Commons: section 1(3), House of Commons Disqualification Act 1957.

(**b**) Members of certain grades of the Civil Service (i.e. professional and administrative) are permitted no political activities whatever.

(**c**) Other grades are permitted limited activities, such as the following:

> (*i*) Lower executive and clerical grades may take part in local government and political meetings, subject to an approved code of conduct; and

> (*ii*) Industrial grades may participate in any political activities (except, of course, standing for Parliament).

Over and above all these is the requirement that civil servants should remain politically neutral in the sense that they must serve the government which happens to be in office at any particular time.

The Privy Council

22. The Privy Council

The Privy Council (PC) originates in the medieval King's Council. This was a sort of inner council of advisers to the king, and formed the basis not only of the modern Privy Council, but the Cabinet as well. With the rise of democracy, and system of accountable government, the Cabinet rose to prominence as the chief policy-making governmental body. However, the PC still retains some important functions:

(**a**) *Judicial.* The PC remains the highest court of appeal for Commonwealth nations (though few such nations nowadays use it), and for certain domestic courts and tribunals, e.g. ecclesiastical courts. Its judicial functions are, since 1833, exercised by a Judicial Committee, whose members are Lords of Appeal in Ordinary (Law Lords) or ex-Law Lords, presided over by the Lord Chancellor.

(**b**) *Delegated legislative powers.* The PC has powers to make Orders in council (a form of delegated legislation). These include the making of laws for colonies, establishing new government departments or transferring power from one to another, and imposing conditions on the employment of civil servants. Their authority to make such orders arose originally from the royal prerogative; nowadays, such authority largely arises from statutes.

(c) *Advisory*. The PC has retained certain of its advisory functions, in particular, in connection with those prerogative powers which are not political in character, e.g. the establishment of new cities, or of universities, by Royal Charter. Even in the political domain, the PC has some residual authority, so that, for instance, where the political machinery breaks down, or a situation not falling within established convention occurs, the PC's advice may be sought, e.g. whether the PM's request that the Queen dissolves Parliament should be granted (*see* 7).

23. Membership

The PC consists of persons who hold, or have held, political, judicial or ecclesiastical office. These include the Lord President of the Council, Lord Chancellor, Law Lords, and ex Law Lords, the two archbishops of the Church of England, peers, and a number of British and Commonwealth statesmen.

In the case of British statesmen, this customarily includes opposition leaders, as well as the PM and senior Cabinet members. Privy Councillors are addressed as 'The Right Honourable . . . '; they are appointed by letters patent. There are around 300 or so Privy Councillors.

The armed forces

24. Historical basis

The historical basis of the armed forces lies in the feudal levy of knight service, whereby the king's tenants supplied knights for the king's use, in return for their tenure of land. Alternatively, such tenants could pay a sum of money (known as scutage or shield money) towards the maintenance of an army by the king. Such levies were not popular amongst the feudal lords, nor in Parliament, particularly during the seventeenth century, and so they were abolished by the Tenures Abolition Act 1660. The Bill of Rights 1689 forbade the maintenance of an army by the king without Parliament's approval: henceforth, the army would be maintained by funds granted by Parliament.

The Royal Navy, on the other hand, has always been within the scope of the royal prerogative (*see* 13). Nowadays, however, this is largely circumscribed by statutes applying to all of the armed forces, and the navy is funded by money granted by Parliament. The Royal Air Force was created by statute in 1917.

25. Legislative basis

Whatever their origins, all three of the armed forces (as well as the women's services, the Ulster Defence Force and Reserve Forces) are now on a statutory basis. Until 1955, the various statutes authorising the armed forces had to be re-enacted by Parliament every year. Since that year, however, an annual resolution of both Houses of Parliament has been sufficient to authorise the Crown to maintain the armed forces for one year at a time. (This is one of the reasons why, by convention, Parliament must meet at least once a year: *see* 3.) Since 1981, a single Act, the Armed Forces Act 1981, has applied to all three of the armed forces.

26. Common law and military law

Members of the armed forces are subject both to military law and the ordinary law of the land. They are, however, outside the scope of the common law in a number of situations.

(a) They may be dismissed at the pleasure of the Crown, and have no rights (with regard to dismissal) under the employment Protection Acts 1975-78.

(b) They are immune from personal liability in tort in respect of death, injury or damage inflicted upon other servicemen, so long as this occurs in the course of their duties.

(c) Like civil servants, they are not able to stand for election to Parliament: House of Commons Disqualification Act 1975.

(d) A serviceman remains liable for any criminal offences or wrongs other than those committed against his colleagues while on duty. Before 1966 this might have involved him in both the civil courts and a court martial (military court). Under section 25 of the Armed Forces Act 1966, however, a serviceman convicted by a court martial cannot be tried in a civil court for an offence which is substantially the same as the offence for which he has been court martialled (the rule against double jeopardy).

(e) A different situation, as far as the serviceman is concerned, arises when he is confronted with the choice of obeying orders (as he must, under military law) when this involves the commission of an offence; or refusing to obey them, and face a court martial.

The *Manual of Military Law* (the official source book of military law) states that if an order is 'manifestly illegal', a serviceman may refuse it. On the other hand, it does not accept that 'superior orders' should be a defence to a criminal charge. The view of the ordinary courts is best summed up by the words of Willes J who said in *Keighley* v. *Bell* (1966): ' . . . an officer or soldier acting under the orders of his superior – not being necessarily or manifestly illegal – would be justified by his orders.'

This dilemma is partly solved, at least, by the fact that appeal from a court martial lies to the Courts Martial Appeal Court (a division of the Court of Appeal), and thence to the House of Lords.
(f) Apart from disobeying orders, there are many offences under military law which do not exist at common law. For instance, section 1 of the Sexual Offences Act 1967 (which removes the penalties for the offence of buggery, when committed by a male aged twenty-one years or more with a consenting male also aged twenty-one or more and in private) does not apply to the armed forces. Such conduct remains an offence under section 66 of the Army Act 1955, and section 66 of the Air Force Act 1955, which provides that a serviceman guilty of 'disgraceful conduct of an unnatural kind' is guilty of an offence, and section 37 the Naval Discipline Act 1958, which makes similar provision in respect of sailors.

27. Control and deployment of the armed forces
Constitutionally, the sovereign is Supreme Commander of all of the armed forces, as part of the royal prerogative (*see* 13). Thus, whilst the discipline and financial provisions for the armed forces is governed mostly by statute, their actual control and deployment is a matter for the Crown, which in practice means the government. It is within the scope of the prerogative to utilise the armed forces for the suppression of any threat to the peace and security of the realm, whether from outside or within the country. Thus, the keeping of the Queen's peace remains a part of the royal prerogative: *R* v. *Home Secretary, ex p. Northumbria Police Authority* (1987). Similarly, the question whether or not to declare or end war is a matter for the discretion of the Crown: *R* v. *Bottrill, ex p. Keuchenmeister* (1947): *see* 13:14(b)(ii). In either case, the deployment of the armed forces might be (and in the case of war obviously will be) invoked. In practice, however, the Crown has usually turned to Parliament for the grant of particular statutory powers to deal with emergency situations, particularly during the two World Wars. These, and the remaining prerogative (common

law) powers available to the Crown to deal with emergencies, are dealt with below.

The deployment of members of the armed forces to maintain order in peace time (except under special statutory provisions) is nowadays extremely rare. It did occur during the coal strike in 1921, however, when troops were deployed to persuade striking miners in South Wales to return to work. In Northern Ireland, troops have been in use for peace-keeping purposes for twenty years, but this has been authorised by the Northern Ireland (Emergency Provisions) Act 1973 (*see* **29**, below).

Emergency powers

28. The prerogative

As noted in **27**, above, the peace and defence of the realm are the responsibility of the government, and the basis of the government's power in these areas is the royal prerogative. However, in practice, statutory powers have become increasingly important in this area and, in keeping with the principle established in *Attorney-General* v. *De Keyser's Royal Hotel Ltd* (1920) (*see* 13), this has meant that the Crown has had to rely in the statutory powers concerned, since as Lord Reid put it in the *Burmah Oil* case (1965): (*see* 13:18), the prerogative is 'not lost by disuse, but only available for a case not covered by statute'. Apart from the general prerogative of keeping the peace and waging war (mentioned in **27**, above) the following specific prerogatives probably do still exist:

(a) *Seizure of private property.* It is still a part of the prerogative for the Crown to seize private property where it is necessary for the defence of the realm. This was acknowledged in the *Case of Saltpetre* (1607), at a period when many of the King's prerogatives were being denied him! Typically, this prerogative involves the requisitioning of vehicles or vessels for use as troop-carriers, etc. Its exercise is not dependent on a formal declaration of war, as witnessed in the Falklands crisis of 1981. However, the Crown is (subject to any statutory dispensation which may exist) obliged to compensate the owners of private property requisitioned or deliberately destroyed: *Burmah Oil Co. Ltd* v. *Lord Advocate* (1965).

(b) *Martial law.* This is unknown in modern Britain. It is even doubtful whether the Crown is empowered by the prerogative to declare martial law at all, at least in times of peace. Martial law is usually understood to mean the suspension of ordinary law and courts of law, and the temporary government of a country by military tribunal. The general view seems to be that it is hard to envisage an emergency sufficiently serious to justify such a step. However, in times of war, it is possible for martial law to prevail. Indeed, the situation during 1914-18 got quite close to a state of martial law, with special military tribunals set up and empowered to try civilians for newly created offences at least for a short time (*see* 30, below).

29. Statutory powers to deal with peace time emergencies

There are several Acts of Parliament currently in force which equip the government with powers to deal with peace time emergencies, some of them involving deployment of the armed forces.

(a) *The Emergency Powers Act 1920.* This Act, as amended by the Emergency Powers Act 1964, provides that the Crown may declare a state of emergency. This declaration is made by a proclamation which remains in force for one month only (though it can be renewed): section 1(1) EPA 1920. Parliament must be informed, and, if not in session, summoned within five days: section 1(2) EPA 1920. Subject to Parliament's approval, the Crown may make Orders in Council for dealing with the situation, including such measures (which may involve the deployment of troops) as seem necessary for maintaining the peace, and securing public services and safety. (Such powers do not, however, include the imposition of martial law.) A state of emergency may be declared if it appears to the government that essential services, such as the supply or distribution of food, fuel, water or lighting have been, or are about to be, threatened. Such a threat may be natural or man-made. The powers were first used during the general strike of 1926. More recently, they were used in the power workers' strike of 1974.

(b) *The Emergency Powers Act 1964.* This act was passed partly to amend the EPA 1920. However, section 2 of the 1964 Act contains an important new provision. Essentially, it empowers the Crown to deploy members of the armed forces for the maintaining of essential services. Unlike the 1920 Act, however, this does not require that a state of emergency be declared, and does not, therefore, require Parliament's approval. This provision, in fact, re-enacted in permanent form a piece of war-time emergency legislation, the Emergency Powers (Defence) Acts 1939-40. It was used during the firemen's strike of 1977, when troops were deployed for fire-fighting purposes.

(c) *Northern Ireland.* Mention has already been made (at **27** above) of the Northern Ireland (Emergency Provisions) Act 1973 which authorises the deployment of troops for peace-keeping purposes in Northern Ireland.

(d) *Terrorism.* Under the Prevention of Terrorism Act 1989 the government has certain special powers to deal with terrorism. These include:

> (*i*) The power to proscribe an organisation. Membership or support of such an organisation is an offence. Organisations so far proscribed by the Home Secretary include the Irish Republican Army, and the Irish National Liberation Army.
>
> (*ii*) The power to exclude individuals from Great Britain, or from Northern Ireland, or from the UK as a whole: section 3.

30. Statutory powers to deal with war-time emergencies

In both of the major wars in which the UK has been involved this century, statutory powers were largely relied upon by the Crown. With some exceptions (*see* **29**, above) such powers lapsed at the end of each of the wars concerned, with the repeal of the acts in question. Accordingly, more recent military adventures (such as the Falklands and Gulf Wars) have not invoked war-time provisions, and were conducted under existing prerogative powers (*see* **27** and **28**, above).

(a) *Defence of the Realm Acts 1914-15.* The 1914 Act placed the UK virtually under martial law (*see* **28**, above). Special military tribunals were empowered to try certain offences: this situation was changed, however, by the 1915 Act, which reinstated normal trial procedures. The 1915 Act also conferred upon the government 'such powers as are necessary for the efficient prosecution of the war'. These did not include the power to impose any new charge on the public (e.g. by way of taxation): *Attorney-General* v. *Wiltshire United Dairies Ltd* (1922). However, the government was relieved of any liability (both civil and criminal) arising from anything done in the course of the war, provided it was done for the defence of the realm or in the public interest: Indemnity Act 1920.

(b) *Emergency Powers (Defence) Acts 1939-40.*

> (*i*) The 1939 Act had the general purpose of conferring upon the executive the power to make such regulations 'as appear necessary for securing the public safety, the defence of the realm, the maintenance of public order and the efficient

prosecution of the war', and for 'maintaining supplies and services essential to the life of the community': section 1. Unlike the 1914-15 Acts, this Act conferred upon the government the power to impose charges, subject to Parliament's approval (which could be given *ex post facto*). One particularly important and controversial regulation passed under these powers was Regulation 18(8), which empowered the Home Secretary to intern any person whom he had reasonable grounds for believing to be of 'hostile origin or association'. In *Liversidge* v. *Anderson* (1942) the House of Lords held that, provided there was no evidence that he had failed to act in good faith, the Home Secretary's decision could not be challenged, and that he could not be compelled to disclose his reasons.

(*ii*) The Emergency Powers (Defence) Act 1940 empowered the Crown to make regulations 'requiring persons to place themselves, their services, and their property at the disposal of His Majesty'. Unlike the prerogative power to seize property, which (at lease since the *Burmah Oil* case) may involve the duty to pay compensation to affected individuals, the powers conferred under this Act placed the Crown under no obligation to compensate.

[Note: the War Damage Act 1965 which took effect retrospectively, effectively reversed the *Burmah Oil* decision as far as the conduct of the Crown in the prosecution of a war is concerned.]

Progress test 12

1. What is the executive? What are the main functions of the executive, and what persons and bodies are involved in these? (1-3)

2. Describe the chief features of executive authority in terms of: (a) its nature; and (b) its origins. (4)

3. Outline the main systems of control which limit the exercise of executive authority. What difference does the origin of a particular executive power make in this regard? (5-6)

4. What are the main functions of the Prime Minister? (9-10)

5. Describe the composition, functions and workings of the Cabinet. What is meant by the 'collective responsibility' of the Cabinet? (11-13, 15)

6. Summarise the origins and background of the various Departments of State, describing some of the major ones. **(17)**

7. What are the functions of the Privy Council today? Who are the members of the Privy Council? **(22–23)**

8. In what ways are members of the armed forces outside the scope of the ordinary law of the land? **(26)**

9. Describe the main powers available to the Crown to deal with Emergencies: **(a)** in peace-time; and **(b)** in time of war. **(28–30)**

13

The monarchy and the royal prerogative

The monarchy

1. The monarchy

As was noted at 1:13, the system of government in the UK is said to be monarchical. In other words, the Head of State is a hereditary monarch (currently Queen Elizabeth II), as opposed to a president. However, the Queen does not actually rule in the sense of wielding any real governmental power. We have what is known as a constitutional monarchy, that is, one where the authority of the monarch is limited by the laws and conventions which make up the constitution.

Thus, for example, legal sovereignty (the authority to make laws) now rests with Parliament (*see* 4), and even most executive functions are nowadays carried out by ministers of the Crown, and not by the Queen herself, whose role is largely titular and/or ceremonial. It was not always thus, however. Historically, the monarch wielded a great deal of power, and up until the time of the Stuarts many English monarchs asserted their right to rule absolutely. It was largely due to the assertion of this right by the Stuart kings that the constitutional developments of the seventeenth century, culminating in the revolution of 1688 and Bill of Rights the following year, occurred, leading to the sovereignty of Parliament and constitutional monarchy we know today.

It will be obvious from the above that English kings wielded power long before Parliament existed, or indeed any of the present organs of the government. These powers were not derived from any constitution or other legal source in the strict sense. Rather, they derived from an assumption of authority, based on the belief that the king, by virtue of his royal birth, was somehow superior to others and endowed with a God-given right to rule (the 'Divine Right of Kings'). The authority thus vested was known as the royal prerogative. It still exists (though in vastly changed form), and remains an important feature of our constitution. The modern prerogative is discussed below.

2. The succession and title

One of the purposes of the Act of Settlement 1700, was to settle the matter of the royal succession. Thus, succession to the throne is limited to the Protestant heirs of Princess Sophia, Elector of Hanover (granddaughter of James I).

Upon the death of the king (or queen, where she is the monarch rather than the monarch's spouse), his successor immediately accedes to the throne. Hence the saying, that 'the king never dies'. (This occurs even if the successor is an infant; in such cases a Regent will be appointed under the Regency Act 1953 to discharge most of the king's functions.) The same will apply if the king abdicates (voluntarily gives up the throne), as occurred in 1936, when Edward VIII abdicated. The requirement that the successor be a Protestant also extends to his spouse; in 1978 for instance Prince Michael of Kent was obliged to renounce his own right of succession when he married a Roman Catholic.

The official title of the reigning monarch has been changed from time to time since the Act of Settlement, to accommodate (for instance) the union of England and Wales with Scotland (1707) and Ireland (1800), and, in this century, the acquisition of independence by various Commonwealth nations. Such changes have been affected by various Acts of Parliament or by royal proclamation made under an enabling Act. The current Act is the Royal Titles Act 1953. Under this Act, the current monarch, Queen Elizabeth II, bears the official title, Elizabeth II, by the Grace of God of the United Kingdom of Great Britain and Northern Ireland and of her other Realms and Territories Queen, Head of the Commonwealth, Defender of the Faith.

3. The sovereign and Royal Family

It is usual, when speaking of the monarchy, to refer not only to the king or queen regnant (i.e. reigning queen, as opposed to simply the wife of a king) but to the Royal Family as a whole. Thus, the Royal Family consists of the following:

(a) *The sovereign.* For historical reasons the king or queen regnant is also referred to as the sovereign. This is because he or she is the Head of State, that is, all governmental powers historically flow from the monarch. Nowadays, of course, the Queen plays a very limited role in government, though it remains the case that many important executive powers are carried out in her name, as in the administration of justice. (Parliament does not act in the name of the sovereign, though the Queen does have a limited role in the legislature, and her assent to bills is a necessary feature of the legislative process.)

(b) *The sovereign's spouse.* Queen Elizabeth's husband is Prince Phillip, the Duke of Edinburgh.

(c) *The princes and princesses 'of the blood'.* These are important, since they have a right to the succession (though this may be a very distant one). The heir apparent (i.e. the person with the immediate right to succession, who will accede to the throne on the Queen's death), is the eldest son of the sovereign, who by custom enjoys the title of Duke of Cornwall, and may be installed as Prince of Wales. The current heir to the throne is Prince Charles, Prince of Wales. Since the succession to the throne is linear, Prince Charles's son William is the next in line after him (rather than, say, his sister, who is nevertheless a 'princess of the blood'). The Queen's eldest daughter is entitled to (and does) enjoy the title, Princess Royal. By the Royal Marriage Act 1772, members of the Royal Family require the sovereign's consent to marry; their spouses are commonly regarded as forming part of the Royal Family also, though they have no constitutional functions as such.

4. Finance of the monarchy
The monarchy is mainly financed in two ways.

(a) *The Civil List.* Since the Civil List Act 1952 (as amended in 1972 and 1975) an annual sum is granted by Parliament for the financing of the monarchy, known as the Civil List. Money is allocated to members of the Royal Family, to meet the expenses they necessarily incur in the discharge of their official duties, and for the upkeep of the royal household servants, etc. The money allocated to the use of the Queen herself is known as the 'Privy Purse'.

(b) *Departmental allocations.* The upkeep of the royal palaces, the royal yacht *Britannia*, and other such artefacts used by the Royal Family in their official capacity is the responsibility of central government. Thus the appropriate government department will provide the necessary funds, so that (for example) the Department of the Environment maintain the royal palaces.

Legally, the monarchy is meant not to be a drain on public funds, and the money which is thus allocated or provided in the Civil List is meant to derive from the income from crown property. Since the reign of George III it has been customary for the sovereign to surrender the hereditary income from royal estates, and it is from this income that the funds used to finance the monarch are supposedly drawn. The administration of royal estates is now the responsibility of Crown Estate Commissioners: Crown Estate Act 1961.

Nevertheless, there has recently been growing concern over expenditure of public money by the Royal Family, and with the amounts involved in the Civil List in particular. Accordingly, there have been calls for the abolition of the Civil List, or at least for it to be limited to those members of the Royal Family who are in the immediate line of succession.

There is nothing to prevent the Royal Family from owning private property, and amassing wealth from investments, etc. Some members of the Royal Family, particularly those with few official duties, may hold full-time employment.

5. The sovereign's official functions

As her title suggests (*see* 2, above), the Queen is not simply the sovereign of the UK. Mention has already been made of the fact that as the Head of State, executive and judicial powers are carried out in her name. She remains sovereign of the colonies and of those Commonwealth nations which have not become republics (such as Canada), as well as Head of the Commonwealth of Nations. She is also Supreme Commander of the Armed Forces, and Head of the Established Churches of England and Scotland. As such, the Queen has many official functions to discharge. These are broadly as follows:

(a) *work relating to the government of the nation* (e.g. weekly audiences with the prime minister, signing Royal Commissions).
(b) *Ceremonial occasions* (e.g. the State Opening of Parliament).
(c) *Making and receiving Commonwealth visits.* These are not mutually exclusive, however, in that, for example, the Queen will consult the British prime minister on a question relating to Commonwealth matters.

6. Sovereign and Crown

Whilst this might, on the face of it, seem a curious distinction to draw, it is normal to use the terms the sovereign and the crown differently. It remains the case that legally, much executive power is in the hands of the sovereign. However, by virtue of conventions, the sovereign has little real power since:

(a) She must act on the advice of the prime minister or (occasionally) some other minister; and
(b) Many powers are in practice exercised by the government.

We therefore speak of the Crown in either of these situations, and of the sovereignty when referring to the Queen in her personal capacity. Thus, most executive powers are exercised by the government, or by individual government ministers, in the name of the Crown. It should also be remembered that many executive powers and functions have actually been removed from the sovereign by Parliament and are nowadays exercised by Parliament itself (e.g. the power to impose taxation) or have been delegated by Act of Parliament to a particular minister in the government of the day. (This category includes a vast number of powers which are the subject of administrative law: *see* 14 onwards.)

The royal prerogative

7. The prerogative

Mention has already been made of the fact that, whilst most governmental powers were originally exercised by the sovereign himself, few are nowadays so exercised. Nevertheless, such powers are exercised by, or on the advice of government ministers in the name of the Crown. These powers are said to constitute the prerogative, which has therefore been defined as 'the residue of discretionary and arbitrary authority which at any time is legally left in the hands of the Crown' (Dicey, *An Introduction to the Study of the Law of the Constitution*).

The three key elements of the prerogative according to Dicey are, therefore:

(1) It is residual in nature. That is, it is what remains after the law (in the form of statute and common law decisions) has whittled it down.
(2) Accordingly, the scope of the prerogative has diminished. Prerogatives cannot be created or extended. As Lord Diplock put it in *BBC* v. *Johns* (1965), 'It is 350 years and a Civil War too late for the courts to extend the royal prerogative by judicial decision.'
(3) It consists of 'discretionary and arbitrary authority' and is in the hands of the Crown and no one else.

Whether or not all of these elements are as true now as they were in Dicey's time is discussed below.

8. Classification of prerogatives

Like parliamentary privilege (which it resembles in certain ways) the prerogative consists of a variety of powers, rights and immunities. Hence, we speak of various prerogatives.

Broadly, there are two categories of prerogatives:

(a) *Personal prerogatives.* These are enjoyed by the sovereign in her personal capacity. Generally, they consist of rights and immunities, rather than powers. For example:

> (*i*) *'The King never dies.'* As was mentioned at **2**, above, the monarchy is a constant feature of the British Constitution, and when one sovereign dies, his (or her) heir immediately succeeds him.
>
> (*ii*) *'The king can do no wrong.'* This means that the sovereign cannot be proceeded against in a court of law and is immune from all civil and criminal liability. In addition, the Sovereign is not liable to pay income tax, even on her own personal income. As with the whole question of the Civil List (*see* **4** above) this has provoked controversy of late, and proposals have been made by some MPs that this immunity should be abolished, at least as far as the Queen's personal income is concerned.

In addition to these, the sovereign is said to be always legally capable (*see* **2**, above) and his person is inviolable (it is high treason to assault the sovereign, or attempt to assassinate him). These are very ancient prerogatives indeed.

(b) *Political prerogatives.* These are the prerogatives which involve governmental power in one form or another. Accordingly, most are nowadays exercised by government ministers, in the name of the Crown. Some important political prerogatives are still exercised by the sovereign. However, the sovereign is obliged to act on the advice of the prime minister or (occasionally) some other minister, by convention.

Some of the most important prerogative powers which are formally exercised by the sovereign are as follows:

> (*i*) The appointment of ministers (including the prime minister).
>
> (*ii*) The summoning and dissolution of Parliament.

These important prerogatives are not governed by law but by conventions so that, for instance, the Queen should appoint as ministers those persons whom the prime minister requests. The prime minister himself, of course, is (by convention) the leader of the political party which enjoys the support of the House of Commons.

9.   Prerogative and the Crown

As we saw, most prerogatives, and particularly those involving any real political power, are actually exercised by government ministers, in the name of the crown.

These prerogatives, too, can be classified into two categories:

(a)   *The prerogative in relation to home affairs*; and
(b)   *The prerogative in relation to foreign affairs.*

In connection with such prerogatives, we speak of the Crown (or nowadays even the government) as the chief participant.

Amongst the most significant prerogatives in relation to Home Affairs (over and above the personal prerogatives discussed above) are the following:

(*i*)   *The defence of the realm, and declarations of war and peace.* (This obviously has implications for foreign affairs also, since not every war involves the actual defence of British territory, e.g. the Gulf War in early 1991.) In addition, deployment of the armed forces generally.

(*ii*)   *Judicial prerogatives.* Whilst the judiciary itself is independent of government, certain functions of a broadly judicial character remain within the scope of the prerogative. For example, certain kinds of judicial proceedings can only be brought by the Attorney-General (who is a government minister) or with his consent. Similarly, the prerogative of mercy (pardoning of convicted criminals) is, in practice, a power which is in the hands of the Home Secretary. Until the abolition of capital punishment in the UK in 1965, the prerogative of mercy included the power to commute the death penalty to life imprisonment. Some colonies (Bermuda and Hong Kong) have retained the death penalty: in those colonies, this aspect of the prerogative of mercy is exercised by the colonial governor.

(*iii*)   *The grant of honours.* Most honours (such as knighthoods, peerages, etc.) are in the gift of the prime minister. A few (the Orders of Merit, the Garter, and the Thistle) are dispensed by the sovereign personally.

(*iv*)   *National security and the Queen's peace.* Whilst most aspects of these are now regulated by statute, the underlying basis of governmental power in these areas remains the prerogative.

Thus, it has been held that normal legal requirements can in some cases be circumvented where these areas are involved: *Council of Civil Service Unions* v. *The Minister for the Civil Service* (1984) and *R* v. *Home Secretary ex p. Northumbria Police Authority* (1987). (These are discussed below.)

(*v*) *Ecclesiastical affairs.* The appointment of the archbishops and bishops of the Church of England is done by the Crown, acting under the prerogative.

The prerogative and foreign affairs – 'Act of State'

10. The prerogative in foreign affairs

The conduct of foreign affairs – that is, relations between the UK and foreign countries, including the making of treaties – forms part of the prerogative. Generally speaking, foreign affairs are conducted by, or (in the case of the UK) on behalf of, the Head of State. Accordingly, foreign affairs are sometimes referred to as 'Acts of State'. Indeed, in some countries (such as the USA), the government department responsible for such affairs is known as the Department of State Affairs (or something similar), usually headed by a Secretary of State.

Whilst the UK's foreign affairs are mostly conducted by the government in the name of the Crown, they too may be referred to as 'Acts of State'. That phrase, however, has come to acquire a somewhat more restricted meaning with a more specifically legal context.

11. Act of State

As noted in **10**, above, the phrase 'Act of State' may be used when speaking of any exercise of its prerogative in relation to foreign affairs by the government. Legally, however, 'Act of State' has come to be used as the title of a kind of defence which can be raised by the government so as to obtain immunity from any legal liability arising from loss of injury caused to persons or property by its conduct in relation to foreign affairs.

To operate as such a defence, 'Act of State' must be specifically claimed by the government in any proceedings brought against it or its servants or agents. Thus, the government must have approved the action beforehand, or be prepared to ratify it after the event. The effect of this is that, in so doing, the government is accepting that the action complained of falls within the broad scope of official government policy. For this, of course, they are politically (though not legally) accountable by virtue of the convention of ministerial responsibility (*see* 12:15).

12. Act of State as a defence

Strictly speaking, Act of State is not a defence as such. When successfully invoked, a plea of Act of State means that the Crown is immune from any legal liability arising from its actions, because, since they fall within the scope of established prerogative powers, they cannot be challenged in a court of law. In fact, there is an even more obvious reason why Acts of State cannot give rise to legal liability. An act of State is an exercise, by the government, of its prerogative in relation to foreign affairs. In other words it involves conduct on the part of the British government, which by its nature occurs outside British territory and therefore beyond the usual jurisdiction of the British courts. As Fletcher Moulton LJ put it in *Salaman* v. *Secretary of State for India* (1906) an Act of State is 'essentially an act of sovereign power and hence cannot be challenged, controlled or interfered with by courts'.

As the cases show, however, the courts have confined the use of the defence of Act of State to those situations which can genuinely be said to have involved *only* foreign affairs.

13. Cases on Act of State

Act of State is pleaded by the Crown so as to avoid liability for loss or damage suffered by some person at the hands of the government. Such persons may fall into various categories; an examination of these demonstrates the limits and scope of the doctrine.

(a) *British subjects, within British territory.* It is well established that action by the Crown which causes loss to a British subject, and which occurs within British territory (even if this is overseas) is not an Act of State and is therefore not immune from legal liability. Thus, when British naval officers ordered the destruction of the plaintiff's Newfoundland lobster factory he could recover compensation in the British courts, since he was a British subject, and the action took place on British territory (Newfoundland being a colony at the time: *Walker* v. *Baird* (1892).)

The general principle here is that, whilst the Crown (by virtue of the prerogative) has certain powers over its subjects, it owes them its protection in return: this includes the protection of the courts.

Thus, it is well established that the Crown may, in time of war or other emergency, requisition private property belonging to its subjects: *Case of the King's Prerogative in Saltpetre* (1637). However, the subject concerned is entitled to bring his case before the common law courts, to see that the Crown has not exceeded the scope of its prerogative powers. He should not be prevented from so doing by a plea of Act of State.

(b) *Aliens within British territory.* The position of aliens will depend upon whether they are friendly or hostile.

(*i*) *Friendly aliens.* A friendly alien who is temporarily in Britain or British territory is in the same position as a British subject, by virtue of what is known as 'local allegiance'. Thus, whilst aliens do not enjoy the legal right to enter and remain in the UK, if they are permitted to do so, they are entitled to the same legal protection as subjects, and enjoy many of the same legal rights (such as property rights, rights to make contracts, etc.) as British subjects. (They do not, however, enjoy the right to vote in general elections.)

Accordingly, when an American citizen was arrested in connection with suspected illegal drilling and his property and money confiscated, he was entitled to go to the courts to obtain their return. The government could not plead Act of State so as to justify their retention: *Johnstone* v. *Pedlar* (1922).

(*ii*) *Enemy aliens.* These are citizens of a country currently at war with the UK. Such persons have no rights in the UK: indeed enemy aliens have not infrequently been subject to internment (imprisonment without trial) for the duration of the war. Accordingly, the Crown can claim Act of State in an action for such detention brought by an enemy alien at the end of hostilities: *R* v. *Bottrill, ex p. Kuechenmeister* (1947).

(c) *Aliens abroad.* It is settled law that an alien who suffers loss due to the conduct of the Crown or its agents in a foreign country cannot proceed with an action for compensation in the British courts: *Buron* v. *Denman* (1848). Such a person may, of course, pursue his claim through diplomatic channels, in the hope of an *ex gratia* payment, but the British government will, by virtue of its being an Act of State, be under no legal liability to compensate him for his loss.

14. The problem of British subjects abroad

Until fairly recently this posed no real problem, since the

general principle was that the Crown owed its protection to all its subjects, wherever they were. However, that principle was applicable to a time when no clear distinction between subjects and citizens (or nationals) arose. The term subject is an historic one: it refers to the relationship between the sovereign and his people. This relationship was a two-way one, in which by virtue of the prerogative, the sovereign had authority and power over them but, reciprocally, subjects were entitled to the protection of the Crown. Hence certain prerogatives (such as the authority to declare war) involve both elements: wars are waged so as to protect subjects from outside interference but will involve a certain loss of liberty or property on their part.

British subjects are those persons, wherever they live, who owe allegiance to the Queen. On acquiring independence from British rule the former colonies and dominions understandably wished to consolidate their new status by conferring their own nationality on their people. However, such people did not necessarily cease to be British subjects, since, in many cases, the newly independent countries were not republics, but looked to the Queen as their sovereign (e.g. Canada, and Australia).

Thus, a situation arose where, not only did many British subjects reside permanently in foreign countries, but they were also not British citizens, having the nationality of the country where they permanently lived. This problem was further compounded when, in 1948 the UK for the first time passed its own Nationality Act, conferring the status of citizens of the UK and Colonies on those who had been born within the UK or its colonies, or who were descended from a British citizen. (The British Nationality Acts of 1981 and 1989 have amended the rules relating to citizenship still further.) This complex situation formed the background to the case of *Nissan* v. *Attorney-General* (1970).

15. *Nissan* v. *Attorney-General* (1970)

In this case, British troops were despatched to Cyprus, which had recently acquired independence from British colonial rule, to help keep the peace at the request of the Cypriot government. In due course they were assimilated into a United Nations peace-keeping force. In the meantime, however, the troops had caused damage to property belonging to the appellant, who was a citizen of the UK and Colonies. The question for the House of Lords was whether the Crown's claim that this was an Act of State should prevent the appellant from proceeding with a claim for compensation in the British courts!

The House of Lords held that he should be able to proceed on the following alternate grounds:

(1) *Per* Lord Reid: ' . . . a British subject – at least if he is also a citizen of the UK and Colonies – can never be deprived of his legal right to redress by any assertion that the acts of which he complains are Acts of State.'

(2) *Per* Lord Pearce: (Lords Morris, Wilberforce and Pearson concurring) the specific acts complained of (i.e. the damage caused by the troops) were not, despite the Crown's claim, Acts of State at all.

The prerogative and the courts

16. Statute and the prerogative

For many years, Parliament has been involved in the process of gradually whittling down the prerogative. Thus, many statutes have removed prerogative powers from the hands of the Crown and either simply abolished the prerogatives concerned, or transferred them to some other body (possibly Parliament itself, or a specific minister). In either case, the prerogative concerned ceases to exist, since even if the power or function involved is conferred on to a government minister, it has become in the process a statutory, rather than prerogative, power or function. An example of a prerogative being abolished by statute can be seen in the Crown Proceedings Act 1947, which abolished the Crown's immunity from liability to proceedings in contract and tort (though not the sovereign's personal immunity). Examples of the transfer of powers away from the prerogative and their conversion into statutory powers are numerous; such matters as taxation, the power to legislate and many others have been affected in this way.

Alternatively a statute may cover the same ground as a prerogative by conferring, say, an identical power on some person or body, or by providing for a similar immunity or other legal procedure. The general rule is that a prerogative power and a statutory provision covering the same ground cannot co-exist; that is, the court must apply one or the other. Accordingly, due to the doctrine of parliamentary sovereignty it is the statute which will prevail and be applied by the courts.

The following points should be noted:

(a) The prerogative is not abolished except by express words to that effect (as in the Crown Proceedings Act 1947, for example). Where a statute does not expressly abolish a prerogative, but merely covers the same ground, the prerogative is not impliedly repealed as a statute would be but merely suspended. This is so because the statute itself may be repealed, which might result in a gap in governmental authority if the prerogative had ceased to exist. Thus, where legislation covering prerogative powers is repealed (as occurred with some war-time legislation) the prerogative again begins to operate.

(b) The implication of (a) above is that whilst legislation of the kind discussed is in force, the Crown is bound by its terms and cannot claim to be acting under prerogative powers to hide behind the prerogative by way of defence.

In *Attorney-General* v. *De Keyser's Royal Hotel Ltd* (1922), the army, acting under the authority of the Crown, requisitioned the plaintiff's hotel for use as a military headquarters. They claimed they were entitled to do this under prerogative powers. However, the Defence of the Realm (Consolidation) Act 1914, re-enacting earlier statutory provisions, laid down procedures for the payment of compensation in cases of requisitioning. The House of Lords therefore held that the Crown was obliged to pay compensation in accordance with these provisions. Since the statute covered powers of requisitioning, the Crown could not claim to be acting under a prerogative power which entitled them to seize property without the obligation to compensate its owners.

The line is a fine one, however, and unless the statute concerned covers the prerogative quite clearly, the courts will probably accept the continued existence of the prerogative concerned. In *R* v. *Home Secretary, ex p. Northumbria Police Authority* (1987) a police authority sought to challenge the Home Secretary's decision to make riot-control equipment available to police forces. The Authority claimed that the issue of equipment was governed by section 4 of the Police Act 1964 which empowers police authorities to supply 'such vehicles, clothing and other equipment as may be required'. The Home Secretary contended that another section of the Act (which referred to training and related matters) empowered him to supply riot-control equipment. In addition he claimed he was in any case empowered to supply the equipment under his prerogative power to maintain the peace. The Court of Appeal accepted the Home Secretary's claim, holding that, despite the provision of section 4, the Home Secretary's prerogative powers were intact, and that these included the power to provide the equipment in question.

17. Prerogative and the courts

One of the most significant developments in recent years has been the extent to which the courts are prepared to challenge the use of prerogative powers by the Crown.

In relation to Home Affairs (unlike Foreign Affairs, where the doctrine of Act of State applies), there is no presumption that the prerogative as a whole is non-justiciable. In other words, it is within the jurisdiction of the courts to examine a purported exercise of prerogative power. However, until quite recently, the courts used such a jurisdiction somewhat sparingly, and were only prepared to look at the prerogative concerned, and to determine whether the Crown, in acting, had in fact acted within its scope. Thus, the courts confined themselves to determining the existence and scope of a prerogative.

This judicial reluctance led some to the conclusion that the use of prerogatives was not subject to the important principles of judicial review, which involves an examination by the court of executive or administrative action, so as to determine whether it is lawful or not. It is now clear, with hindsight, that this was not entirely correct.

(a) Even as early as the seventeenth century the courts were prepared to examine the purported use of prerogative powers and decide upon their lawfulness. Thus, in the *Case of Proclamations* (1616) the court established the principle that 'the King hath no prerogative save that which the law allows him' (*per* Coke CJ) and the King's power to make or suspend laws without Parliament's approval was removed by the court. Thus, the existence and scope of a prerogative was (and is) a question of common law for the court to decide.

(b) Accordingly, in determining the limits of a prerogative, and deciding whether, in acting, the Crown was exceeding those limits the courts have, in practice, been applying at least one of the principles of judicial review to the use of prerogative power.

(c) However, it has become clear in recent years that, by virtue of their nature, certain prerogative powers cannot be made subject to judicial review. It is now established, however, that this is not due to the fact that they are prerogatives, or involve powers derived from the prerogative, but is due to the particular nature of the power concerned.

18. Judicial review of the prerogative

There have been several recent examples of the courts examining a prerogative and, having determined its scope and limits, concluding that the government, in purportedly exercising a prerogative, has actually exceeded its scope. To that extent at least, a prerogative is subject to the jurisdiction of the courts.

(a) *Burmah Oil Co. Ltd* v. *Lord Advocate* (1965). The government had authorised the destruction, by military personnel, of the plaintiff's property in Burma (then a British colony) to prevent it falling into the hands of the Japanese army, with whom Britain was at war. They claimed that, not only were they entitled (by virtue of the prerogative power to defend the realm) to destroy the property, but also that by virtue of the same prerogative, they were exempt from the need to compensate the plaintiffs. The House of Lords rejected this. A distinction has to be drawn between 'battle-damage' (i.e. damage caused during actual fighting) which was an inevitable consequence of war, and deliberate destruction such as this. Where deliberate destruction was concerned, the Crown enjoyed a limited power, namely to take and/or destroy the property. The prerogative did not extend to denying compensation to the owners, and the Crown was obliged, if it took property, to 'take and pay'.

> [Note: The War Damage Act 1965 provided that the Crown should not be liable to pay compensation in respect of damage or destruction of property caused by acts lawfully done during or in contemplation of war, thus nullifying the *Burmah Oil* case decision.]

(b) In *Laker Airways Ltd* v. *Department of Trade* (1977) the Court of Appeal applied the principle laid down in *Attorney-General* v. *De Keysers Royal Hotel Ltd* (*see* **16**, above). However, the court went further, holding that even where a statutory provision does not entirely cover a prerogative (thus preserving the prerogative in question) the residual prerogative power must not be used in a way that runs counter to the statute, or enables a minister to thwart its purpose. (Lord Denning went even further in suggesting that a prerogative could never be used 'unreasonably' or 'mistakenly', whether a statute covered it or not.)

(c) The most significant decision in recent years has been that of the House of Lords in *Council of Civil Service Unions* v. *Minister for the Civil Service* (1984) (the CCSU case).

19. The *CCSU* case

Industrial action at the Government Communications Headquarters (GCHQ) had aroused anxiety on the part of the government that, so long as employees there remained members of trade unions, there was a risk that activities might be disrupted. Since these activities included surveillance of foreign intelligence communications, it was felt that a risk to national security might result. Accordingly, it was agreed that employees at GCHQ should no longer be permitted to be members of trade unions, and the Minister (i.e. the Prime Minister, Margaret Thatcher) issued instructions to that effect under the Civil Service Order in Council 1982, whose authority (somewhat unusually) derived from the prerogative, rather than from statute.

The Council of Civil Service Unions, on behalf of their members at GCHQ, brought proceedings for judicial review, claiming that on previous occasions the Minister had consulted them in matters relating to their employment, so that they were entitled to such consultation on this occasion. In failing to consult before taking her decision, they claimed, the Minister had acted improperly. The Minister claimed that because the Order in Council had been made using prerogative powers, her action was non-justiciable. Further, her action was also non-justiciable on the grounds that national security was involved.

The House of Lords held that there was no general rule that powers derived from the prerogative were non-justiciable and (*per* Lords Scarman, Diplock and Roskill) the same was also true of the prerogative generally. However, the House agreed that certain prerogative powers were by their nature, non-justiciable (i.e. not subject to the jurisdiction of a court of law). This is for the following alternative reasons:

(a) The exact limits of a prerogative power can not be defined by reference to its objects or to the procedures involved so as to make it a suitable one for judicial review (*per* Lords Fraser and Brightman); or
(b) The subject matter of a prerogative is such that it is non-justiciable (*per* Lords Scarman, Diplock and Roskill).

According to Lord Roskill, such prerogatives included:

(*i*) The making of treaties;

(*ii*) The defence of the realm;

(*iii*) The grant of honours;

(*iv*) The prerogative of mercy;

(*v*) The dissolution of Parliament; and

(*vi*) The appointment of ministers.

In the instant case, since the Minister had indicated by affidavit that national security (defence of the realm) was involved, the House felt the decision could not be challenged.

20. Summary – non-justiciable powers

The *CCSU* case appears to have established that there is no general rule that the exercise of prerogative powers in relation to home affairs is non-justiciable. However, it was agreed that certain powers were not justiciable. An attempt must be made to establish some guidelines for this.

(a) Lords Fraser and Brightman returned to the fact that many prerogative powers cannot be satisfactorily defined in terms of objects and procedures, so that judicial review is not possible. For example, the prerogative of mercy. The Home Secretary is empowered to advise the sovereign to pardon a convicted criminal as an act of mercy, at his discretion. It was held in *Hanratty* v. *Lord Butler of Saffron Waldon* (1971) that the Home Secretary's decision not to pardon posthumously a man who had been hanged for murder could not be challenged in the courts. The man had been properly tried and his appeal heard in the court. In other words, all the relevant judicial procedures had been complied with. Since (as Lord Diplock put it) 'mercy begins where justice ends', there was no further scope for his family to challenge the Home Secretary's decision legally. The prerogative was not limited by any required procedures, nor was its object capable of definition, so that one could not say of the Home Secretary that he acted improperly from any legal point of view (though one might, of course, disagree with his decision).

(b) Lords Scarman, Diplock and Roskill suggested that the subject-matter of some prerogatives made them non-justiciable. This is actually not all that different from what Lords Fraser and Brightman said, but does look at the matter from a slightly different point of view. For example, the grant of honours was referred to by

Lord Roskill. It is obvious that this is non-justiciable, because the grant of honours involves no legal rights or duties (or indeed, legal issues of any kind). To be justiciable, an issue must be essentially legal in character. It must involve legal rights or at least legitimate expectations which the courts can enforce. Since no one can claim a right to an honour it is hard to see how, say, the failure of the Crown to enoble an individual could be challenged in a court of law. (Obviously, if a minister took a bribe to award an honour he would be guilty of corruption; the question of the individual's entitlement, however, remains non-justiciable.)

The analysis of the majority of the House has been followed in subsequent cases. In *R* v. *Secretary of State for Foreign and Commonwealth Affairs, ex p. Everett* (1989), the Court of Appeal held that the Secretary's refusal to issue a passport could be challenged, despite the fact that this was a prerogative power. Whilst accepting that some prerogatives (including those referred to by Lord Roskill) were non-justiciable, the Court did not regard the issue of a passport to be one of them. As Taylor LJ put it, ' . . . the powers of the court cannot be ousted merely by invoking the word "prerogative".'

21. Grounds for judicial review

In the *CCSU* case, Lord Diplock sought to summarise the grounds on which prerogative powers could be challenged, if at all. The possible grounds (which already apply to statutory powers) are as follows.

(*i*) *Illegality.* A person or body acts illegally where they *exceed* their powers. This is clearly applicable to statutory powers; it is also applicable to prerogative powers where the limits of that power, its objects and the procedures involved, are discernible. This is true of some, but not all, prerogative powers.

(*ii*) *Irrationality.* A body acts irrationally where it uses its powers unreasonably, such as where it ignores relevant evidence before acting. This applies to the use of statutory powers. According to Lord Diplock, however, it is hard to see how this applies to prerogative powers which are (according to Dicey) 'discretionary and arbitrary' in nature. Accordingly, prerogatives are unlikely to be challenged on the grounds of irrationality.

(*iii*) *Procedural impropriety.* This arises where a body fails to observe required procedures. These include not only statutory procedures, but common law ones, such as the rules of natural justice, including the duty to consult where this arises (as in the *CCSU* case). This can be used to challenge the use of prerogative powers. (For a more detailed discussion of these three grounds, particularly in relation to statutory powers, *see* 15).

The prerogative and conventions

22. Conventional control

Whilst judicial control of the prerogative to any large extent is a comparatively recent development, conventions have for a long time exerted control on the use of prerogative powers. Furthermore, even in connection with those prerogatives which are non-justiciable and therefore not subject to judicial review at all, conventional control arises. Thus, for example, by convention the sovereign must give her consent to bills; dissolve Parliament at the request of the prime minister; appoint the ministers of the PM's choice, etc. Regarding the Crown (the government), the most significant conventions which are used to control ministers' use of prerogative powers are those of ministerial responsibility (*see* 3 and 13). Accordingly, constitutional conventions remain an important (possibly the most important) system of controls on prerogative powers.

Progress test 13

1. What is meant by 'the monarchy'? On what basis is succession to the throne established? **(1–3)**

2. Briefly describe how the monarchy is financed. **(4)**

3. Define 'the prerogatives'. What are the key elements of the prerogative today? **(7)**

4. How might one classify the various prerogatives which exist? What are the most important prerogatives in relation to Home Affairs? **(8–9)**

5. What is meant by 'Act of State'? In what circumstances, and against whom can this be pleaded by the Crown? **(10–13)**

6. Outline the position of British subjects in relation to the exercise of the prerogative, where the conduct of the Crown affects their person or

property. What developments have affected this position in recent years? **(14–15)**

7. What affect might the enactment of a statute have on a prerogative? **(16)**

8. Outline the development of the law whereby the exercise of a prerogative power may be subject to judicial review. On what grounds might a prerogative be challenged? **(17–21)**

14

Administrative law

General

1. Administrative law

Administrative law is concerned with the system of rules whereby the exercise of governmental power is controlled. In particular, it involves the system of legal rules, principles and procedures by which such powers are controlled in the courts and is generally known as judicial review of administrative action. However, a study of administrative law entails a consideration of other means of control which exist: it also covers the nature of administrative authorities and the sorts of powers they wield.

2. Executive and administrative functions

In chapter 12 we examined the nature of executive authority, with particular reference to central government. Those persons and bodies which make up central government, or which are subject to its immediate control, include the monarch; the PM; Cabinet and other government ministers; the Civil Service; the Privy Council; and the armed forces.

In general, references to the executive (for example, as one of the three main organs of government) are to the central government and to the Prime Minister, Cabinet and other government ministers in particular. As mentioned in chapter 5, however, there are other bodies which wield executive authority, albeit in a more limited sphere, which are not part of, or under the direct control of, central government. These are the police, public corporations, and local councils.

The essence of executive authority is that it entails the framing of policy and the exercise of discretion (*see* 12). At its highest level (as with the PM and the Cabinet), it is the policies thus framed which form the basis of legislation, and which are put to Parliament in the form of government bills (*see* 7). At lower levels, it might take various forms, depending on the body concerned. For instance, a Chief Constable of Police might initiate a policy concerning policing in his area, such as the use of more constables on foot patrol to combat street crime, and so on. Such policy-making, however, cannot serve any purpose in a vacuum. If an executive body wishes to see its policies put into effect, it must have some actual authority, or power, with which to do so.

In the UK such powers derive from one of two sources:

(a) *The royal prerogative.* Prerogative powers are exercised (in varying degrees) by the sovereign personally, by the government (the Crown), and by the Privy Council (*see* 13).

(b) *Statute.* By far the most numerous powers are statutory in origin. Such powers are enjoyed by all of the bodies mentioned at 2, above, with the exception of the sovereign, whose powers (which are in any case limited in scope) remain prerogative in nature. (When a statute conferred powers upon Her Majesty in Council, this refers to the Privy Council.) Thus, the Crown (the government) exercises both prerogative and statutory powers, whereas the police, public corporations and local councils tend to exercise only statutory ones.

Statutes passed for the purpose of conferring such powers on executive bodies are known as enabling Acts. They enable the authority concerned to put into effect the policies embodied in the Act – in other words to administer those policies and objectives. During the passage of a bill of this kind Parliament will have carefully considered the policies and objects involved. In passing the Act then, it will, in effect, be endorsing these policies and objects.

3. Executive and administrative distinguished

One can readily see from the above that it is not easy to draw a clear distinction between executive functions and administrative ones – one flows into the other, since in order to put its policies into practice, an executive body must be given the power to do so.

Perhaps the simplest way to understand the distinction – and at the same time, to put administrative law into perspective – is to consider the approach taken by judicial review (the most significant subject of administrative law). Basically, the courts will not examine the fundamental policy of an executive body, but only how it is put into effect, and whether that is done in accordance with legal constraints, including those contained in the enabling Act. In other words, it is the administration (the putting into effect) of the policy which can be challenged, rather than the policy itself: hence judicial review of administrative action.

4. Discretionary powers

As noted at **2** above, it is a feature of executive authority that it should involve a degree of discretion. This is obviously necessary in the interests of good government, so that changing circumstances and social needs, or the exigencies of an emergency, can be met. As Lord Diplock put it in *Secretary of State for Education and Science* v. *Tameside Metropolitan Borough Council* (1976), 'The whole nature of administrative discretion is that it involves more than one course of conduct about which there is room for reasonable men to hold differing opinions as to which is to be preferred.' This does not mean, however, that the discretion permitted to executive bodies is unlimited. In particular, the process of embodying administrative discretion in statutory form, by its nature, imposes upon such a body certain constraints. It is the task of the courts to apply and interpret Acts of Parliament, so as to give effect to Parliament's intentions (since Parliament is sovereign). In doing so, however, the courts invariably have regard to certain fundamental principles as the proper way to give effect to Parliament's intentions. With regard to administrative powers, the most significant of these are as follows:

(a) A body may only do what Parliament has authorised it to do, either expressly, or by clear implication.

(b) Any mandatory procedures (including safeguards against arbitrary use of powers) contained in the enabling Act must be complied with.

(c) Powers should be used only for the purposes and objects authorised by Parliament.

In addition to the above principles (which are really no more than particular aspects of statutory interpretation) the courts insist that fundamental principles of common law (largely embodied in the rule of law) are also complied with, with the result that administrative discretion is further limited in the following ways:

(d) A person should not suffer any loss (whether of life, liberty or property) or other disadvantage (such as loss of livelihood) except in accordance with fundamental requirements of fairness. (What the Americans call 'due process of law'; in the UK, in relation to administrative powers, this means the rules of natural justice: *see* 16.)

(e) Powers should not be used arbitrarily; a body exercising administrative power should consider all the circumstances of the matter.

Thus, referring to Lord Diplock's *dictum* (above), it is true that administrative discretion involves choices about which reasonable people might differ, and therefore act differently. But there comes a point beyond which, for one reason or another, a reasonable person would not act. That is the point at which discretionary power is limited (*see* 15).

5. Discretionary powers and duties

It is chiefly with the control of discretionary powers that administrative law is concerned. As indicated above, a discretionary power is one which leaves a great deal of choice, as to when and how to exercise it, on the part of the person or body to whom it is conferred.

A duty, on the other hand, involves obligation: a person charged with a duty must discharge it, at least in the circumstances provided for in the enabling Act. In practice, there are two kinds of duty which might arise under statute. Both kinds, however, are almost invariably accompanied by discretionary powers so that, in effect, duties and powers tend to accompany each other.

(a) Sometimes a statute will impose upon an administrative authority a very broad duty. For example, local education authorities are, under the Education Act 1944, under a duty to 'provide a comprehensive system of education' in their areas. Obviously, a certain amount of discretion will be left to them in discharging this duty, and (subject to further statutory requirements contained in the Education Act 1988), such things as the type of schools, location of schools, appointment of teachers, and so on, are a matter for the authority's discretion. Similarly, at common law, the police are under a broad duty to enforce the law. However, the question of how to deploy his men, and even whether or not a prosecution should be brought in a particular case, is a matter for the discretion of the chief constable.

This does not mean, however, that such broad duties cannot be enforced. In *R* v. *Metropolitan Police Commissioner, ex p. Blackburn* (1968) the Court of Appeal held that the police were under a duty to enforce the law generally, and whilst they had a discretion whether or not to prosecute in a particular case, they were acting unlawfully in failing to enforce a particular law (in this case the law relating to illegal gambling). Accordingly, they could be compelled to discharge their duty to enforce the law by an order of *mandamus*, the appropriate means whereby a court can compel a body to do its duty (*see* 18).

(b) The other kind of duty is more specific, and may well take the form of a procedural requirement. This, too, can be enforced by the courts by virtue of the principles of judicial review (*see* 15).

Thus, for example, an authority may have the discretion to do something, as it sees fits. However, if it proposes to do so, it might be required by the enabling Act to hold an inquiry, to give notice, or to provide consultation, before reaching its final decision. These procedural requirements are in the form of duties. Conversely, an authority may be under a duty to act, but only in certain circumstances. The question whether or not those circumstances have arisen is one for that body to decide; this aspect of its function is a form of discretion.

Generally, the existence of a discretionary power in an Act can be recognised by the use of permissive language (such as, 'The minister may, if he thinks fit . . . '). A duty, on the other hand, can usually be recognised from the use of obligatory language, as in 'A local authority shall, when authorising a development, give notice . . . '.

It is probably fair to say that the greatest degree of discretion is permitted to government ministers, especially when acting in the name of the Crown. This is largely due to the fact that ministers exercise prerogative as well as statutory powers; also because ministers are in any case responsible to Parliament for their conduct: *Liversidge* v. *Anderson* (1942). This does not mean, of course, that the exercise of discretionary powers by ministers, whether prerogative powers or statutory ones, cannot be challenged in the courts. It is frequently the case, however, that the exercise of a statutory power by a minister will have a prerogative element. (Examples of this arise in connection with national security, defence, etc. *see* 12 and 13.) Since prerogative powers are broad and general in nature, they are not circumscribed by the detailed limitations which one tends to find in an Act of Parliament and, furthermore, some prerogatives are simply non-justiciable. The actual scope for challenge of prerogative powers, therefore, is rather less than that for statutory ones (*see* 13).

6. Examples of administrative powers

Administrative powers, most of which involve some element of discretion, are very numerous and wide-ranging in scope. The following are just a few of the broad powers available:

(a) *The imposition of charges, including taxation.* It has already been noted that the imposition of taxation and the expenditure of public money by central government must be authorised by Parliament. Local councils, too, are empowered by statute to raise money by way of local taxation with which to meet their expenditure, or at least a part of it (*see* **23**, below). Councils, and other authorities, are also empowered to make charges for particular services (e.g. public transport, sports facilities, etc.)

(b) *Public works.* Obviously, government is under a general duty to ensure adequate provision of housing, roads, transport, sports facilities, etc. How it goes about this is largely a matter of discretion. To facilitate the provision of public works, powers have to be available for their building and maintenance. In addition, 'ancillary' powers, whereby the necessary land for development purposes can be acquired, must be provided.

(c) *Regulatory powers.* Many administrative powers are regulatory in nature, and bodies and officials at all levels are empowered to ensure agreed standards are met (e.g. under Public Health Acts, Public Safety Acts, etc.)

(d) *Licensing.* In some ways closely relating to regulatory powers, many bodies have licensing powers (e.g. Magistrates' powers to grant liquor licences; police inspectors' powers to grant firearms certificates; the grant of gaming licences by the Gaming Board of Great Britain and street trading licences granted by local councils).

The above are just a few of the powers found in current legislation; others are discussed elsewhere in this chapter. However, there are two very important categories of powers, which merit special treatment:

(1) Powers of delegated legislation.
(2) Powers invested in tribunals and inquiries (known generally as 'adjudicative' powers).

Powers of delegated legislation

7. Delegated legislation

As its name suggests, this is a variety of law-making. Unlike the legislative powers of Parliament (which give rise to original or primary legislation), powers of delegated legislation are conferred upon executive bodies, usually for limited, defined purposes, and normally by statute (though there are a very few powers of delegated legislation which derive from the royal prerogative). As such, delegated legislation is not sovereign and may, unlike an Act of Parliament, be challenged in a court of law. We may therefore also speak of delegated legislation as subordinate legislation.

8. The nature and purposes of delegated legislation

Delegated legislation is a useful tool in the administration of the nation's affairs, since it does not challenge Parliament's sovereignty, yet has the force of law on those to whom it applies, and is relatively easy to pass. Thus, for instance local council by-laws are a form of delegated legislation. By-laws may be passed, for example, prohibiting the dropping of litter in council-maintained streets, with provision for penalties (usually fines) for offenders. Thus, a local council can implement its environmental cleanliness policies with the force of law.

Typically, delegated legislation will be passed in relation to such things as the following:

(a) *Local affairs, for which a local council is responsible.* Local needs may differ (e.g. depending on whether the area is an inner-city one or rural). Delegated legislation is well-suited to meeting these differing needs.

(b) *Emergencies.* Delegated legislation is often used to deal with emergencies, whether natural or man-made. For such situations, it is often more appropriate than an Act of Parliament, being speedier. ('It is impossible to pass an Act of Parliament to control an epidemic of measles or an outbreak of foot and mouth disease as and when it occurs': Donoughmore Committee Report.) Mention has already been made of some of the powers of delegated legislation used in war-time emergencies (*see* 12).

(c) *To implement or bring into force statutory provisions.* Quite frequently a statute, or certain parts of a statute, do not come into force when it receives the royal assent, but at a date to be determined by the relevant minister, often by means of delegated legislation. Similarly, certain provisions of a statute require that further rules, etc. be implemented in the form of delegated legislation (e.g. the provisions in the Police and Criminal Evidence Act requiring that the Secretary of State introduces Codes of Practice).

It should be noted, however, that there are two areas which normally fall outside the scope of any powers of delegated legislation:

(*i*) *Power to amend or set aside an Act of Parliament.* Since Parliament is sovereign, and powers of delegated legislation are only subordinate, it follows that it is not possible for anyone, by means of delegated legislation, to amend or set aside an Act (as opposed to actually implementing it: *see* **(c)**, above).

To this general principle, however, there is an exception. Section 2(6) of the European Communities Act 1972 empowers the government or any government minister to make regulations (delegated legislation) for the purposes of implementing Community law (such as directives): this may involve changing existing statute law.

(*ii*) *Power to levy any public charge (taxation).* The principle that the executive cannot impose a charge on the public (i.e. taxation) without the authority of Parliament in the form of primary legislation (i.e. an Act of Parliament) was mentioned at 7. In fact, there have been a few exceptions to this principle, too. The Emergency Powers (Defence) Act 1939 conferred upon the government the power of imposing taxes for the purpose of prosecuting the war, subject to parliamentary approval given by means of resolution: *see* **12:29**. This power lapsed, however, in 1946.

More recently, section 5 of the European Communities Act 1972 empowers the Treasury to amend certain duties (but not general taxation) in accordance with EC law, by means of delegated legislation.

9. Varieties of delegated legislation

There are different varieties of delegated legislation; these are usually classified according to how and by whom they are made.

(a) *Orders in Council.* This is the broad term given to delegated legislation made by the Queen in Council (i.e. the Privy Council). Powers to make Orders in Council are usually granted by statutes (e.g. the Emergency Powers legislation discussed in 12), but some Orders in Council derive from the Prerogative (*see* discussion on the *CCSU* case at **13:19**).

(b) *Ministerial regulations and orders.* As their name suggests, these involve powers to make rules, regulations, etc., conferred by Parliament upon government ministers. They are very numerous and wide ranging; the important powers conferred upon ministers by section 2(4) of the European Communities Act 1972 are discussed above and at 5.

(c) *Local authority by-laws.* As noted earlier, local councils are empowered (mostly under the Local Government Act 1972) to make by-laws with respect to their areas. Such powers are also enjoyed by other public bodies having control over particular areas or activities (e.g. British Rail, which is empowered to issue by-laws for the management of railways).

(d) *Compulsory purchase orders.* Local councils are empowered by the Acquisition of Land Act 1981 to issue 'compulsory purchase orders' (CPOs) whereby they are authorised to acquire land for development purposes. Such orders are a variety of delegated legislation, in that they involve the same procedures, broadly speaking. (*See* **22**, below.)

(e) *Other type of delegated legislation.* Many other bodies are empowered to make delegated legislation, usually involving rules applicable to their own activities. For instance, the Rules Committee of the Supreme Court may implement Rules of Supreme Court, governing procedures in courts of law: section 85 of the Supreme Court Act 1981. The 'Measures' (acts) of the General Synod of the Church of England also fall into the category.

(f) *'Statutory Instruments'.* This does not actually refer to a separate category of delegated legislation.

The Statutory Instruments Act 1946 provides that where, under that Act or any subsequent Act, any power of delegated legislation is conferred upon Her Majesty in Council, or upon any minister of the Crown, and is referred to either as an Order in Council or a statutory instrument, then the provisions of the Act apply. These provisions relate to the publication and procedures whereby such delegated legislation is made. Statutory Instruments are published in documentary form, by the official government publisher (like statutes) and catalogued according to number and year (e.g. SI 1978, No. 100). (The procedural requirements are dealt with at **10**, below.)

10. Procedures and safeguards

(a) *Orders in Council and ministerial regulations.* These forms of delegated legislation are made by the government, or by government ministers. As part of the procedure under which they are implemented, however, they are generally subject to the procedure known as 'laying before Parliament'. There are two varieties of this procedure:

(*i*) The negative resolution procedure. Under this procedure a piece of delegated legislation takes effect, subject to annulment.

Annulment is a resolution of either of the two Houses of Parliament to the effect that the delegated legislation concerned should not take effect (the negative resolution). This procedure applies to Statutory Instruments (*see* **9**, above). A negative resolution must usually be made within 40 days of publication of the Statutory Instrument, if it is to be annulled.

(*ii*) The affirmative resolution procedure. Under their enabling Acts, certain ministerial regulations must be laid before Parliament for its positive approval (affirmative resolution) before taking effect.

(*iii*) In addition, both Houses of Parliament have special committees for the purpose of scrutinising proposed delegated legislation.

(b) *By-laws.* These are made by local councils and other bodies. The most significant procedural safeguard here is that a by-law must be approved by the relevant minister. Local government by-laws are also subject to other controls and, in particular, they must be published at least one month prior to ministerial confirmation: section 236(4), Local Government Act 1972. Furthermore, by-laws are subject to challenge in the courts (*see* **11**, below).

(c) *Other.* Some kinds of delegated legislation (such as compulsory purchase orders made by local councils, and some orders made by ministers) can only be made after consultation with interested parties, or some form of inquiry, is held.

11. Judicial controls

Since they are subordinate to Acts of Parliament, pieces of delegated legislation have no greater status than any other administrative action taken under statutory authority, so far as the courts are concerned. Accordingly, delegated legislation can be challenged in the courts by means of judicial review:

(a) If a piece of delegated legislation is made in contravention of statutory procedures, it can be struck down (procedural impropriety): The *Aylesbury Mushroom* case [1972]: *see* 15: **10(b)(iii)**.

(b) Delegated legislation can be challenged on the grounds of irrationality. In *Kruse* v. *Johnson* (1898), for instance, it was held that a by-law which was 'unequal in its operation as between different classes' or which involved 'oppressive or gratuitous interference with the rights of the subjects' was void (*per* Lord Russell). Similarly, a by-law which forbade the playing of any music, singing or preaching in any street was held to be so arbitrary as to be unreasonable, and therefore void, in *Monro* v. *Watson* (1887). Under section 235 of the Local Government Act 1972 the power to make by-laws is exercisable 'for the good rule and government of the whole or any part of their area'; this is interpreted as meaning 'in the public interest'. A by-law which does not serve the public interest (such as those in the above cases) could be successfully challenged.

(c) In addition, a local authority by-law can be challenged if it is uncertain or vague as to its objects or terms: *Nash* v. *Finlay* (1901). The same principle has been applied to a ministerial regulation: *McEldowne* v. *Forde* (1971). However, the regulation in question was an extraordinary one, relating to the troubles in Northern Ireland, and having implications for civil liberties. (In any case, the challenge was unsuccessful.) In general, it is accepted that ministerial regulations and Orders in Council cannot be challenged on these grounds.

(d) It is debatable whether delegated legislation can be challenged on the grounds of breach of natural justice. The better view is that it can not. Any requirements for a hearing, notification, etc. will normally arise from the enabling Act itself, and a failure to comply can be challenged on those grounds. It is hard to see, therefore, what scope for challenge would remain on the grounds of breach of natural justice. As Megarry J put it in *Bates* v. *Lord Hailsham* (1972), ' . . . these considerations [of natural justice] do not seem to me to affect the process of legislation, whether primary or delegated.'

Adjudicative powers: tribunals and inquiries

12. Adjudicative powers

It is not uncommon for an administrative authority to be required to act, from time to time, in a manner which can broadly be described as adjudicative or judicial. What this generally means is that the authority concerned will resolve disputes or hear claims brought by individuals, involving questions of law as well as fact. A licensing authority, for instance, might take such a decision in a particular case. Nevertheless, such authorities remain administrative in nature.

On the other hand, there is nowadays a large number of special bodies whose work is virtually exclusively adjudicative in nature. Such bodies are invariably the creation of statute, and are therefore known as statutory tribunals.

13. Statutory tribunals

As noted above, these are bodies established by statute for adjudicative purposes. There are two broad categories of statutory tribunals:

(a) *Administrative tribunals.* Despite the title administrative, these bodies are adjudicative in nature. This is the largest category of statutory tribunals. A few examples of some of the better known ones will indicate the breadth of their jurisdiction.

(*i*) *Industrial tribunals.* Originally set up in 1965 to resolve disputes arising from the Contracts of Employment Act 1963 and Redundancy Payments Act 1965, their jurisdiction was extended by subsequent legislation, such as the Race Relations Act 1976, Sex Discrimination Act 1975, and Employment Protection (Consolidation) Acts 1975–78. Their jurisdiction covers such matters as discrimination at work and unfair dismissal.

(*ii*) *Immigration appeal tribunals.* Established under section 12 of the Immigration Act 1971, its function is self-explanatory.

(*iii*) *Commissioners of Income Tax.* These sit as a tribunal to determine disputes relating to taxation.

(*iv*) *Rent and housing tribunals.* Known in fact as Rent Assessment Committees, they have the power to determine rents for tenants within the protection of the Housing Act 1980.

In addition to the above, there are many tribunals which hear matters concerned with health, social security and other benefits.

(b) *Domestic tribunals.* These are tribunals established to hear disputes involving a particular profession or organisation. They are frequently disciplinary bodies, such as the Professional Conduct Committee which hears disciplinary matters involving doctors, or the British Boxing Board of Control.

14. Composition and procedure of tribunals

Whilst the basic procedure adopted by tribunals is similar to that utilised in courts of law, there are certain differences. In particular, tribunals are generally somewhat less formal than courts of law, with less reliance on detailed rules of procedure. However, the adversarial method is adopted, and legal representation is normally permitted to both parties. Hearings are held orally, and (usually) in public.

The composition of statutory tribunals varies considerably. One feature which they tend to have in common, however, is the fact that lay persons sit on such tribunals, sometimes along with professional judges or other legally qualified persons (as with the industrial tribunals). The Commissioners of Income Tax, however, do not. Along with their relative informality, this is one of the chief advantages of tribunals, since although their members are often lay-persons (in the sense of not being lawyers), they are in fact chosen for their expertise in the subject matter concerned, or as representative of the interests involved (e.g. employers and trade unions in industrial tribunals).

The other advantages of tribunals are the relative speed with which they operate, and the fact that proceedings before them are less costly than court proceedings.

15. Control of tribunals: the Tribunals and Inquiries Act 1971

The controls on the activities of tribunals are mainly contained in the Tribunals and Inquiries Act 1971.

(a) *Appeal.* A right of appeal from the decision of most tribunals is provided for under section 13 of the Act. Appeal is generally to the High Court on a point of law. (In the case of the Employment Appeal Tribunal, which itself consists of High Court judges, appeals are made to the Court of Appeal.) From the decision of the High Court, appeal to the Court of Appeal, and ultimately the House of Lords lies, in the usual way.

(b) *Membership.* The members of tribunals are appointed or approved by the Lord Chancellor: section 7. Members cannot be dismissed except with the consent of the LC. This means that, like judges, members of tribunals enjoy a degree of independence from the executive.

(c) *Reasons.* A tribunal which falls within the scope of the supervisory powers of the Council on Tribunals (*see* below) must, if requested, furnish a statement, either written or oral, of the reasons for the decision unless to do so would prejudice national security: section 12.

(d) *The Council on Tribunals.* This body was set up by section 1 of the 1971 Act. Its purpose is to keep under review the constitutions and workings of all scheduled tribunals, and to report on these matters to the Lord Chancellor and Secretary of State (both annually, and as required by the latter). The Council's reports are laid before Parliament by the Lord Chancellor and Secretary of

State in the Lords and Commons respectively. The Council also advises the Lord Chancellor and relevant ministers as to the appointment of members to tribunals.

(e) *Supervisory jurisdiction of the High Court.* This refers to the application of the normal principle of judicial review to the activities of tribunals (*see* 15). It has been held that even those tribunals which are not the creation of statutes (such as the Disciplinary Committees of Universities and the Criminal Injuries Compensation Board, which were established by the royal prerogative) are subject to the supervisory jurisdiction of the High Court: *Glynn* v. *Keele University* (1972) and *R* v. *Criminal Injuries Compensation Board, ex p. Lain* (1967).

16. Statutory inquiries

It is quite common for a statute to require that, in certain circumstances, an inquiry must be held before administrative action can be taken. A typical example of this arises from the Town and Country Planning Act 1971, section 9 of which requires the minister to allow interested persons an opportunity to be heard before a planning scheme can be approved by him. Such local inquiries are very common; major schemes, though less common, may also include similar requirements (e.g. proposals to build power stations, etc.).

Unlike tribunals, such inquiries are not adjudicative in nature, though they may have to act judicially in the broad sense that the chairman is obliged to hear both sides of the argument. However, judicial procedures are not a requirement, so that the chairman's refusal to permit cross-examination is not, in itself, necessarily grounds for challenging an inquiry's recommendation: *Bushell* v. *Secretary of State for the Environment* (1981). Accordingly, statutory inquiries often amount to a fact-finding exercise, to enable a minister to be properly informed as to facts, views and so on before taking action.

This does not mean that statutory inquiries are not subject to supervision. Their procedures are, to some extent at least, governed by the Tribunals and Inquiries Act 1971 and, in particular, section 2 (requiring the giving of reasons on request) applies. Any decision taken by a minister after an inquiry has reported to him, and made its recommendations, can be challenged if, for example, the minister has failed to give due consideration to the report: *Coleen Properties Ltd* v. *Minister of Housing and Local Government* (1971).

Administrative authorities

17. Administrative authorities

Administrative authorities are those bodies which are entrusted, either by statute or at common law (usually by virtue of the royal prerogative), with functions of a public nature (i.e. functions which serve the interests of the public, as opposed to private profit or the interests of shareholders). For the most part, such bodies exist solely for such purposes (e.g. local councils), but it is quite possible for a private company or other body to discharge a limited number of functions which may be described as public, e.g. the supply and distribution of water, electricity, etc. Provided that they discharge public functions, then, all such bodies fall within the classification of administrative authorities, and within the scope of administrative law, since their activities will be subject to various forms of regulation and control, and in particular to judicial review (*see* 15). The variety of administrative authorities therefore defines the scope of administrative law, since any functions (particularly powers) derived from statute or from the prerogative (provided these are justiciable in nature: *see* 13) are subject to judicial review, thus making all the bodies which exercise such powers the concern of administrative law.

18. Varieties of administrative authorities

Administrative authorities are associated with the executive branch of government. Thus, central government itself may be said to involve a number of administrative authorities: the Crown; ministers; the Privy Council and the armed forces (*see* 12). However, central government also comprises one of the primary organs of government, and its functions are more than merely administrative, in that it is the policies of central government which rule the country and form the basis of most Acts of Parliament. Furthermore, many of the functions of central government are derived from the prerogative, and are therefore original in nature, unlike the powers of other administrative authorities, which are conferred upon them (delegated) by Parliament and which may therefore be described as secondary in nature. To describe the bodies which make up central government simply as administrative authorities, therefore, is misleading. Nevertheless, the government and individual government ministers in particular are granted extensive administrative powers by Parliament and may, to that extent at least, be regarded as administrative authorities.

In addition to central government there are other kinds of bodies concerned with administrative functions, and since these bodies do not exercise original powers, it is perfectly appropriate (with one exception) to describe them simply as administrative authorities, or as public authorities. These are as follows:

(1) Local councils;
(2) The police and police authorities; and
(3) Public corporations.

The exception noted above involves private companies which, along with their other profit-making activities, do provide some public functions or services. Such bodies have become increasingly common since the Thatcher government initiated its programme of privatisation and increased competition in 1979. They include the water companies and private electricity company (known as Powergen). Obviously, the private, profit-making side of their activities is outside the scope of this book. As far as their public functions are concerned, these are subject to much the same system of controls as are the public corporations (*see* below).

The general nature and functions of central government has been dealt with at 12. The following is a brief summary of the nature and functions of the remaining varieties of administrative authorities.

Local councils

19. Local government
Britain has had some form of local government for a very long time. Indeed local government has existed at least since Norman times, when a local administrator, the sheriff ('shire-reeve') governed local affairs in the shires (counties). He was joined by the Justices of the Peace (JPs) who enjoyed (and still do) some administrative functions, as well as their judicial ones. In addition, the more important towns (particularly those with military or trading significance, which were known as boroughs) appointed for themselves councils to govern many of their local affairs.

Thus, a pattern for a system of local government was established which, loosely speaking, formed the basis of the modern system. This derives from the Local Government Act 1972.

20. Local councils today

The Local Government Act 1972 established the modern system of local councils in England and Wales (Scotland and Northern Ireland have their own, broadly similar, systems). London, however, was not included; its system of local government derives from the London Governments Acts 1899–1963 and Local Government Act 1985.

Like its historical model, the system established by the 1972 Act was a two-tier one, involving two units of local government, as follows:

(a) *The counties.* Geographically, the largest unit of local government is the county. Under the 1972 Act, the country was divided into counties, including six metropolitan counties in the major conurbations (except for London). These metropolitan counties, however, were abolished by the Local Government Act 1985.

(b) *The districts.* Each of the counties are divided into a number of districts. These include a number of towns, which for historical reasons, continued to be known as boroughs (*see* 19, above). Their status (in local government terms), however, is the same as the districts.

Each county and district in England and Wales has its own council, which is an elected body of an executive character. The functions of these councils are local in nature, and shared between county and district councils, each having responsibility for certain aspects of local government.

(c) *London.* London has always remained separate from the rest of the country as far as local government is concerned. Under the London Government Act of 1899, the metropolis was divided into London boroughs (roughly the equivalent of districts elsewhere), and in 1963, a London County Council was established (roughly the equivalent of a county council for London). This was replaced in 1972 by the Greater London Council. The GLC, however, was abolished by the Local Government Act 1985. Thus, most of London's affairs are governed by the London borough councils independently. There are important exceptions, such as transport, which is administered by a special body, London Regional Transport: London Regional Transport Act 1983. The city of London has its own system of local government, forming a kind of county within London, and having its own councils.

21. The functions of local councils

The functions and powers of local councils derive from the Local Government Act, and from many other statutes. Certain functions are discharged by county councils, others by district councils; the remaining functions are shared between the two. Many of these functions involve the provision of public services of one sort or another. However, a local council may not in every case provide the service itself; for example, refuse collection. Since 1982, councils have been required by law to put out tenders for refuse collection and, where a private company can provide the service more economically than the council's own labour force, the private company must be contracted to do so. However, the council itself remains responsible for the actual provision of the service. The thinking behind such requirements is to ensure the provision of economical services by stimulating competition, whilst retaining local accountability.

The following are some of the most important functions discharged, and services provided by local councils, or for which local councils are responsible.

(a) *County councils.* The functions of county councils include the provision of education and social services; transport and highways; refuse disposal; police and fire services (for this purpose, several counties are usually amalgamated into one police or fire authority: *see* 28, below); and planning policy.

(b) *District councils.* Their functions include housing and local planning; roads and transport (in urban districts); refuse collection; local licensing; and (where applicable) coastguards.

(c) *Shared functions.* Both county and district councils are involved in maintaining parks, libraries and other public amenities.

There are also parish councils, but these have few functions (and even fewer powers) of an administrative nature, though they may act as pressure groups in local matters. They have responsibility for the upkeep of local paths and cemeteries.

22. Specific powers of local councils

To enable them to discharge their functions, and govern generally in their areas, local councils are endowed with certain specific statutory powers.

(a) *Delegated legislation.* Mention has already been made of the power of local councils to make by-laws.

(b) *Compulsory purchase orders*. These are a form of delegated legislation in that a similar procedure (including ministerial confirmation) applies. The power to compulsorily purchase property arises under the Acquisition of Land Act 1981 and certain other Acts: in either case, the procedures laid down in the 1981 Act must be complied with.

(c) *Contracts*. Local councils have legal personality, being public corporations. As such, a local council has the capacity to enter into legally binding contracts with other authorities or with private persons.

(d) *Legal proceedings*. Under section 222 of the Local Government Act 1972, a local authority is empowered, where it thinks fit, to bring legal proceedings, both civil and criminal, in the interests of local inhabitants. Thus, a local council may initiate proceedings in a case where an individual is unable to proceed due to a lack of standing (*see* 17:4). For example, under the Control of Pollution Act 1974, local authorities may bring proceedings in cases of public nuisance, as in *Hammersmith London Borough Council* v. *Magnum Automated Forecourts Ltd* (1978).

(e) *Taxes*. District councils (and London borough councils) are empowered to impose local taxes, to meet at least part of their financial requirements. This is dealt with below.

23. Local government finance

It is obvious that, in order to provide the services discussed at **2**, above (which they are required to do, by law), local councils need to raise money. This is done in three ways: local taxes; grants and loans; and charges.

(a) *Local taxes*. A proportion of local government expenditure is met by means of local taxes, levied by district councils. A new system of local taxation, known as the Council Tax, is to take effect during 1993. Under this system, every domestic property in a council's area will be valued, and each inhabitant will (unless exempted) pay an annual sum in accordance with that valuation. Business premises are subject to a similar charge, except that this does not depend on the number of employees.

Under the new system, the powers enjoyed by the Secretary of State to 'cap' local taxes (i.e. dictate the maximum they can raise by that means), established in the Rates Act 1984, have been retained.

(b) *Grants and loans*. Grants are made annually to local councils by central government. These are the block grant and the rate-support grant which are designed to enable local councils to meet their expenditure requirements which cannot be met by local taxes. In order to prevent over spending by local councils, the Secretary of State is empowered to control the amounts paid to each authority: Local Government Finance Acts 1982–88. A local council whose grant is less than it wishes cannot simply raise the extra money by local taxes, due to the Secretary of State's other powers referred to at (**a**), above.

In addition to the above, the government may make a one-off grant of money to a local council for the purpose of financing a particular development or venture. Local councils may also raise money to finance such ventures by means of loans, including loans from other councils.

(**c**) *Charges.* A limited amount of revenue is raised by local councils through charges made by them for certain services and facilities (e.g. public transport, admission to museums, library charges, etc.).

24. Controls on local councils

(**a**) *Judicial controls.* Being public authorities, exercising statutory powers, local councils are subject to judicial review. (This is dealt with at 15.)

(**b**) *Governmental control.* Local government falls within the area of responsibility of the Secretary of State for the Environment. Mention has already been made of his powers in relation to the control of local government finance. In addition to these, he has the following powers:

(*i*) Ministerial confirmation is necessary in order for local councils to implement by-laws, [compulsory purchase orders] and certain development schemes.

(*ii*) The Secretary has certain powers to take over the functions of local councils, where the council concerned is failing to discharge its functions properly. (For example, he may 'call in' a planning application and decide it himself: Town and Country Planning Act 1971.)

(*iii*) Inspections and inquiries. Ministers are empowered to arrange for the inspection of certain local services, and for the holding of a local inquiry (e.g. planning and development).

(**c**) *The audit.* This is an important control on local government expenditure. An Audit Commission, whose members are appointed by the Secretary of State, arranges for auditors to scrutinise the accounts of every local authority to ensure that each item of expenditure is lawful and necessary. With regard to unlawful expenditure, the auditor is able to bring proceedings in the court and may, if the claim is upheld, order the individual responsible for the unauthorised expenditure to repay it, and even disqualify him from local government. The auditor reports to the Secretary of State, so that unnecessary or excessive expenditure is brought to light, and may be considered by the Secretary in the next round of grants, etc. (*see* (b) above).

(d) *The local ombudsman.* Since 1974, there has been a Commission for Local Administration, whose members (known as local ombudsmen) are empowered to investigate complaints of maladministration in local government. The system was based on the Parliamentary Commissioner for Administration model, established in 1967 (*see* **31**, below).

Public corporations

25. Public corporations

These are bodies set up for the discharge of public functions, usually by statute. As noted at **17**, above, some such functions are nowadays discharged by private companies. As far as these functions are concerned, such companies enjoy similar powers and are subject to the same system of controls. Such corporations are sometimes known as quangos (quasi autonomous non-governmental organisations). As their name suggests, they enjoy relative independence since, not being part of the Civil Service, they do not fall within the direct responsibility of any government minister, and are therefore not subject to direct parliamentary scrutiny as such. Furthermore, the use of a quango means that expertise and management skills from specialised fields in private industry and commerce can be imported into public services.

According to Hood Phillips, there are two main varieties of public corporations:

(a) *Managerial.* Some corporations exist for the purposes of managing public concerns. These are of two kinds:

(*i*) Industry and commerce (e.g. British Coal; British Rail; the electricity boards etc.).

(*ii*) Social services (e.g. health authorities; the BBC; development corporations).

(b) *Regulatory and advisory.* These include:

(*i*) Bodies which regulate private enterprise (e.g. the Independent Broadcasting Authority).

(*ii*) Bodies which advise the government (e.g. the Nature Conservancy Council). Some bodies advise ministers as just one of their various functions (e.g. the Audit Commission; English Heritage).

(*iii*) Miscellaneous bodies, such as those established to monitor and enforce legislation. Two examples of this are the Equal Opportunities Commission and the Commission for Racial Equality, established in 1975 and 1976 respectively, which monitor and enforce the laws on sexual and racial discrimination (*see* 9).

26. Status and controls

Public corporations vary tremendously in their structure, membership, etc. Generally, a public corporation will be run by a board and headed by a chairman (rather like a private business) all of whom are appointed by the Crown, in accordance with the Act which created the corporation.

Such differences as exist are not especially significant since all public corporations have one thing in common: they enjoy legal personality in their own right and enjoy the same powers, capacities and liabilities as any other artificial legal person. They are also subject to various controls. These are, broadly, as follows:

(a) *Parliamentary controls.* It was mentioned above that public corporations are not the direct responsibility of any ministers, not being part of central government or the Civil Service. This does not mean, however, that Parliament does not debate the activities of public corporations. Furthermore, insofar as many of the public corporations do not finance themselves, but require the grant of public money to meet their expenses, their activities come under parliamentary scrutiny. The system of select committees is used for this purpose.

(b) *Judicial controls.* As mentioned above, the conduct of public corporations is amenable to judicial review. This is based on the fact that, as the creation of statute, the legal powers available to a public corporation are limited to those actually conferred upon it by the statute in question. It may not lawfully exceed those powers (act *ultra vires*), or use them irrationally or improperly (*see* 15).

The police and police authorities

27. The police

Whilst it might seem strange to think of the police and policemen as administrative authorities, it is not inaccurate. Like any other public authority, they are endowed with powers which are often discretionary in nature. We saw at 10 that a PC, when deciding whether or not to arrest an individual, is using a discretionary power, which must be exercised in accordance with the normal requirements, applicable to all administrative discretion: *Holgate-Mohamed* v. *Duke* (1984). Similarly, the decision by a chief officer of police to impose conditions upon the organiser of a procession, in accordance with section 12 of the Public Order Act 1986 involves the exercise of a discretion, which can be challenged by means of judicial review.

However, in practice the police are seldom the subject of judicial review, at least by comparison with other public authorities. There are several reasons for this.

(a) In relation to many of their powers, alternative statutory and common law safeguards and procedures exist. Thus, for instance, the abuse of certain powers will result in the inadmissibility of evidence, disciplinary proceedings, etc., under the Police and Criminal Evidence Act 1984 (*see* 10). Similarly, a person who has been wrongly arrested and detained may obtain damages by means of a private-law action for false imprisonment.

(b) In relation to detailed operational matters, the courts tend to allow the police a wide discretion. Thus, for example, the decision whether or not to refer a particular case to the Crown Prosecution Service for prosecution is one for the discretion of the police, and the courts will not normally intervene (though they will intervene in a decision not to investigate any cases involving a particular offence: *R* v. *Metropolitan Police Commissioner, ex p. Blackburn* (1968), *see* 5, above).

28. Police forces and authorities

In the UK, there is no national police force. Police constables belong to one or another regional police force, each of which (with the exceptions of the Metropolitan and City police in London) is administered by a local police authority. Each police authority represents a county, or amalgamated county councils who appoint its members, e.g. the Thames Valley Police Authority which covers

Buckinghamshire, Berkshire and Oxfordshire. It is the police authority which actually employs the police constables in its area, including the chief constable, though appointments to the rank of chief constable, deputy chief constable and assistant chief constable must be approved by the Home Secretary: section 7, Police Act 1964. (In London, there is no police authority, and the chief constables for the City and Metropolitan forces are appointed by the Home Secretary, and are servants of the Crown.) Other constables (PCs) are appointed by the chief constable himself.

It is the duty of each police authority to secure an adequate and efficient police force in its area: section 4(1), Police Act 1964. To that end, it has powers to determine the size of the force, and the equipment (including vehicles and buildings) available to the force, though the Home Secretary may provide funds for the purchase of special equipment to meet particular needs. Whilst the police authority has no power to make, or intervene in, operational decisions (these are the responsibility of the chief constable), it does exercise a monitoring function, and may require the chief constable to submit a report of police activities, over and above the annual report required by law: section 12, Police Act 1964. In addition, a police authority may, with the approval of the Home Secretary, demand the retirement of a chief constable (or deputy or assistant chief constable), 'in the interests of efficiency': section 5, Police Act 1964. Being a public authority, its conduct may be challenged in the courts. As well as the police authorities, there exists an Inspectorate of Constabulary, which scrutinises police forces and reports its findings to the Home Secretary.

Maladministration and the ombudsman

29. Maladministration

A discussion on executive and administrative powers and duties and their control would be incomplete without some mention of maladministration and the ombudsmen.

As previously noted, the main concern of administrative law is with judicial review of administrative action. This involves an examination, by the court, of the legality of a public authority's conduct. However, public authorities are invariably subject to other forms of scrutiny and control, many of which are discussed in this chapter. In particular, there is a need to scrutinise the activities of public authorities so as to ensure that they act efficiently, even where their conduct is not unlawful (and not, therefore, subject to judicial review), since (amongst other things) public money is involved. Such inefficiency, (along with other forms of bad practice, such as excessive delays in dealing with individuals' affairs, discourtesy, incompetence, bad advice, etc.), is sometimes described as maladministration.

30. The Parliamentary Commissioner for Administration

This official was created in 1967, by an Act of Parliament (Parliamentary Commissioner Act 1967). Since the office was modelled on a Scandinavian one, the Scandinavian term for him, *Ombudsman*, is frequently used.

The function of the Commissioner is to investigate complaints of maladministration in most of the central government departments and some of the larger public corporations: Schedule 2. Such complaints must be made in writing to an MP, and referred to the Commissioner by him. Communications to or by the Commissioner in the course of an investigation are subject to legal privilege: section 10, 1967 Act (and *see* 8). The Commissioner has a discretion whether or not to investigate a complaint: this cannot be challenged. At the end of each investigation the Commissioner reports to the department concerned and to the MP: if he finds maladministration to have occurred, this report will include recommendations for dealing with the problem. (He also reports annually to Parliament, before whom all his case reports are made available.) He has no sanctions with which to back-up his recommendations, however, and the elimination of maladministration depends largely on co-operation in the department concerned, and on pressure from Parliament. The work of the Commissioner, therefore, is complementary to other remedies, including, in particular, ministerial responsibility.

The Parliamentary Commissioner may not investigate a matter in respect of which a judicial remedy exists, except where it would not be reasonable to require the complainant to seek such a remedy: section 5, Parliamentary Commissioner Act 1967.

31. Other Ombudsmen

Despite his relative 'lack of teeth', the Parliamentary Commissioner has been reasonably successful, with the result that the model established in 1967 has been applied to other areas.

(a) *National Health*. The National Health Service Re-organisation

Act 1973 (and the National Health Service (Scotland) Act 1972) provided for Health Service Commissioners for England, Wales and Scotland. Complaints concerning the Health Service are made direct to the Commissioner, and not through an MP. The Commissioner reports to the Secretary of State for Health, rather than to Parliament.

(b) *Local Government.* The Local Government Act 1974 extended the 'ombudsman' principle to local government, with the establishment of two Commissioners for Local Administration, one each for England and Wales, to be appointed by the Crown (Local Government Act 1974 s.23). The Local Commissioners hear complaints of misadministration in connection with local authorities and (except in London), police authorities. Complaints must be referred to the Commissioner by the authority concerned: as a further safeguard, the Commissioner may, if an authority fails to refer a complaint, investigate it anyway.

Progress test 14

1. What is meant by administrative law? Briefly describe the field covered by this subject. **(1–3)**

2. What are the fundamental procedures relating to administrative powers which the courts have regard to? In what other ways is administrative discretion generally limited by the courts? **(4)**

3. Distinguish discretionary powers and duties, commenting on the relationship between these. What kinds of administrative duties generally arise? **(5)**

4. Outline some of the most common forms of powers available to administrative authorities generally, indicating the sorts of purposes for which these might be used. **(6)**

5. What is meant by 'delegated legislation'? In relation to what sorts of circumstances are powers to make delegated legislation typically granted? **(7-8)**

6. What varieties of delegated legislation exist, and how are these: **(a)** created; and **(b)** controlled? **(9–11)**

7. Describe the typical composition and procedures of an administrative tribunal. What are the main varieties of tribunals which exist? **(13–14)**

8. How are tribunals supervised? **(15)**

9. What are the main purposes of statutory inquiries, and how are these controlled? **(16)**

10. Describe the main varieties of administrative authorities. What do these have in common? **(18)**

11. Briefly describe the modern system of local government, indicating the main functions of local councils and their powers. **(19–22)**

12. In what ways is the conduct of local councils subject to control? **(24)**

13. How can the major public corporations be classified? What is the legal status of public corporations, and how are their activities controlled? **(25–26)**

14. Who, or what, is the 'ombudsman'? What are his/her functions, and how does he/she implement these? **(29–30)**

15

Judicial review of administrative action

General

1. Judicial review

This is the process whereby a court of law examines the conduct of a body to establish whether or not that body has acted lawfully, in the sense of acting within the scope of its lawful powers. Judicial review is not confined to constitutional and administrative law (it could be applied, for example, to the conduct of a private company) but it is in relation to administrative law that it has grown spectacularly in recent years.

As a consequence of this growth, judicial review has become a complex topic which has several aspects: these must be addressed separately. Broadly, they are as follows:

(a) The grounds on which judicial review may be granted (or refused) by a court of law.

(b) The procedures whereby judicial review may be applied for, and any requirements which the law makes of the person seeking judicial review.

(c) The judicial remedies which may result from a successful application for judicial review, and their effects.

This and the following chapter deal with the grounds on which judicial review may be granted or refused: the procedures and remedies are dealt with in 17 and 18.

2. The nature of judicial review

It is a fundamental principle – indeed, an aspect of the rule of law – that persons or bodies in authority may only wield power over others by virtue of some lawful authority. Thus, where a public authority, whether it is a government department, a minister, a local authority or a policeman, wishes to exercise power in such a way as to affect the rights or expectations of an individual, they must point to some legal source of that power. The sources of such powers – which we may call executive or administrative powers – are the prerogative and statute.

Thus, subject to the exceptions noted at 13:**19** (i.e. those prerogatives which are non-justiciable), it is now fair to say that all governmental powers may be controlled by means of judicial review. However, it remains true that statutory powers, by their nature, are likely to be subject to certain requirements not applicable to prerogative powers. Thus, for example, a statute which grants certain powers to an administrative authority might require that authority to adhere to certain procedures (such as giving notice to affected parties, holding an inquiry etc.) before acting. Accordingly, the broad grounds for judicial review apply (with the exceptions noted above) to governmental powers of all kinds. In practice, however, some aspects of these may apply only to certain – usually statutory – powers.

Judicial review can also be distinguished from other proceedings, both civil and criminal, as follows:

(*i*) *Civil proceedings.* Whereas civil proceedings arise where a person's private rights or interests are infringed, judicial review is concerned principally with the public interest, and an individual's private interests are secondary. In particular, judicial review invariably involves the conduct of a public authority; the defendant in a civil action will frequently be a private person (though it may also be a public authority).

Procedurally, too, there are differences. Judicial review involves a two-stage procedure in which a judge scrutinises a person's initial application. Normal civil proceedings, on the other hand, are initiated by a writ, which can be readily obtained, and involve no initial scrutiny.

(*ii*) *Criminal prosecutions.* In some respects, judicial review resembles a criminal prosecution, in that both are public in nature (and may be brought by the Attorney-General), and both involve a two-stage procedure. In connection with serious criminal matters at least, committal proceedings, at which the prosecution's case is scrutinised, occur before the actual trial; judicial review also involves a two-stage procedure.

However, the function of the court in connection with judicial review is wholly different from its function in criminal matters. In general, criminal statutes or rules of common law are prohibitive (as in the biblical edict, 'Thou shalt not kill'). Thus, a criminal trial addresses the question, Has the defendant trangressed or broken the law by disobeying the edict in question? Judicial review, on the other hand, is concerned with permissive statutes, that is, ones conferring powers upon public authorities. There are often discretionary in nature (as in 'The minister may, if he thinks fit . . . '). The question is therefore not whether the minister (or other public authority) has disobeyed the statute, but whether he has exercised the powers conferred thereby properly, within the limits and for the purposes which Parliament intended.

In *CCSU* v. *Minister for the Civil Service* (1984), Lord Diplock identified three broad grounds for judicial review:

(a) *Illegality*. Both prerogative and statutory powers may be challenged on this ground.
(b) *Irrationality*. As Lord Diplock put it, 'It is hard to see how this could apply to prerogative powers.'
(c) *Procedural impropriety*. In principle, both prerogative and statutory powers may be reviewed on this ground. In practice, however, statutory powers are more frequently susceptible to challenge. In particular, statutory powers can be reviewed on the grounds that statutory procedures are not complied with (*see* 11, below). Such procedures will seldom apply to prerogative powers: however, the common law requirements of natural justice do apply here.

Illegality

3. Illegality and the doctrine of *ultra vires*

Ultra vires means beyond the powers. The clearest case of illegality as a ground of judicial review occurs when an administrative authority acts beyond its powers. In other words when it exceeds the scope of those powers granted it by Parliament or arising from the prerogative.

A classic case of illegality occurred in *Attorney-General* v. *Fulham Corporation* (1921). Here the Chancery Division held that when the Corporation provided laundry facilities purportedly under powers granted to it by the Wash-House Acts 1846-78 it was acting *ultra vires*, since those Acts only authorised the provision of 'bathing and washing facilities'. A laundry was a 'completely different venture'.

In *Burmah Oil Co. Ltd* v. *Lord Advocate* (1965), a case involving the illegal use of prerogative powers, it was held that, whilst the government was acting lawfully in destroying the personal property of British subjects in time of war, it was nevertheless obliged to pay and was therefore acting illegally in claiming the power to do so without compensating the owners (*see* 13:18).

As we have also seen that sometimes the courts have to consider the effects of a statutory provision upon prerogative powers. Here, the general rule is that the statute will be enforced and the prerogative power will therefore be limited by the terms of the statute: *Attorney-General* v. *De Keysers Royal Hotel Ltd* (1922).

4. Further aspects of illegality

(a) Cases involving public authorities which manifestly exceed their lawful powers are the most obvious instances of illegal behaviour, and of *ultra vires* actions. Such cases are not all that common however, since there is invariably some legal basis – often statutory – for the purported exercise of power by a public authority. Whether or not such a body has acted illegally, therefore, is largely a matter of interpretation.

For instance, in *Westminster Corporation* v. *London & North-Western Railway Co.* (1905), the corporation was empowered to build public conveniences by the Public Health Act 1901. They decided to build some conveniences underground; to provide public access to these they planned to build subways. Coincidentally, these subways would enable pedestrians to pass under Parliament Street, a busy thoroughfare in London. The Railway Company objected, claiming that the building of subways was not authorised by the Act, and was therefore illegal.

Following a principle laid down in *Attorney-General* v. *Great Eastern Railway Co.* (1880) the House of Lords held that the provision of subways was not illegal since it was a perfectly reasonable use of the Corporation's statutory powers. As Lord Selborne stated in the earlier decision, the law 'ought to be reasonably . . . understood and applied and whatever may fairly be regarded as incidental to or consequential upon those things which the legislature has authorised ought not, unless expressly prohibited, to be held by judicial constriction to be *ultra vires.*'

(b) It is sometimes the case that in taking an action in the first place, an administrative authority is acting illegally. Thus, for instance, where a statute empowered a local authority to refer rent valuations to a tribunal in cases referred by tenants, it was held that the authority acted illegally in referring a case by itself: *R* v. *Paddington and St Marylebone Rent Tribunal ex p. Bell Properties* (1949).

Similarly, if an authority is empowered to act only where certain factual circumstances exist, any action taken in the absence of those circumstances is illegal. For example, where a tribunal was empowered to assess the rent of an unfurnished property, it would have been illegal for it to do so in relation to a furnished one: *R* v. *Fulham, Hammersmith and Kensington Rent Tribunal, ex p. Zerek* (1951).

Perhaps the clearest example of this kind of situation arises in connection with a private citizen's powers of arrest. Under section 24 of the Police and Criminal Evidence Act 1984, a private citizen may arrest someone he suspects of having committed an arrestable offence only where an arrestable offence has, in fact, been committed (unlike a police constable, who may arrest someone where he merely suspects such an offence has been committed). If no offence has been committed, then any attempt by a private citizen to arrest a person would be illegal: *Walters* v. *W.H. Smith & Co.* (1914).

(c) There is, in administrative law, a principle known as *delagatus non potest delegare.* Roughly translated, this means that where powers are conferred (delegated) to a body by statute then that body may not, unless the statute authorises it (expressly or by necessary implication), delegate those powers to someone else. In other words, if Parliament confers decision-making powers on a person or body, that person or body must make his own decision, and not leave it to someone else. Thus, where an Act conferred the power to suspend dock workers found guilty of misconduct to a dock board, the board acted illegally in permitting a port manager to suspend workers: *Barnard* v. *National Dock Labour Board* (1953). (Another way of looking at such a case is to say simply that the port manager acted *ultra vires* since no power of suspension had actually been conferred upon him.)

One area where the courts have taken what appears to be a soft line on this is where a civil servant acts in accordance with the wishes of the minister responsible for his department or ministry. Here, ' . . . the act of the official is, of course, the decision of the minister. The minister is responsible,' *per* Lord Greene, *Carltona* v. *Commissioners of Works* (1943). In other words, powers are not normally delegated to civil servants: rather they act on behalf of the minister, in his name. Thus, even where a civil servant takes action in connection with powers granted by statute to a minister this will not necessarily, by itself, offend against the rule *delegatus non potest delegare* and will not, therefore, be illegal.

Irrationality

5. Irrationality

According to Lord Diplock in the *CCSU* case irrationality refers to the unreasonable use of discretionary powers, as formulated in the case of *Associated Provincial Picture Houses Ltd.* v. *Wednesbury Corporation* (1948) by Lord Greene MR. In general, according to Lord Greene, the decision of a public authority is to be regarded as unreasonable if ' . . . the court considers it to be a decision which no reasonable body could take. It is not what the court thinks is unreasonable, which is a different thing altogether.' In other words, the courts should not simply impose their own views as to what is a good administrative decision: they should only interfere if, viewed objectively, a decision can fairly be described as unreasonable. As Lord Diplock stated in *Secretary of State for Education and Science* v. *Tameside Borough Council* (1976), 'The very concept of administrative discretion involves a right to choose between more than one possible course of action upon which there is room for reasonable people to hold differing opinions as to which is to be preferred.'

Accordingly, the courts are slow to find that an authority has acted unreasonably unless there is some specific reason for doing so. This normally relates to the manner in which the decision has been reached, rather than the decision itself.

[Note: this should not be taken too far, however, and an authority's decision might well be found to be reasonable notwithstanding some minor flaw in the decision-making process. *See* **9(c)** below, for instance.]

Thus, according to Lord Greene:

Lawyers, familiar with the phraseology, often use the word 'unreasonable' in a rather comprehensive sense. It has frequently been used as a general description of the things that must not be done. For instance, a person entrusted with a discretion must, so to speak, direct himself properly in law. He must call his own attention to the matters which he is bound to consider. He must exclude from his consideration matters which are irrelevant to what he has to consider.

These are discussed in more detail below.

6. Must direct himself properly in law

(a) A good example of an authority which failed to direct itself properly in law and was, as a result, acting irrationally, occurred in *Perilly* v. *Tower Hamlets London Borough Council* (1973). The Greater London Council (General Powers) Act 1947, empowered the Tower Hamlets Council to allocate 'pitches' to traders in street markets. When a pitch fell vacant, the Council should fill it by the grant of a licence 'as soon as reasonably possible'. The applicant's mother, who had traded from a pitch in a street market for some years, died, and the applicant applied for her pitch some days later. However, in the meantime another person had applied, and the Council, thinking that the Act required it to grant a licence on a first-come-first-served basis, granted it to that person. The Court of Appeal held that the relevant section gave a discretion to the Council to decide applications on their merits. They had misinterpreted the phrase 'as soon as reasonably possible' and were wrong in thinking themselves bound to allocate pitches on a first-come-first-served basis. Accordingly, they had acted unreasonably.

(b) Sometimes an authority, in misdirecting itself as to the law, ends up acting in a manner which is contrary to the intentions of Parliament as to the purpose for which the discretion was granted. For example, in *Padfield* v. *Minister of Agriculture, Fisheries and Food* (1968) the Agricultural Marketing Act 1958 established a system for the collection and distribution of milk and dairy products throughout the country. Producers in the south-east of England complained that they were getting a poor deal from the system. Under the Act, the Minister had the discretion of referring such complaints to a committee of investigation. In this case, the Minister did not do so. The House of Lords held that he had acted unreasonably in not doing so, since it was clear from the Act that in cases of this kind he should. *Per* Lord Reid:

> Parliament must have conferred the discretion . . . to the Minister with the intention that it should be used to promote the policy and objects of the Act. If the Minister, by reason of his having misconstrued the Act, or for any other reason so uses his discretion so as to thwart or run counter to the policy and objects of the Act, then our law would be very defective if persons aggrieved were not entitled to the protection of the courts.

(c) *Error of law on the record.* Historically, a superior court had the power to quash the decision of an inferior court where an error of law appeared on the record of that court's proceedings, irrespective of whether the inferior court had exceeded its jurisdiction (i.e. acted illegally, irrationally etc.). In 1952, the doctrine of error of law on the face of the record was applied to the decision of an administrative authority: *R* v. *Northumberland Compensation Appeal Tribunal, ex p. Shaw* (1952). In 1969, however, the House of Lords effectively reduced the doctrine to history, holding that where an administrative authority commits an error of law in reaching its decision, it acts without jurisdiction and therefore unlawfully: *Anisminic* v. *Foreign Compensation Commission* (1969).

7. Must call his attention to matters he is bound to consider

An administrative authority may be bound to consider certain matters by virtue *either* of the enabling Act concerned, or of the common law.

(a) *By virtue of the enabling Act.* A clear example of a body acting irrationally by virtue of its having failed to consider matters required by statute is *Coleen Properties Ltd* v. *Minister of Housing and Local Government* (1971). Under the Housing Act 1957, local councils had power to acquire land where this was 'reasonably necessary' for a development. Such acquisition had to be approved by the Minister. A council proposed to acquire land for clearance purposes. In consequence of objections by residents, an inspection was made in accordance with the Act. The inspector recommended that the acquisition was not necessary, since the buildings were sound. The Minister nevertheless approved the scheme. The Court of Appeal found that he failed to have sufficient regard to the inspector's report, and was therefore acting unreasonably.

(b) *By virtue of the common law.* It is perfectly possible for a line of cases to establish that it is unreasonable for an authority to disregard certain matters which should be taken into consideration when making a decision. Possibly the best example of this arises in connection with a local authority's responsibility to ensure that its actions do not give rise to an unjustified burden on its rate (now council tax) payers. The leading case on this point is *Prescott* v. *Birmingham Corporation* (1955). An Act empowered the Corporation to impose 'such fares and charges as they think fit' for bus travel. The Corporation decided to permit pensioners to travel free; the result was that the bus service would incur a loss, which would have to be made up by an increase in rates. It was held that the Corporation owed a fiduciary duty to its rate payers and should take their interests into consideration when making decisions of this kind. In order to avoid an unwarranted financial burden falling on rate payers, the authorities should fix fares in accordance with ordinary business principles. This principle was also applied in *Bromley London Borough Council* v. *Greater London Council* (1982) by the House of Lords. (It should be noted that, under the Local Government Finance Act (1989) and subsequent legislation, the government can cap local taxes: i.e.; once the proposed rates for a given year have been agreed, the Secretary of State for the Environment may prevent a local council from imposing any increase in council tax.)

8. Must exclude irrelevant matters

The classic case in this point is *Roberts* v. *Hopwood* (1925). The Poplar Council decided to pay its employees a standard wage, in accordance with the political ideals of the majority (ruling) group. This wage was also higher than the national average which, due to a fall in the cost of living, had also fallen. The court held that, notwithstanding the fact that the enabling Act conferred what seemed to be a very wide discretion on the Council, its decision was unreasonable since it had taken irrelevant considerations (namely political ideals) into account.

The *Bromley* case (*see* **7**, above) also illustrates this principle. In the Court of Appeal, the Greater London Council's claim that they were bound to follow an election promise was held to be an irrelevant consideration.

9. Further points on irrationality

(a) It is important to note that since irrationality (or unreasonableness) is a 'comprehensive' term (*per* Lord Greene), it should not be surprising to find that conduct which can be described as unreasonable or irrational may sometimes also be considered illegal, in the sense used in **3**, above. For instance, in *Congreve* v. *Home Office* (1976), the Home Secretary was empowered by the Wireless Telegraphy Act to revoke TV licences in certain circumstances. A licence holder sought to avoid an imminent increase in the licence fee by taking out a new licence prior to the expiry of his old one. The Home Secretary threatened to revoke his licence. The Court of Appeal held that this was not a proper use of the Secretary's power of revocation, and he had evidently misdirected himself as to the meaning of the Act. In so doing, however, he had also ascribed to himself powers which Parliament has not in fact granted so that, if he had carried out his threat, he would have been exceeding his powers, i.e. acting illegally. Thus an unauthorised decision may be both irrational and illegal.

(b) Similarly, where a body considers irrelevant matters, it will often be at the expense of matters it should have considered. Thus, in *Roberts* v. *Hopwood* (above), the Council not only considered irrelevant matters, but failed to have regard to the national average wage, which the court found it should have considered.

(c) It should be remembered that unreasonableness or irrationality must be viewed, in each case, in relation to the relevant Act and to its objects. A failure by a public authority to have regard to some matters which its should have considered will not necessarily render its decision *ultra vires* provided it is acting in accordance with the overall purpose of the enabling Act. Thus, in *Pickwell* v. *Camden London Borough Council* (1983) an authority was found to have acted quite reasonably when, in order to ensure that public services were not disrupted, it settled a wages dispute with its employees without waiting for the resolution of a national dispute, the result of which, in normal circumstances, it should have considered. As Lord Penzance stated in *Howard* v. *Boddington* (1877), the court must consider the importance of the provision which has been disregarded and the relevance of that provision to the general object which is to be served by the act.

(d) Sometimes a statute actually refers to reasonableness. In *Secretary of State for Education* v. *Tameside Borough Council* (1976), the Education Act empowered the Secretary to intervene if the defendant Council was acting unreasonably. It was held by the House of Lords that he could only intervene if the Council acted unreasonably in the sense used by Lord Greene in the *Wednesbury* case (above). Thus, where a statute uses the term unreasonable (or similar) in connection with administrative bodies, the courts will apply the comprehensive meaning used at common law.

Procedural impropriety

10. Procedural impropriety
   According to Lord Diplock, this involves two distinct branches:

(1) Failure to observe procedural rules laid down in the relevant Act; and

(2) Failure to observe basic rules of natural justice

(These are common law rules, not found in any Act.)

11. Statutory procedures

In principle, where Parliament lays down a procedure for an administrative authority to follow, then its failure to follow it can be challenged in the courts. However, that principle will only apply where it can be shown that it was Parliament's intention that the procedure must be followed: in other words is *mandatory*.

(a) Some procedures are said to be 'directory' only. Failure to observe such a procedure will not of itself render a decision void. Thus in *Howard* v. *Secretary of State for the Environment* (1975), a statute provided that the grounds for an appeal be given. Failure to supply the grounds, it was held, did not invalidate the appeal, since the requirement was directory (i.e. for information) rather than mandatory.

(b) In determining the scope and extent of a mandatory procedure, the court will have regard to the overall purpose of the Act. The following are examples:

(*i*) *Grunwick Processing Laboratories Ltd v. ACAS* (1978). Here the Employment Protection Act 1975 required that the views of employees should be sought in connection with recognition of a trade union at the applicant's laboratories. It was held that, by failing to ascertain the views of a significant number of employees, ACAS had failed to comply with procedural requirements.

(*ii*) *Lee* v. *Department of Education and Science* (1967). The Education Act 1944 provides that, prior to making a change in the local education system, the authorities should notify interested parties. Such parties are required by the Act to raise any objections that may have within three months. A local authority introduced a scheme for such a change. It was announced at the end of the week and objectors were given till early the following week to complain. The court held that the Secretary's argument that this was within three months should not prevail. Not only was the procedure laid down a mandatory one, its purpose was to enable objectors a reasonable period – up to three months – in which to complain. In failing to allow such a period, the authority were acting contrary to the purpose of the Act.

(*iii*) *Agricultural, Horticultural and Forestry Training Board* v. *Aylesbury Mushroom Co. Ltd.* (1972). A minister was required to consult employers in the relevant fields before introducing training schemes. Prior to introducing an agricultural scheme he consulted with the National Farmers Union, but not with the Mushroom Growers Association. It was held that he had not consulted widely enough and had therefore failed to observe the statutory procedures properly.

11. Rules of natural justice

The concept of natural justice is an old one, and is fundamental to most legal systems. What this entails, however, will inevitably differ according to the kind of legal system involved and, in particular, trial procedures. For example, in systems where religious laws and religious courts predominate (such as in some Islamic countries), natural justice is frequently related to 'divine' or religious law.

In the UK, the USA and most Commonwealth nations, the legal system is based on the common law, and the trial procedure is adversarial in nature. In other words, the two parties in dispute (whether they be the State and individual in a criminal trial; private citizens in a civil action; or private citizen and administrative authority in an application for judicial review) must actually fight the dispute by producing evidence and argument, cross-examining witnesses, and citing relevant authorities. The judge takes no part in the presentation of the case: his function is to decide which side wins by presenting the better argument (rather like a referee or umpire in a sporting contest).

For such a method or procedure to work effectively and fairly, two basic rules must be observed:

(1) Both parties to the dispute are to be given an equal chance to give their version of events. In order for them to do so, and so that they can adequately prepare, each must have some idea of the case against him. (In administrative law this rule is known in Latin as *audi alteram partem.*)

(2) Like the referee or umpire in a sporting contest, the judge must be a neutral and impartial person, who has no vested interest in the outcome of the trial beyond seeing to it that justice is done. (This rule is known as *nemo judex in causa sua.*)

These broad principles, whose purpose it is to ensure that the system works fairly, are the basis of two rules of natural justice. In recent years they have become particularly important in relation to administrative law. Although breach of these rules is nowadays treated as an aspect of procedural impropriety, the topic is a large one, and is therefore dealt with in a separate chapter.

12. Emerging areas

The established grounds on which the conduct of administrative bodies or officials can be challenged by means of judicial review are discussed above. As with all other areas of English common law, these are constantly being developed and added to.

Two emerging areas which have been the subject of judicial decisions or comment in recent years are proportionality and misfeasance in a public office.

(a) *Proportionality.* Under this principle, a decision can be challenged on the grounds that the loss or harm caused by it outweighs any good caused, or is out of proportion to the wrongdoing or harm it seeks to prevent. It is particularly relevant to cases where a body is empowered to punish someone, or to deprive them of property (e.g. a licence).

Thus, for instance, in *R* v. *Barnsley Metropolitan Borough Council, ex p. Hook* (1986) a market trader had his licence revoked as the result of an argument with an official. As well as being in breach of natural justice, it was suggested that this punishment was out of proportion to the wrongdoing the applicant had committed.

Lord Diplock referred to proportionality as a possible ground for judicial review in the *CCSU* case (above). The general view, however, seems to be that proportionality is an aspect of irrationality, insofar as it may be raised as a ground for challenging a public authority's decision.

(b) *Misfeasance in a public office.* Strictly speaking, this is a tort (a private wrong). However, its ingredients are that a person holding public office abuses his or her position with intent to injure another person: *Jones* v. *Swansea City Council* (1989). Since the powers possessed by a public authority must only be used for the public good, it follows that such conduct must be unlawful, since the official concerned would, in so acting, be doing so for a purpose unauthorised by Parliament (as in *Padfield* above), and/or would be taking extraneous considerations into account (as in *Robert* v. *Hopwood*) quite apart from the element of bad faith involved.

Progress test 15

1. What is meant by judicial review of administrative action? On what grounds (broadly speaking) might judicial review be granted, and how does it differ from other legal proceedings? **(1–2)**

2. What is meant by 'illegality' in connection with judicial review? Is it possible for the exercise of prerogative power to be illegal? **(3–4)**

3. Outline Lord Greene MR's formulation of the unreasonable use of powers, as given in *Associated Provincial Picture Houses Ltd* v. *Wednesbury Corporation* (1948). How has the law on irrationality developed since this case? **(5–9)**

4. What is meant by 'error of law on the record'? **(6)**

5. In what circumstances might an authority's failure to have regard to relevant matters *not* render its decision *ultra vires*? How far is it true to say that, when evaluating administrative action, the court is looking at the decision-making process, rather than the decision itself? **(9)**

6. What is meant by 'procedural impropriety'? What forms might this take? **(10–11)**

Procedural impropriety: breach of natural justice

General

1. The rules of natural justice – background

We have already noted that there are two rules of natural justice applicable to administrative law.

(*i*) *Audi alteram partem* (literally, 'hear the other side'); and

(*ii*) *Nemo judex in causa sua* (literally, 'no man should judge in his own cause'. It is also called the rule against bias).

(a) As we have already seen, the rules are intimately connected with the fundamental nature of the English legal system, and in particular with the adversial system of trial procedure. It will therefore not be surprising to note that, historically, the rules were consistently applied by superior courts to review decisions in the lower courts. This procedure was facilitated by the prerogative writs (which still survive as prerogative orders) which provided the mechanism by which a court could control the decision of an inferior court.

Thus, in *Dimes* v. *Grand Junction Canal* (1852), (still a leading authority), the question for the House of Lords was whether the decision of a Lord Chancellor who had shares in the defendant company should be allowed to stand. The House held it should not:

> . . . it is of the first importance that the maxim that no man is to be a judge in his own cause should be held sacred. And that is not to be confined to a cause in which he is a party, but applies to a cause in which he has an interest. This will be a lesson to all inferior tribunals to take care that not only in their decrees they are not influenced by personal interest, but to avoid the appearance of labouring under such an influence, *per* Lord Campbell.

(b) It was clear from fairly early times that the rules of natural justice were capable of being applied to tribunals other than courts of law. For example in *Dr Bonham's case* (1610), the decision of a board of physicians to fine a doctor for practising medicine without the board's licence was successfully challenged on the ground that the board had an interest in the matter (i.e. it was in breach of the rule, *nemo judex in causa sua*).

The massive expansion of administrative authorities which has occurred during the nineteenth and twentieth centuries brought with it an extension of the application of the rules. By the middle of this century, the matter was exercising the courts, who began to take a more restrictive approach, giving rise to what Professor H.W.R. Wade in his book *Administrative Law* calls the 'retreat from natural justice'.

2. The retreat from natural justice: judicial and administrative functions

(a) We have seen above that the rules of natural justice were felt to be requirements not only where the decisions of courts of law were concerned but also, at least in certain circumstances, where the decisions of other authorities, including administrative authorities, were involved.

Thus, in *Cooper* v. *Wandsworth Board of Works* (1863) the Board's decision to pull down a man's home when the man had failed to get the Board's consent, as required by statute, was quashed on the grounds that the Board had not heard the man's side of the case. As Erle CJ stated: 'It has been said that the principle that no man should be deprived of his property without being heard is limited to a judicial proceeding, and that a board pulling down a house cannot be said to be a judicial act. I do not agree with that.'

In other words, the courts were able to apply the principles of natural justice to the action of administrative authorities by taking a broad view of what was meant by judicial proceedings or decisions. Thus, where an administrative authority was required to consider an appeal or apply questions of law as well as ones of fact, this was sufficiently judicial to require them to observe the rules of natural justice: *Board of Education* v. *Rice* (1911). (This was particularly necessary where the rule *audi alteram partem* was concerned, since the requirement to hear both sides in itself involved a judicial type inquiry.)

(b) However, in 1947 the House of Lords held that if the function of a public authority following statutory procedures was essentially administrative in nature, then it could not be judicial. Accordingly, therefore, natural justice was not a relevant consideration in connection with purely administrative functions.

In *Franklin* v. *Minister of Town and Country Planning* (1948), the Minister attended a public meeting where his proposals to establish a new town at Stevenage was being discussed. At the meeting, he indicated that he intended to designate Stevenage under the New Towns Act 1947 and it was pointless for protesters in the audience to complain. Shorly afterwards, the statutory procedure provided for under the Act was set in motion. This involved a local inquiry, at which the objectors expressed their views. The Minister was required to consider the report of the inquiry (amongst other things) before deciding on the matter. He eventually confirmed his original proposal. The objectors sought a judicial review, claiming that the Minister's mind had already been made up and that he was therefore biased against the objectors. They also argued that he had failed to consider relevant matters, namely the report or a part of it.

The House of Lords held that, unless they could actually show, by means of the evidence, that the Minister had failed to follow statutory procedures, they should fail. When taking his final decision, the Minister was acting in a purely administrative capacity, and that decision itself could not be challenged on the grounds of a breach of natural justice. Any bias displayed by him at the earlier meeting was not evidence of a failure by the Minister to follow the proper procedures. It was merely an instance of departmental bias, i.e. a Minister expressing the agreed policy of the department for which he was responsible, and therefore of the government itself.

This important decision was followed by the Privy Council in 1951 in *Nakkuda Ali* v. *Jayaratne*, where it was held that the grant of licences by a controller of textiles was purely administrative, and by the High Court in 1953, where it was held that a taxi driver's licence could be revoked without the need for a hearing, since the grant and revocation of licences was a purely administrative function: *R* v. *Metropolitan Police Commissioner ex p. Parker* (1953).

The new approach

3.   The new approach

The result of decisions like those discussed in 2, above was that application of the rules of natural justice – particularly the rule *audi alteram partem* – became severely limited. However, the pendulum swung in the opposite direction in the 1960s, so that in *Re HK* (1967), Lord Parker CJ, speaking of the application of the rules to an immigration officer's decision, commented, 'It is not as I see it a matter of acting or being required to act judicially, but of being required to act fairly.'

The case which, more than any other, brought about this new approach, was *Ridge* v. *Baldwin* (1964). The chief constable of the Brighton Police Force was prosecuted with two other constables for certain criminal offences, of which he was acquitted. The other policemen, however, were convicted, and during the trial the judge made comments concerning his qualities of leadership. Despite his acquittal, the Watch Committee decided to dismiss him: he was not told of their reasons for doing so, nor was he invited to attend the meeting at which the decision was taken, in order to make representations. At the request of his solicitor a further meeting was arranged at which representations were heard, but the Committee declined to change the original decision.

The House of Lords held that his dismissal was invalid. Regarding the scope of natural justice, they agreed that in a case of this sort the applicant was entitled to know the reasons why he was faced with dismissal, and to have an opportunity of making representations of his own. In short, he was entitled to a fair hearing.

According to Lord Reid, three situations might arise:

(*i*) *A master who seeks to dismiss his servant.* Here, the law of contract applies, and a master can dismiss his servant without a hearing or the giving of reasons as he chooses. Whilst he may be in breach of contract in so doing, his conduct cannot be challenged by means of judicial review on the grounds of procedural impropriety.

(*ii*) *A person holding public office 'at pleasure'* (such as a government minister). Such a person can be dismissed without a hearing and will have no legal redress whatsoever.

(*iii*) *A person who holds office under statutory provisions which lay down the grounds on which he may be dismissed.* In this case, the official cannot be dismissed without being told the cause and being given the opportunity to challenge it. If he is not, he may seek judicial review.

Ridge v. *Baldwin* itself fell into this third category, since the Watch Committee's powers to appoint and dismiss police constables were laid down by the Municipal Corporations Act 1892, section 191 of which provided that the Committee could dismiss any constable they thought 'negligent in the discharge of his duty or otherwise unfit'.

4. Licensing cases

One of the effects of the 'retreat from natural justice' in cases like *Parker* (*see* 2, above) was that such activities as licensing came to be regarded as purely administrative with the result that the view was adopted that licences could be refused or revoked without reasons being given.

Following *Ridge* v. *Baldwin*, however, the new approach began to be applied to licensing cases. Thus, in *R* v. *Gaming Board for Great Britain, ex p. Benaim and Khaida* (1970) it was held that where the Board refused the grant of a gaming licence to the applicant, they had to give at least the broad grounds for their decision, though not every detail of their reasons for refusing the licence. The Court of Appeal approved Lord Parker's dictum in *Re HK* (above) finding that, provided the Board had given the applicants a reasonable chance to state their case, they had acted fairly.

In *McInness* v. *Onslow Fane* (1978), Megarry VC in the Chancery Division adopted the analysis of Lord Reid in *Ridge* v. *Baldwin*, applying it to a licensing case. According to Megarry VC there were three possible situations involving licensing, each of which should be treated differently.

(*i*) *Forfeiture cases.* Where a public authority is empowered to revoke a person's licence. Such cases are tantamount to interfering with a person's existing rights: it can be presumed that such a step should only be taken for good cause. Accordingly, a person whose licence is revoked is normally entitled to a hearing. A case of this kind is *Congreve* v. *Home Office* (1976).

(*ii*) *First-time application cases.* Here nothing is being taken away from the applicant, though his suitability for a licence may have to be determined. An applicant has a hope but no more: the licensing authority will not normally be obliged to grant a hearing to an unsuccessful applicant.

(*iii*) *The expectation cases.* Such cases generally involve the renewal of a licence. This category differs from the others in that the applicant does not have an existing right which is taken away, but equally, has more than a mere hope that he will be granted a licence for the first time. Instead, he has a 'legitimate' expectation' of receiving something – in this case a licence – based (normally) on previous conduct, i.e. the fact that a licence has been granted on previous occasions.

The development of this analysis and, in particular, the

concept of 'legitimate expectation' has been further developed in recent cases, and has come to be established as an appropriate test for determining whether or not an administrative authority is required to observe the requirements of natural justice, especially whether to permit a hearing.

Legitimate expectations

5. Rights and legitimate expectations

Following Megarry VC's analysis in *McInness* v. *Onslow Fane* (4, above) the courts have developed the concept of 'legitimate expectation', so that now a person who is affected by administrative action will be entitled to a hearing before any decision is reached where he meets either of the following criteria:

(1) He has a legal right to a hearing; or
(2) He has a legitimate expectation to a hearing.

The legal right to a hearing will normally arise where the statute under which the administrative authority is acting provides for a hearing. A legitimate expectation can arise in two ways. As Lord Bridge stated in *Re Westminster Council* (1986), 'The courts have developed a relatively novel doctrine in public law that a duty of consultation may arise from the legitimate expectation of consultation aroused either by a promise or by an established practice of consultation.' Thus it may arise in two ways:

(a) *From what has already happened* . In *Council of Civil Service Unions* v. *Minister for the Civil Service* (1984), the Minister, i.e. Margaret Thatcher, the Prime Minister, sought to change the conditions of service of civil servants working in a secret government installation. She did not consult the civil servants, nor their representative unions, before doing so. The House of Lords held that, whenever such changes had taken place in the past, consultation had taken place, so that the civil servants had a legitimate expectation to consultation in this case. (However, for other reasons the Minister's decision was not, in the event, overturned.)

(b) *From an undertaking given by an administrative authority*. In *Attorney-General for Hong Kong* v. *Ng Yuen Shiu* (1983) the respondent had entered Hong Kong from China illegally. Some years later, the Hong Kong government wished to deal with the problem of illegal immigration, and announced that if persons who had already entered illegally came forward, each case would be treated on its merits. The respondent was subsequently detained pending deportation, without a hearing. He challenged this decision, claiming it was in breach of natural justice.

The Privy Council held that in consequence of the Hong Kong government's assurance that every case would be treated on its merits, he had a legitimate expectation to a hearing before any decision as to his status was reached. (This case also shows that a person can have a legitimate expectation of a hearing if other people in the same situation as him – here illegal immigrants – have been granted a hearing.)

On the other hand, a person does not have a legitimate expectation to a hearing in order to challenge a decision to enforce the law, even if he has been permitted (because the authority have turned a blind eye) to break the law in the past. In *Cinnamond* v. *British Airports Authority* (1980), taxi drivers had for some time been parking in prohibited areas in London airport, despite by-laws which were meant to prevent this. When the Authority finally decided to enforce the by-laws without permitting them any hearing, the drivers were unsuccessful in their attempt to challenge that decision.

(It should be noted that the above cases all involved the right to a hearing, i.e. the rule, *audi alteram partem*. It is in relation to this rule that most problems arise. In connection with the rule *nemo judex in causa sua* it could be said that anyone whose interests are affected by a decision has a legitimate expectation that the decisions will be taken impartially.)

Audi alteram partem

6. *Audi alteram partem*
Meaning hear both sides, this rule is also referred to as the right to a fair hearing. We have already discussed the circumstances in which a person is entitled to a hearing before an administrative decision affecting him is taken (*see* 4 and 5, above). The problem which remains is in deciding what, exactly, is meant by a fair hearing.

Fundamentally, the rule requires that a person is entitled to know the case against him and to have the opportunity of giving his own side of the case. In practice, however, these requirements can take various forms. They do not necessarily impose upon an administrative authority the obligation to hold a full-scale quasi-judicial inquiry every time a decision is to be taken (unless, of course, the enabling Act or some other statute imposes such a duty on the authority). As Lord Denning stated in *Selvarajan* v. *Race Relations Board* (1976), 'The investigating body is the master of its own proceedings. It need not hold an [oral] hearing. It can do everything in writing. It need not allow lawyers. It need not put every detail of the case against a man. Suffice it that the broad grounds are given.'

Each case is different, however, and must be treated on its own merits. As the cases indicate, in some circumstances, a person may have a legitimate expectation to no more than knowing the case against him. In others, he may legitimately expect a formal hearing, possibly even legal representation.

7. Examples of the rule in practice

The following cases show how the rule *audi alteram partem* works in practice.

(a) In *CCSU* v. *Minister for the Civil Service* (1984) *(see* 13:19, above for facts) it was held that the Minister's failure to consult was a breach of the rule *audi alteram partem*. This was because, having consulted the civil servants on similar matters previously, the Minister's conduct had given rise to the legitimate expectation on the part of the civil servants that they would continue to be consulted on matters concerning the terms of their employment in the future.

(b) In *R* v. *Home Secretary ex p. Tarrant and others* (1985) a prison Board of Visitors ruled that a prisoner who faced serious disciplinary charges should not be permitted legal representation in the hearing which took place. The High Court ruled that this was a breach of natural justice. In this case, the prisoner was, in effect, facing criminal charges and would, if found guilty, face an extended period of imprisonment through loss of remission. In such circumstances, a person had a legitimate expectation to legal representation, just as he would have if he faced proceedings in a criminal court.

(c) On the other hand in *Maynard* v. *Osmond* (1977), where a police constable faced disciplinary proceedings, it was held that he was not entitled to legal representation. Provided that the statutory requirements under the Police Act 1964 (which provided for a hearing) were complied with, there had been no breach of natural justice, since where disciplinary proceedings in professional bodies such as the police were concerned, there was no general right to legal representation. (Note also *R* v. *Gaming Board for Great Britain; McInness* v. *Onslow Fane*; discussed at 4, above.)

(d) Finally, *Re HK* (1967). An immigration official became suspicious as to whether an immigrant boy was entitled to enter the UK. Having sought to confirm his suspicions by questioning the boy and having him medically examined he had him detained. This was not a breach of natural justice: the boy had been given an opportunity to give his side of the story and no formal hearing was required.

Nemo judex in causa sua

8. *Nemo judex in causa sua*

Meaning no man should be a judge in his own cause, this rule is sometimes referred to as the rule against bias. As noted at **5**, above it is arguably a more fundamental rule than *audi alteram partem* since, though a person may not always be entitled to a hearing, he will normally have a legitimate expectation that the person or body taking an administrative decision affecting him will be unbiased.

In practice, the rule may be violated in two ways:

(1) Where the decision-maker has an interest – usually pecuniary – in the matter; and
(2) Where there is a real risk of bias on the part of the decision-maker.

9. Interests

The classic case here is *Dimes* v. *Grand Junction Canal Ltd* (1852) (*see* 1, above, for facts). The Lord Chancellor's decision was taken in breach of the rule *nemo judex in causa sua* simply because he had a financial interest (shares) in the defendant company.

A more modern case which shows the scope of the rule, and which is famous in its own right is *R* v. *Sussex Justices ex p. McCarthy* (1924). The applicant faced criminal proceedings before the justices, arising from an accident. The clerk, whose job it was to advise the magistrates on points of law, was a solicitor from the firm which had been retained by the other party involved in the accident in a civil action between that party and the applicant, also arising out of the accident. The court held that even though there was no evidence that the clerk had actually influenced the magistrates' decision, it could not stand, since the clerk, who clearly had an interest in the case, could have done so. As Lord Hewart CJ stated, 'It is of fundamental importance that justice should not only be done, but should manifestly and undoubtedly be seen to be done.'

10. Bias

Cases of actual bias are very difficult to prove (*see*, for example, *Franklin* v. *Minister of Town and Country Planning see* 2, above). Accordingly, in Lord Denning's words in *Metropolitan Properties Co. Ltd* v. *Lannon* (1969), 'in considering whether there is a real likelihood of bias, the court does not look at the mind of the chairman (of a committee) or whoever it might be. It does not look to see if there was a real likelihood that he followed one side or the other. The court looks at the impression that would be given to other people – if right-minded people would think there was a real likelihood of bias.'

In this case, a committee had to assess the rents charged in a block of flats owned by the applicants. The committee's chairman lived with his parents in a flat owned by another company in the same group as the applicants. This, the Court of Appeal held, contravened the rule against bias, since right-thinking people would think there was a real likelihood of bias on the part of the chairman, and this bias would taint the decision of the committee as a whole. (Note: where the decision complained of is that of a committee, it is not necessary to show that each member is biased. It is sufficient that a single member who is in a position to influence the decision as a whole is *biased* in the sense given above.)

11. Departmental bias

We have already noted the *Franklin* case (*see* 2, above), where departmental bias was established. Departmental bias may arise where a minister, having agreed with his officials and with government colleagues what his department's policy on a matter should be, adheres to that policy to the detriment of an individual, or group, despite the latter's objections. As the *Franklin* case shows, departmental bias does not in itself offend against the rule *nemo judex in causa sua* and should not in this context be treated as bias at all. Indeed, one should really refer instead to 'departmental policy'.

Another case on the point is *Schmidt* v. *Home Secretary* (1969). Schmidt, an alien member of the notorious Church of Scientology, was refused leave to remain in the UK. Schmidt challenged the decision, alleging that the Secretary should have indicated his reasons for expelling him, and claiming that his failure to do so showed bias on his part. The court rejected this claim, upholding the Secretary's exercise of his discretion. His view that Scientology was a harmful creed, which was the basis of his policy to refuse leave to enter or remain in the UK to alien Scientologists, had been endorsed by Parliament, and was therefore no more than departmental bias. The fact that it operated to the disadvantage of Scientologists did not amount to bias in the legal sense of the term.

Breach of natural justice

12. Breach of natural justice

There are two issues to be considered in the event that an administrative authority acts in breach of natural justice:

(1) Whether its decision is thereby rendered void or merely voidable; and

(2) Whether an appropriate remedy is forthcoming.

(a) *Void or voidable.* Historically, where a lower court acted in breach of natural justice, its decision was said to be voidable (as opposed to void). That is, its decision stood until successfully challenged in a higher court. For example, in *Dimes* v. *Grand Junction Canal Co.* (1852) the House of Lords pointed out that the Lord Chancellor's decision was not void (i.e. a nullity from the start) even though it was taken in breach of the rule against bias. This is because the decision of a court of law is the law until overruled: if it were otherwise, the law would be uncertain. (This problem did not arise when – rarely – a court acted illegally, since an illegal decision clearly cannot be the law, and is therefore void from the beginning.)

The concept of void/viodable is also seen in connection with the law of contract, where a party to a contract may in some circumstances legally avoid his contractual obligations (i.e. the contract is voidable).

Since certain administrative functions are judicial in nature (a fact that was very important in relation to natural justice at one time – *see* 1, 2, above), attempts have sometimes been made to introduce the concept of void/voidable into cases involving breach of natural justice. It is submitted that the better view nowadays is that the distinction between void and voidable has no real significance in relation to breach of natural justice. As Megarry VC stated in *Hounslow Borough Council* v. *Twickenham Garden Development Ltd* (1977):

> A decision reached by a tribunal wholly outside its jurisdiction and in complete defiance of natural justice is about as void as anything can be, but if nobody who is entitled to challenge or question it chooses to do so, it remains in being. Yet to describe such a decision as being voidable is to use that word in a sense that is not only special but likely to mislead.

(b) *Appropriate remedy.* Far more significant (in practice) than the void/voidable debate is the issue concerning remedies, specifically those remedies which a court may award at its discretion and which are particularly important in administrative law, since they include the so-called public law remedies. It is possible for an applicant for judicial review to succeed in showing a breach of natural justice, but he denied one of these remedies because the court, in its discretion, thinks it inappropriate to award it. The result of this is that to all intents and purposes the decision taken in breach of natural justice is not actually reversed by the court.

(*i*) *Glynn* v. *Keele University* (1971). The applicant, a student at Keele, was reported to the Vice-Chancellor for misbehaviour. He was told he would be punished. He requested a hearing at which to challenge that decision. After consultation with colleagues, the Vice-Chancellor decided to allow a hearing, and wrote to the applicant informing him of this. The applicant was abroad when the letter arrived at his residence, and did not return until after the date set for the hearing had passed, with the result that he did not, in the event, give his side of the case.

The Court of Appeal held that, whilst the original decision of the Vice-Chancellor to punish him had been taken in breach of natural justice (since no hearing had occurred), Glynn had been given every opportunity to challenge the decision subsequently. Accordingly, at the end of the day, no injustice had occurred, and so the court would not award the remedy sought. (The nature of these remedies and other cases involving their discretionary nature, are dealt with in 18.)

(*ii*) A somewhat similar case was *Chief Constable for North Wales* v. *Evans* (1982). Because of rumours concerning his private life, Evans (a probationary police constable) was asked to resign by the Chief Constable. He applied for judicial review, claiming breach of the rule *audi alteram partem*, and seeking (amongst other things) an order re-instating him.

The House of Lords held that whilst the Chief Constable's decision had been taken in breach of natural justice, they would not grant the order sought. It was not for the court, they said, to 'usurp the function' of the Chief Constable: it was a matter for him to decide what sort of people were suitable to serve as constables in his force, as provided for by statute.

(Note: This decision comes perilously close to reviving the old distinction between judicial and purely administrative functions.)

13. Validating clauses in statutes
Sometimes a statute will provide that a decision cannot be challenged in a court, despite what would otherwise amount to a breach of natural justice on the part of the decision-maker.

For example:

(a) Section 82, of the Local Government Act 1972 provides that decisions taken by a local authority shall not be legally invalid despite being taken by a council which includes a disqualified person. (A person may be disqualified, for instance, if he has a financial interest in the matter.) Normally, of course, such a decision would be in breach of the rule *nemo judex in causa sua* and could be successfully challenged in court. Because of section 82, it cannot.

(Note: a disqualified person who takes part in such a decision may himself be guilty of an offence.)

(b) Similarly Licensing Acts have sometimes provided that where a licensing magistrate is disqualified by reason of having an interest in a licensing matter, a licence actually granted is not invalid for that reason: *R* v. *Barnsley Justices* (1960).

Progress test 16

1. In what sense might the rules of natural justice be described as 'intimately connected' with the fundamental nature of the English legal system? **(1)**

2. Describe the development of the 1940s and 50s which have been described as the 'retreat from natural justice'. **(2)**

3. On what basis have the courts determined whether or not observance of natural justice (and particularly the right to a hearing) is applicable to administrative action since 1964? **(3–5)**

4. What is meant by *audi alteram patem*? Give examples of this rule in practice. **(6–7)**

5. In administrative law, what is meant by 'bias'? **(8–10)**

6. What are the effects of a breach of natural justice on an administrative decision? How might the discretionary nature of some legal remedies affect this? **(12)**

Applications for judicial review

The new procedure

1. The new procedure

The procedure whereby a person aggrieved of administrative action applies for judicial review of that action is a new one, deriving from two recent sources:

(1) Rules of the Supreme Court (RSC), Order 53 (1977); and

(2) The Supreme Court Act 1981 (giving statutory basis to the 1977 rules).

Prior to 1977 no single procedure for applications for judicial review existed, and the procedure involved could vary according to the remedy sought and the court where the hearing took place. Indeed, it was even possible for a person seeking more than one remedy to be required to apply for them separately.

The main reform which resulted from the above changes was the introduction of a single procedure for all applications for judicial review (albeit a two-stage procedure) which is applicable irrespective of which remedy is sought. Moreover, the new rules provide that all applications for judicial review must be made in the Divisional Court of the Queen's Bench Division of the High Court.

2. A single procedure

The Supreme Court Act 1981 (section 31 effectively enacts RSC, Order 53 rule 1 (1977)) provides a single procedure for all applications for judicial review.

(a) Section 31(1) provides that an application for one of the so-called public law remedies (i.e. an order of *mandamus, prohibition* or *certiorari*) must be made in accordance with the new rules, by the procedure known as an application for judicial review.

(b) Sections 31(2) and 31(4) provide that other remedies such as a declaration, an injunction and damages, may be awarded to an applicant for judicial review where the court thinks it appropriate, or where (in the case of damages) the court is satisfied that, had the action been begun by writ (in the same way as a normal civil claim), damages would have been awarded.

Thus, a single procedure for all applications for judicial review, irrespective of the remedy sought, is provided for. The first case in which the effects of this can be seen was *R* v. *Inland Revenue Commissioners, ex p. Rossminster Ltd* (1980). Here, an applicant was able to seek an order of *certiorari*, a declaration and an award of damages in one and the same application. This would not have been possible before 1977, when the new rules took effect.

3. A two-stage procedure

The Supreme Court Act 1981 provides that 'No application for judicial review shall be made unless the leave of the High Court has been obtained in accordance with rules of court': section 31(3). There are, therefore, two stages to an application for judicial review:

(1) The 'leave' stage; and
(2) The hearing stage.

The rules of court in question are contained in Order 53 rule 3. This provides that an application must be made *ex parte* (by the applicant, in the absence of the other party) to a judge. This application must include the particulars of the claim, including the relief sought and the grounds for seeking it. It is the function of the judge to act as a kind of filter at this first stage (the 'leave' stage). In particular, section 31(3) provides that leave should not be granted unless the court is satisfied that the applicant has a sufficient interest in the matter to which the application relates. (This aspect is discussed in detail below.) The applicant must also establish a *prima facie* case.

If the court grants leave, it can direct that the grant also has the effect of staying (i.e. halting) the administrative action in question, or, if remedies other than an order of *prohibition* or *certiorari* sought, grant interim relief (usually an injunction) to the same end. Thus, for example, where an applicant alleges that an administrative authority is acting illegally, the court can prevent it from taking any further such action pending the outcome of the hearing itself (the second stage of the procedure).

Whilst the first stage (the 'leave' stage) is clearly intended to filter out cases which lack any real basis, or applications from people or bodies who lack standing, this does not necessarily mean that, where an applicant succeeds in obtaining leave, he may not be shown at the hearing to have no standing.

In *R* v. *Inland Revenue Commissioners, ex p. National Federation of Self-Employed and Small Businesses Ltd (1981)* leave to apply for judicial review was granted to the Federation. The case went eventually to the House of Lords, who decided that the Federation did not have a sufficient interest in the matter to which the application related (*see* **5**, below).

Sufficient interest

4. Sufficient interest and the old law

As noted above, section 31(3) of the Supreme Court Act 1981 provides that an applicant for judicial review must have a sufficient interest in the matter to which his application relates. This requirement may be compared with the old common-law requirement of standing, which applies in English Law generally, though in various guises.

(a) The basic principle is that to bring proceedings before the courts, a person must have *locus standi* (a place of standing). In matters concerning private rights, this is normally straightforward, so that, for example, a person wishing to sue for breach of contract must be a party to the contract; to sue for defamation one must show that one is the victim of the libel or slander concerned, and so on.

(b) Where public rights are concerned, however, things are rather less straightforward. The general rule was that it was left up to a public official to bring proceedings. Thus, for example, the Attorney-General acts on behalf of the public by initiating proceedings. An example of this at common law is public nuisance, which may be defined as a nuisance which affects the convenience and comfort of a significant number of people. However, if an individual could show that he suffers some special damage unique to himself, over and above the inconvenience caused to the public as a whole, he may bring proceedings on his own behalf: *Rose* v. *Miles* (1815).

(c) The problem with judicial review was that, not unlike public nuisance, it involved not only questions of a public character (and in particular questions as to the legality of the conduct of public authorities) but sometimes also private rights as, for instance, when a local authority compulsorily purchases a person's property in excess of its powers, or without having observed statutory procedures. This problem was compounded by the fact that many of the appropriate remedies were discretionary in nature, not to be awarded too freely, so that a great deal of case law was built up about the requirements for standing where any of these remedies were sought. The result was that the law developed piecemeal, with differing requirements of standing according to which was sought.

As Lord Denning has stated in *R* v. *Commissioner of Police for the Metropolis, ex p. Blackburn* (1968) 2QB241 the requirements are such that a sufficient interest is not possessed by 'a mere busybody who is interfering in things which do not concern him, but it includes any person who has a genuine grievance because something has been done or may be done, which affects him.'

The most commonly used phrase, which described such a person (and which is still used) is 'a person aggrieved' of administrative action.

5.   The new law on standing: The *Fleet Street Casuals* case

It is clear that RSC Order 53 and section 31 of the Supreme Court Act 1981 were intended to, and have, opened up the law on standing so that unlawful conduct by public bodies may be more readily challenged. However, it is also clear that the requirement that an applicant for judicial review must have a 'sufficient interest in the matter to which the application relates' must have some meaning so that, broadly speaking, Lord Denning's statement that a 'mere busybody is not included' still applies.

In *R* v. *Inland Revenue Commissioners, ex p. National Federation of Self-Employed and Small Businesses* (1981) the Federation applied for judicial review of the Commissioners' decision to grant an amnesty to numbers of unidentified Fleet Street casual workers whom, they alleged, were guilty of income tax evasion. They claimed to be acting on behalf of their members, and were thus representing large numbers of tax payers in the matter. The amnesty, they argued, was illegal, since it was the Commissioners' duty under the Taxes Management Act 1970 to collect taxes due. The Commissioners claimed they had a discretion in the matter, which they had exercised reasonably (and therefore lawfully) by making the amnesty.

The House of Lords, finding that the Federation lacked sufficient interest, held that, except in obvious cases where an applicant lacked a sufficient interest, the courts should not treat the issue on standing as a preliminary one, to be dealt with only at the 'leave' stage, but should consider it along with all the evidence as to the alleged wrongdoing by the public authority concerned. Thus, the question of standing should be treated as one of the factors to be considered by the court when exercising its discretion at the hearing stage. Since the phrase used in the rules (now section 3 of the Supreme Court Act 1981) was 'sufficient interest in the matter to which the application relates', it was clearly necessary to identify that matter before deciding whether or not an applicant had a sufficient interest in it. Accordingly the two questions could not always be dealt with separately.

In the event, the House refused the application. However, Lord Diplock's judgment is of interest, since it sheds some light on the actual meaning of the term 'sufficient interest', as well as the procedural implications. According to Lord Diplock, it was of great importance that 'flagrant and serious breaches of the law by persons and authorities exercising governmental business' should be checked. He went on, '. . . to revert to technical restrictions on *locus standi* to prevent this that were current thirty years ago or more would be to reverse that progress towards a comprehensive system of administrative law that I regard as having been the greatest achievement of the English courts in my judicial lifetime'.

6. Further cases on standing

(*i*) In *R* v. *Independent Broadcasting Authority, ex p. Whitehouse* (1984) it was held that Mrs Whitehouse, the president of a voluntary watchdog body called the National Viewers and Listeners Association, had a sufficient interest to challenge the IBA's alleged breach of its statutory duty to monitor the contents of television programmes.

(*ii*) On the other hand in *Holmes* v. *Checkland* (1984), an anti-smoking campaigner was held not to have standing when he sought to prevent the BBC from broadcasting a snooker championship which happened to be sponsored by a tobacco company.

(*iii*) In *R* v. *Felixstowe Justices, ex p. Leigh* (1987) a journalist successfully challenged the decision of a magistrates' court to conceal the identity of the justices, not because he personally wished to report the case in question, but on the ground that he represented the press, which was the guardian and watchdog of the public interest in open justice.

(*iv*) Perhaps the most comprehensive statement on standing in recent years is in *R* v. *Secretary of State for the Environment, ex p. Rose Theatre Trust Ltd* (1989). In the course of a development, the remains of an ancient theatre, of great historical significance, were discovered. The Secretary of State, however, refused to use his statutory powers to preserve the site from the planned development. The Trust sought a judicial review alleging he had acted unlawfully. The court held that he had not. However, also in issue was the question of the Trust's standing about which the court made the following observations:

(a) The fact that the Trust had been granted leave to apply for judicial review did not preclude the court, at the hearing stage, from considering the question whether they had a sufficient interest in the matter. Indeed, the court should do so (following the *Fleet Street Casuals* case).

(b) Whether or not an applicant had a sufficient interest was not a matter for the court's discretion, but should be decided on established principles. Clearly, not every member of the public had such an interest. On the other hand, 'sufficient interest' was not confined to direct financial or legal interests only.

(c) An individual did not have a sufficient interest merely because he asserted that he had such an interest. Accordingly, just because a group of individuals got together for a particular purpose did not mean that the group had a sufficient interest where none of the individuals concerned did. In the event, the Trust had no standing.

7. The new law on standing: a summary

Whether an applicant has a sufficient interest in the matter to which the application relates is clearly one of the most important questions arising in connection with judicial review, and with the Order 53 procedure. Equally clearly, it is a question which must be addressed in each case individually so that a general answer, applicable to all cases, is difficult to formulate.

The following points are offered by way of a summary of the law as it has developed since 1977.

(a) The question of standing cannot, except in very obvious cases, be divorced from the merits of the case (i.e. whether the body whose decision is being challenged has acted unlawfully or not). The law requires a 'sufficient interest in the matter to which the application relates': that matter has to be clearly identified. (*See* the *Fleet Street Casuals* and *Rose Theatre* cases, **5** above.)

(b) 'Sufficient interest' means more than merely 'being interested' in the matter. Thus, political pressure groups (like the Rose Theatre Trust) or even representative organisations (like the Federation of Self-Employed) did not have sufficient interests.

(c) The question of 'sufficient interest' must be decided on established principles. The old law required that an applicant be a 'person aggrieved'. It is probably safe to say that this principle will still be used today. However, this does not require that to be a 'person aggrieved' the applicant must have a direct financial or legal interest as such. Thus, a television licence holder has a sufficient interest in programming to challenge the television authority's exercise of its supervisory functions (*see Whitehouse*, above), and a member of the press may challenge an attempt to prevent publication in the press of the identity of magistrates (*see Leigh*, **5** above). A rate payer has a sufficient interest to challenge any action by a local authority, particularly when that involved expenditure: *Arsenal Football Club* v. *Ende* (1977). On the other hand, an income tax payer has no interest in how the Inland Revenue treats another tax payer (*Fleet Street Casuals*, **5**, above).

(d) Since the question of 'sufficient interest' relates to the facts of the case (i.e. the matter to which the application relates), it is fair to conclude that it does not relate to the remedy sought. Thus, the old anomaly whereby the standing required varied according to which remedy was sought has gone, and a single test should now apply.

Public and private law matters

8. Public law matters

One important consequence of the new procedures governing judicial review has been the tendency to make a clear distinction between public law matters on the one hand, and private law matters, on the other. As Lord Diplock put it in *Fleet Street Casuals* (*see* **5**, above), 'Judicial review is a remedy that lies exclusively in public law.'

The basis for this view lies in Order 53 (enacted in the Supreme Court Act 1981) as interpreted by the courts, and in particular by the House of Lords in the case of *O'Reilly* v. *Mackman* (1982). Here, a prisoner sought to challenge the decision of a disciplinary board, alleging it had been taken in breach of natural justice. However, instead of applying for judicial review under Order 53, he brought his claim in the way normally used in civil cases, by writ.

The House of Lords held that the court should not hear such a claim. Where a person sought to establish that the decision of a public body infringed rights which were protected by public law (such as his right to a hearing, the benefits of natural justice, statutory procedures, etc.) then he must use the two-stage procedure provided for in Order 53. Thus, if the matter in issue is a public law one the Order 53 procedure must be adhered to.

9.　Cases on public law/private law matters

(a) *R* v. *East Berkshire Area Health Authority ex p. Walsh* (1984). A nurse sought to challenge his dismissal by the authority, and applied for judicial review, using the Order 53 procedure. The Court of Appeal held that this was a private law matter, for which that procedure was inappropriate. The fact that the applicant's employers (the Health Authority) was a public body did not, in itself, make this a public law matter. Cases of alleged unfair dismissal fall within the scope of employment law, a private law matter.

(b) On the other hand, even where private rights are involved, an allegation that these have been infringed by a public authority acting illegally or irrationally, or in breach of procedural requirements involves a public law matter, for which the Order 53 procedure is the appropriate one: *Guevara* v. *Hounslow London Borough Council* (1987).

(c) However, the authority must be shown to have exceeded its powers or otherwise acted illegally or irrationally, or in breach of natural justice in the sense given by Lord Diplock in the *CCSU* case (*see* 13:19).

It is not enough, for the matter to be a public law one, if an authority has been negligent in the exercise of its statutory functions: *Davy* v. *Spelthorne Council* (1983). (Negligence is, of course, a civil wrong or tort. The law of torts is almost entirely concerned with private law matters.)

(d) It is possible, however, for a person to raise a public law matter in a civil (i.e. private law) dispute by way of defence. In *Wandsworth London Borough Council* v. *Winder* (1985) a council tenant was able to defend himself against the Council's claim for rent arrears by arguing that the Council's recent decision to raise the rent had been unreasonable.

On the other hand, in *Quietlynn Ltd* v. *Plymouth City Council* (1987) it was held that a local authority's allegedly wrongful refusal to issue a licence could not be used as a defence to the *criminal* charge of operating premises without the necessary licence.

10. A criticism of the public law/private law split

It can be seen from the above that the distinction between public law and private law matters has come to significance after 1977. Not everyone has welcomed this development and some eminent judges have expressed their concern about it.

Apart from problems in defining public law matters, the most serious criticism is that the distinction between public and private law tends to lead to a separate system and body of rules applicable to public bodies and officials (i.e. the executive) distinct from that applicable to private individuals. This, it is argued, undermines the rule of law which says that in Britain there are no separate courts for the executive, and everyone is answerable before the same courts. As Lord Wilberforce put it, describing this danger in *Davy* v. *Spelthorne Borough Council* (1984):

> English Law fastens not upon principles but upon remedies. The principle remains intact that public authorities and public servants are, unless clearly exempted, answerable in the ordinary courts for wrongs done to individuals. But, by an extension of remedies and a flexible procedure, it can be said that something resembling a system of public law is being developed.

He continued, however:

> We have not yet reached the point at which mere characterisation of a claim as a claim in public law is sufficient to exclude it from consideration by the ordinary courts: to permit this would be to create a dual system of law with the rigidity and procedural hardship for the plaintiff which it was the purpose of the recent reforms to remove.

Other aspects of the new procedure

11. Delay in applying for judicial review

At common law, it was established that a person should not sleep on his rights and unduly delay before seeking judicial review: *R* v. *Aston University, ex p. Roffey* (1969). Order 53, rule 4 provides that 'an application for judicial review shall be made promptly and in any event within three months from the date when grounds for the application first arose, unless the Court considers that there is a good reason for exceeding the period within which the application shall be made.'

Curiously, the relevant section in the Supreme Court Act 1981 uses slightly different language. Section 31(6):

Where the High Court considers that there has been undue delay in making an application for judicial review, the court may refuse to grant:

(a) leave for the making of the application; or

(b) any relief sought in the application

if it considers that the granting of the relief sought would be likely to cause substantial hardship to or substantially prejudice the right of any person or would be prejudicial to good administration.

It goes on, however, to provide (in subsection 7) that this should be 'without prejudice' to any existing rules concerning time limits.

Accordingly both provisions (namely Order 53, rule 4, and section 31 of the Supreme Court Act) would seem to apply.

The leading case on those provisions is *R* v. *Stratford-on-Avon District Council, ex p. Jackson* (1985). The applicant sought judicial review. Through no fault of her own, she met with delay in obtaining legal aid, with the result that her application for leave was made nine months after the decision concerned. The Court of Appeal held:

(1) Despite the wording of Order 53, which appeared to refer to the hearing stage, the time limit referred to the 'leave' stage.

(2) Although it was essential that an application should be made promptly, the court had a discretion to extend the time limit, and was not bound in the exercise of its discretion by those considerations normally applicable to a civil action, since judicial review did not involve a private dispute which had to be resolved. In this case, the applicant was not at fault, and had acted with a due sense of urgency. Accordingly, leave to apply for judicial review should not be denied by virtue of Order 53, rule 4.

(3) However, a failure to act 'promptly, and in any event within three months' (as provided by Order 53, rule 4) could be described as an 'undue delay' within the meaning of Section 31(6) of the

Supreme Court Act. Accordingly, such a failure might at the hearing stage be taken into consideration by the court, as grounds for exercising its discretion to refuse the relief sought.

12. Other provisions

The remaining rules found in Order 53 are largely technical. Briefly summarised, the most import ones are as follows:

(a) *Rule 5.* This provides that it is the Divisional Court which hears the application itself.

(b) *Rule 7.* This provides that, in addition to or instead of the relief sought, the court may make an award of damages, provided that the court is satisfied that, had the action been one begun by writ, damages would have been awarded.

(c) *Rule 9* provides:

(*i*) The court may, as well as quashing an administrative decision, remit the matter to the authority concerned for reconsideration.

(*ii*) Where the court refuses judicial review, it may, where the relief sought is damages, a declaration or an injunction nevertheless hear the case as if it were a normal civil action, and decide it accordingly.

[Note: the converse does *not* apply, of course, and a court cannot grant a judicial review to a party who brings a normal civil claim: *O'Reilly* v. *Mackmem* (*see* **8**, above).]

13. Criticism of the new procedure

Lord Wilberforce's criticism of one aspect of the new procedure – the distinction it has brought about between public and private law matters – has already been noted (*see* **9**, above).

Briefly, the other main criticisms of the procedure can be summarised as follows:

(a) The rigidity resulting from the mandatory two-stage procedure (*see* **3**, above).

(b) The need to apply for the leave of the court.

(c) The difficulty in defining public law matters (*see* **7**, **8**).

(d) The shortness of the time limit (*see* **10**, above).

(e) The absence of any statutory statement as to the grounds for judicial review.

(f) The imprecise nature of the requirement for a 'sufficient interest' (*see* **4**, **5** above).

Progress test 17

1. Summarise the main features of the procedure whereby judicial review is applied for, as it has been since 1977. How does this differ from the old (i.e. pre-1977) procedure? (**1–3, 11–12**)

2. What is meant by the phrase 'sufficient interest'? Give examples of the courts' approach to the interpretation of this requirement. (**4–7**)

3. Distinguish: (**a**) public law; and (**b**) private law. What is the significance of this distinction in connection with an application for judicial review? (**8–10**)

4. What criticisms of the new procedure for applications for judicial review might be made? (**13**).

18

Judicial remedies in administrative law

General

1. Judicial remedies

It is said that English Law is concerned with remedies, rather than rights. This is reflected in the Latin Maxim *ubi remedium, ibi jus* (where there is a remedy, there is a right). Certainly, until very recently, it was the availability of an appropriate remedy which determined the question whether or not a person could pursue a claim in the courts in respect of any grievance he may have had. This requirement manifested itself in a rigid system called the forms of action whereby an aggrieved individual had to shape his claim so that it fell into one or other of these forms of action (e.g. trespass, *assumpsit*, etc.).

Since the nineteenth century the law has become more concerned with the enforcement of rights, and with the provision of a suitable remedy for a person whose rights have been interfered with. This has been brought about largely by the enactment of various rights in statutory form, and the use by the common law courts of equitable remedies. These are discretionary in nature and until the nineteenth century were available only in the Court of Chancery.

In the case of administrative law the courts are not concerned solely with the rights of the individual. The function of administrative law is also to contain the exercise of power by public authorities. Accordingly the courts have utilised a number of special remedies, originally issued under the royal prerogative, which are aimed primarily at the control of power.

Thus, in administrative law, two distinct categories of remedies are available. These are as follows:

(a) *Private law remedies* (including damages and the equitable remedies of injunction and declaration). These are the remedies which are available to the court to award (in an appropriate case) in any civil claim, as well as in administrative law cases.

(b) *Public law remedies.* These are the special prerogative remedies available only in claims against public authorities. They are called *mandamus, prohibition,* and *certiorari.* (There is also the related, but restricted remedy of *habeas corpus.*)

It has already been noted that judicial review is a procedure which is peculiar to public law (*per* Lord Diplock). We have also seen that an application for a public law remedy, or even a private law remedy against a public authority in connection with its public functions, must be made by means of an application for judicial review: Order 53, rule 1; section 31, Supreme Court Act 1981, as applied in *O'Reilly* v. *Mackman* (1984). What this means is that, in practice, whilst all remedies – both public and private – are available to the court in cases involving administrative law, the public law remedies are exclusive to administrative law.

Private law remedies

2. Private law remedies

These are the remedies available to the courts in cases brought by private litigants and which are routinely awarded in cases of breach of contract, tort, etc. There are three of them: damages; injunction; and declaration.

3. Damages

An award of damages is the remedy most commonly awarded to a plaintiff who succeeds in showing that some legal wrong has been committed against him. Unlike injunctions and declarations (which are awarded at the court's discretion) an award of damages is made as of right. However, damages are essentially compensatory: they are designed to compensate the plaintiff who, as a result of the defendant's wrongdoing, has suffered some actual loss or injury. Accordingly, if no such loss or injury has been suffered, the court may award only nominal damages (usually the smallest value coin of the realm, i.e. one pence). However, it should be noted that in some cases the loss or injury will be intangible (e.g. loss of reputation in libel claims). In such cases, damages may nevertheless be very substantial indeed.

Under the Rules of the Supreme Court, damages may be awarded to an applicant who claims them, provided that the court is satisfied that, had damages been claimed in an action begun at the time of the application for judicial review, they would have been awarded: RSC Order 53, rule 7; section 31(4), Supreme Court Act 1981.

4. Injunction

Like a declaration, an injunction is an equitable remedy, which developed in the Court of Chancery. It became available to the common law courts after 1854: Common Law Procedure Act 1854. As with all equitable remedies, it is awarded at the court's discretion, generally in circumstances when an award of damages would not be a sufficient or effective remedy. Thus, injunctions are most commonly used to prevent future wrong doing on the part of the defendant. An injunction takes the form of a court order either forbidding a person from doing something (a prohibitory injunction) or requiring him to do something (a mandatory injunction: these are comparatively rare). Whilst many injunctions are issued to prevent wrong doing which has already begun from continuing, two other kinds of injunctions are worth noting.

(a) *An interim or interlocutory injunction.* This may be granted pending the outcome of the case, but before it has actually been heard. Such an order will frequently be made under Order 53, rule 3 and, if the court so directs, the grant of leave to apply for judicial review can itself operate in the same way as such an order.
(b) *A quia timet injunction.* Exceptionally, the court may make an injunction in respect of illegality which is merely threatened and has not, as yet, actually occurred. This is rare, however, since a declaration (*see* below) is usually sufficient in such cases. Injunctions are not available against the Crown, though they are available against public bodies.

5. Declaration

Also known as a declaratory judgment, this is defined as a determination of the rights of the parties in dispute in relation to a state of affairs which has not yet arisen. Thus, it is appropriate in (though not confined to) a case where illegality is threatened, but has not actually begun at the time of obtaining it. Whilst the declaration does not expressly order the defendant to do or not do something, it is nevertheless an effective remedy, for in 'declaring' what the plaintiff's rights are it is spelling out to the defendant what he is legally permitted to do or not to do. Since it is, like the injunction, a form of court order the defendant who ignores it will be acting in contempt of court (*see* 2:8).

Like the injunction, a declaration is an equitable remedy, awarded at the court's discretion. Unlike an injunction, however, a declaration may be awarded against the Crown (though the Crown cannot be committed for contempt of court): *Dyson* v. *Attorney-General* (1911). Where a declaration (or injunction) is sought against a public authority alleging unlawfulness in connection with its public functions, then the Order 53 procedure must be used: *O'Reilly* v. *Markman* (1984).

6. The role of the Attorney-General

As the chief law officer of the Crown, it is the role of the Attorney-General (AG) to protect the public interest. Thus, he is involved in some criminal prosecutions and actions in public nuisance, where a class of citizens is threatened by a person's behaviour. As such, the AG is empowered to take action against administrative authorities to prevent abuses of power. This will normally occur in a case where no individual has a sufficient interest (standing) in the matter (*see* 17:4), since the AG always has a standing. There are two ways in which the AG may act:

(1) *Ex officio* (by virtue of his office); and
(2) 'At the relation' of an individual who lacks standing himself (the 'relator' action).

7. Relator actions

Where an individual who lacks sufficient interest to apply for judicial review wishes he may refer a case of alleged unlawfulness to the AG, who may himself take action *ex officio*, or be prepared to act 'at the relation' of the individual concerned. There is an important distinction between the two, since when he acts *ex officio*, the AG quite literally takes over the whole case, and proceedings are brought by his office, using public money, instructing counsel to argue the case, etc. In a relator action, on the other hand, the AG only lends his name to the proceedings. It is the complainant himself who is responsible for actually bringing the proceedings, costs, retention of counsel, etc. A relator action may be identified by the phrase *ex rel* which appears after the defendant's name in the law reports, as in, *Attorney-General* v. *Independent Broadcasting Authority, ex rel. McWhirter* (1973).

8. Limits on the role of the AG

There are two important points to note regarding the role of the AG in administrative law:

(a) The AG, whether acting *ex officio* or at the relation of an individual, can only apply for the remedies of injunction or declaration, or both. He cannot obtain damages (since he has suffered no loss), nor can he obtain any of the prerogative orders.
(b) The AG has an absolute discretion whether or not to act. The AG's role is an aspect of the Royal Prerogative and is not justiciable: *CCSU* v. *Minister for the Civil Service* (1984).

In *Gouriet* v. *National Union of Post Office Workers* (1977), the House of Lords held that the AG's refusal to act could not be challenged in court by an individual on any grounds. Furthermore, if the AG declined to act, the individual seeking to make him could not take proceedings himself, lacking as he did *locus standi*.

Public law remedies

9. Background
Historically, the public law remedies have their origins in the prerogative writs, which were the means whereby inferior bodies could be controlled. Initially, the king himself issued such writs to curb the powers of courts and officials. By the sixteenth century, however, they were in constant use by the Court of King's Bench. After the Judicature Acts 1873-76, they became available to the High Court. They were:

(1) *Prohibition;*
(2) *Mandamus;*
(3) *Certiorari;*
(4) *Habeas Corpus;* and
(5) *Quo Warranto.*

The Administration of Justice (Miscellaneous Provisions) Act 1938 made certain changes, so that *quo warranto* ceased to exist, and the other prerogative (with the exception of *habeas corpus*) became known as prerogative orders. The Administration of Justice Act 1960 provided for a new procedure whereby *habeas corpus* could be applied for: it also provides that *habeas corpus* should, in an appropriate case, be granted as of right. The orders of *prohibition, mandamus* and *certiori*, however, are discretionary remedies. Application for these three prerogative orders must now be made by means of an application for judicial review (Order 53, rule 1: section 31, Supreme Court Act 1981).

10. The prerogative orders

As noted above, there are now three of these:

(a) *Prohibition.* This originated in the thirteenth century, as a means of preventing the ecclesiastical courts from exceeding their jurisdiction. Today, the effects of the order remain much the same – to prevent a body from acting illegally – but the order applies to public authorities generally, including inferior courts.

(b) *Mandamus.* This is an order compelling a body to act. Usually, this involves compelling it to do its statutory duty, in a case where it appears not to be doing so. It was first used by the King's Bench to order an administrative authority (a local council) to do its duty in the seventeenth century.

(c) *Certiorari.* This seems to have been used after the sixteenth century as a means of securing the records of proceedings in an inferior court and removing them to the King's Bench, who would then take over the case if some irregularity appeared to have occurred. Accordingly, it developed into a means whereby the King's Bench (later the High Court) could review proceedings in lower courts and quash them, substituting its own decision where necessary. It was first extended to the decisions of administrative authorities in the seventeenth century, and has since become virtually synonymous with judicial review of administrative action.

A few points concerning the prerogative orders should be noted:

(*i*) Since they derive from the royal prerogative, these orders are not available against the Crown. Historically, the order of *certiorari* was not available in connection with ministerial action generally. Nowadays, all three orders are available to a person aggrieved of administrative action, including ministerial action, where such action involves the use of statutory powers. Where a minister is exercising prerogative powers, on the other hand, the prerogative orders cannot be used by the courts to interfere with his action. Here (assuming the prerogative powers are justiciable in the first place) a declaration may be available.

(*ii*) Like the equitable remedies of injunction and declaration, the prerogative orders are discretionary in nature. Accordingly, even where a court finds that an administrative authority has acted unlawfully, it may refuse to make such an order (*see*, for example, *Chief Constable of North Wales* v. *Evans* (1982)).

11. *Habeas corpus*

This ancient prerogative writ was left unchanged by the Administration of Justice (Miscellaneous Provisions) Act 1938; it was, however, changed by the Administration of Justice Act 1960 (*see* **9**, above). Historically, the writ of *habeas corpus* (have the body) is of great significance in connection with personal liberty. It is directed at an individual who holds another in custody, ordering him to produce that other person before a court.

In connection with administrative law this writ is nowadays most commonly applied for and used in cases involving immigration and deportation. A person who is accused of illegal entry, or whose deportation has been ordered, may be held in custody by the authorities concerned. The effect of the writ in such a case is to ensure that a court examines the case against that person, and is able to satisfy itself that required procedures (including natural justice) are being observed.

Habeas corpus is nowadays not normally the appropriate procedure in cases of arrest and detention by the police, since the law (and in particular the Police and Criminal Evidence Act 1984) lays down strict safeguards concerning such detention. Thus, for example, detention by the police is subject to periodic review by a magistrates court: section 43(1), Police and Criminal Evidence Act 1984. Where it is alleged that the police have detained an individual unlawfully, the normal remedy is a common law action for false imprisonment or wrongful arrest brought at the conclusion of any criminal proceedings which occur, or on the individual's release from custody.

Restrictions on availability of remedies

12. Availability of remedies

We have already seen that the remedies appropriate to judicial review are only available to a person with 'sufficient interest in the matter to which the application relates' (i.e. a standing). There are two further restrictions as to the availability of remedies which may mean that an applicant for judicial review is denied relief:

(a) The court may exercise its discretion to refuse an appropriate remedy; and
(b) The possibility of obtaining a particular remedy, or even of challenging an administrative decision, may be excluded by a statutory provision or be limited to a particular period of time.

13. Remedies refused at court's discretion

It has already been noted that all of the remedies available to an applicant for judicial review (other than damages) are discretionary in nature. Since an award of damages requires proof of harm or injury, that will not always be forthcoming, and even if it is, it is not sufficient to overturn an administrative decision which has been taken unlawfully, and therefore has little impact on administrative action as such.

The fact that the courts may refuse to award an appropriate remedy is therefore of great importance. There are two cases, in particular, where despite a breach of natural justice the court refused to grant relief or interfere with the administrative decision involved: *Glynn* v. *Keele University* (1971); *Chief Constable of North Wales* v. *Evans* (1982).

14. Grounds for refusal

Since the grant or refusal of most remedies is discretionary in nature, it is not possible to lay down any binding rules as to when such a remedy might be denied (if it were, then the remedy would cease to be discretionary). It is, however, possible to list some of the principles which have tended to influence the courts in the exercise of their discretion.

(a) *Unreasonable conduct by the applicant himself.* This may include unreasonable delay, though this is now provided for in RSC Order 53, rule 4; section 31(6) of the Supreme Court Act 1981. In *Glynn* v. *Keele University* (1971) the applicant's failure to attend a hearing which was arranged, following a breach of natural justice, was treated as an example of unreasonable behaviour. Similarly, a person may waive his entitlement to a hearing, or agree to be heard by a biased individual. He cannot, later on, complain to the court of that decision.

(b) *Disciplinary matters.* As we saw (12, above) the courts are sometimes loath to interfere with the internal disciplinary affairs of certain bodies, particularly the police. Whist this does not mean that the decisions of such bodies cannot be challenged (where, for instance they are taken improperly) it does mean that the courts are disinclined to avoid remedies like *certiorari* and *mandamus* compelling the body to act in a particular way, lest they 'usurp the functions' of such bodies (*see Chief Constable for North Wales* v. *Evans* (1982)).

(c) *Just and reasonable'*. Certain remedies, particularly the injunction, are only awarded if it is 'just and reasonable' to do so. Thus, the injustice prevented by granting an injunction must be greater than any hardship which may be caused in awarding it. For example in *Morris* v. *Redland Brick Co.* (1977), the House of Lords held that where the defendant's excavating operations undermined the plaintiff's property, threatening it, it would be wrong to issue a mandatory injunction compelling the defendant to take remedial steps where these would have cost more than the value of the property itself.

Similarly in *Miller* v. *Jackson* (1977) (a nuisance case) the Court of Appeal held that, when the defendant's cricket balls were occasionally struck into the plaintiff's premises, causing a small amount of damage, it would be wrong to award an injunction forbidding the playing of cricket in future, since damages would be a sufficient remedy.

15. Exclusion of remedies

By virtue of its sovereignty, it is obviously possible for Parliament to exclude the award of any or all of the available remedies, or even to protect a decision from judicial review altogether. However, the courts are somewhat jealous of their jurisdiction over administrative authorities, and tend to interpret such provisions as narrowly as possible. As Lord Reid stated in *Anisminic* v. *Foreign Compensation Commission* (1969), 'A provision ousting the ordinary jusridiction of the courts must be construed strictly, meaning, I think, that if such a provision is reasonably capable of bearing two meanings the meaning should be taken which preserves the ordinary jurisdiction of the courts'.

Anisminic shows how far the courts are prepared to go in achieving this. A statute provided that 'the determination of any application made [to the Foreign Compensation Commission] . . . shall not be called in question in any court of law'. Anisminic sought to challenge the decision of the Commission, claiming it has made an error of law in the exercise of its functions. The Commission claimed that in accordance with the above provision, judicial review of its decision was excluded.

The House of Lords held that the statute provided that only a determination of an application made to the Commission was immune from judicial review. If, as was alleged here, the Commission had erred in law, then its decision was not a determination at all and could therefore be challenged in a court.

Only a final, legally correct resolution of a dispute could properly be described as a determination.

16. Statutory time limits

As well as the time limits set in RSC Order 53, rule 4, and section 31(6) of the Supreme Court Act 1981 it is not unknown for particular statutes to include strict time limits as to the period in which any challenge of a decision taken under the statute may be made. Thus, for instance, sections 242-45 of the Town and Country Planning Act 1971, provide that any attempt to challenge a planning decision must be made within six weeks. The Acquisition of Law Act 1981 makes a similar provision in respect of compulsory purchase orders.

Such statutory time limits generally operate as partial ouster clauses (i.e. clauses excluding the jurisdiction of the courts) since, as a general rule, no challenge can be made after the statutory time period has elapsed: *Smith* v. *East Elloe Rural District Council* (1956).

Exhaustion of remedies

17. Exhaustions of remedies

In some jurisdictions, there is a rule requiring that, before applying to the courts for relief, an aggrieved individual must exhaust all the available remedies. Strictly speaking, no such rule exists in English law. As Wade puts it, 'a vital part of the rule of law is that illegal administrative action can be challenged as soon as it is taken or threatened'. Thus in *R* v. *Hillingdon Borough Council ex p. Royco Houses Ltd* (1974), it was held that a person could challenge a planning decisions in the courts, where he could obtain an order of *certiorari* if the decision had been improperly taken, irrespective of whether or not he had, at the time, exercised his statutory right of appeal to the minister.

However, a number of judicial *dicta* have drawn attention to the exceptional nature of judicial review, implying that where some alternative remedy exists, the courts should be reluctant to grant a judicial review, save in exceptional circumstances (*per* Lord Scarman in *Preston* v. *Inland Revenue Commissioners* (1985)). It is submitted that such *dicta* can, if misunderstood, tend to obscure the position. The better view is, as Wade puts it, that there is no rule of law requiring that, before applying for judicial review, a person is required to exhaust all other remedies. Nevertheless, some of the considerations already discussed in this and other chapters may produce a similar result in certain situations. Thus:

(a) The court may refuse relief in its discretion, due to the unreasonable behaviour of the applicant (*see* above). Failure to take up an alternative remedy may, in some circumstances, be unreasonable: *R* v. *Epping & Harlow General Commissioners, ex p. Goldstraw* (1983).

(b) The fact that an alternative remedy exists may in some cases be a factor in deciding whether or not the case is a public law one (and therefore suitable for judicial review) or not. In *R* v. *British Broadcasting Corporation, ex p. Lavelle* (1983) the applicant sought to challenge her dismissal. Her contract of employment provided for a grievance procedure involving a domestic tribunal. In holding that this tribunal was the appropriate place to challenge her dismissal, the Court of Appeal appeared to be saying that their alternative remedy must be exhausted before judicial review could be sought. In fact, it was really upholding the principle established in *O'Reilly* v. *Mackman* (1984), that a contractual dispute was a private law matter for which judicial review was unavailable.

(c) As noted above, the courts are reluctant to interfere in internal disciplinary matters of bodies like the police, fire brigade, etc.

(d) Finally, it should be noted that judicial review, as a public law procedure, is such that it should serve the interests of the public to apply it, and not only those of the applicant. If the applicant's own interests are adequately served by an alternative remedy, and the public interest does not require judicial review, the court may refuse an application: *R* v. *Huntingdon District Council, ex p, Cowan* (1984).

Progress test 18

1. Briefly summarise the judicial remedies available to a person aggrieved of administrative action. In what circumstances might 'private law' remedies be appropriate and who might apply for them? **(1–8)**

2. Distinguish: **(a)** prohibition; **(b)** *mandamus*; and **(c)** *certiorari*. In what circumstances might these orders be granted by a court? **(10)**

3. Is it quite possible for an individual to succeed in showing that the conduct of an administrative authority which affects him was unlawful, yet

nevertheless be denied a remedy. Indicate the kinds of situations which might bring this about. **(12–15)**

4. Is there a rule requiring an applicant for judicial review to exhaust all other available remedies? (Give examples and reasons for your argument.) **(16)**

19

The legal liability of public authorities: Crown proceedings and public interest immunity

General

1. Legal Liability

When we speak of the legal liability of public authorities, we are concerned with their liability to ordinary claims brought in the courts by the normal process of litigation and (to a limited extent) criminal proceedings. We are not referring to judicial review, which as, we saw in 7, above, concerns itself with the question whether a body has acted within the scope of its legal (usually statutory) powers. Thus, when discussing the legal liability of public authorities, we are referring to their liability to pay compensation to persons who have suffered loss as a consequence of some wrong doing (usually a tort or breach of contract) or statutory offence (*see* below).

The general principle is that, except for the Crown, public authorities are not immune from liability. Even the Crown, since the Crown Proceedings Act 1947, has been liable to proceedings in contract and tort. The Crown is not, however, liable to criminal proceedings. Nor has the sovereign, personally, lost those immunities which she has historically enjoyed by virtue of the prerogative.

For the purpose of our discussion, the liability of public authorities is dealt with separately from that of the Crown since certain special rules apply to the latter (*see* 6, below).

The liability of public authorities

2. Liability in tort

A tort is a civil wrong, which is redressible by an action for damages. Such wrongs include trespass, negligence, nuisance and defamation.

Legally, public authorities are endowed with 'personality', that is, they enjoy the same legal capacity as an actual person to make contracts, employ other persons, etc. As such, public authorities may be held legally liable for their conduct where this is tortious. Thus, in *Cooper* v. *Wandsworth Board of Works* (1863), the Board was liable in trespass when it pulled down a man's house unlawfully. Similarly, in *Carmarthenshire County Council* v. *Lewis* (1955), a local council was held liable in negligence, and in *Metropolitan Asylum District* v. *Hill* (1881), the district managers of a hospital were held liable in nuisance.

3. The defence of statutory authority

In general, normal principles of liability apply to public authorities, just as they would to private individuals and other bodies. However, in the nature of things, public authorities will almost invariably be acting under some statutory authority, which creates a special situation, rather different to that applicable to private individuals.

With regard to certain torts, and in particular nuisance, it is a defence to show that the authority concerned was acting within the scope of its statutory authority, and that the nuisance caused by it was an inevitable consequence of the exercise of that statutory authority. Thus, in *Hammersmith Railway Co.* v. *Brand* (1869) the Company were not liable to residents who complained about the noise and vibrations caused by trains, since this was an inevitable consequence of running a railway in accordance with statutory authority granted to them. The same principle applied in *Allen* v. *Gulf Oil Refining Ltd* (1988) in connection with an oil refinery. To succeed in nuisance, a plaintiff will have to show not only that the authority's conduct caused interference and/or loss to him, but that the authority was actually acting beyond the scope of its statutory authority: *Westminster Corporation* case (*see* 15:4).

The defence only applies to certain torts, however; notably nuisance. Even where an authority is acting within its statutory powers, it may still be liable for example in negligence. As Lord Blackburn noted, 'It is now thoroughly well established that no action will lie for doing that which the legislature has authorised if it be done without negligence . . . but an action does lie for doing what the legislature has authorised if it is done negligently.'

In relation to negligence, it cannot be said that causing loss or damage is inevitable and, since the defence requires both statutory authority and inevitability, it can be seen that it will not apply to negligent conduct.

4. Liability in contract

Except for the Crown, public authorities are subject to the common law as regards contract, and enjoy no immunity or other dispensations. (The Crown may be liable in contract, but under the Crown Proceedings Act 1947, rather than the common law: *see* below.) Thus, for example, a local authority which enters into a contract with builders or a cleansing firm is liable in the event of breach, just like a private person.

5. Criminal proceedings

To a certain extent, public authorities are liable to criminal proceedings (unlike the Crown, whose immunity from criminal proceedings was untouched by the Crown Proceedings Act 1947). There are certain difficulties attaching to the criminal liability of public authorities, however. These arise principally from the fact that, even though a public authority has legal personality, it has no physical existence and cannot, therefore, have the necessary mental element (intention, etc.) to be guilty of a crime.

Furthermore, a public authority cannot be imprisoned and can therefore only be convicted of an offence which is punishable with a fine.

It is possible, however, for a public authority to be held vicariously liable for the acts of its servants and agents, where this is practicable, or where a statute provides (either expressly or impliedly) for vicarious liability.

Crown proceedings

6. Crown proceedings

The position of the Crown must be considered separately from that of other public authorities. At common law, and by virtue of the prerogative, the Crown enjoyed complete immunity from all proceedings, both civil and criminal. Its immunity from liability in contract and tort was removed by the Crown Proceedings Act 1947. However, since that Act now governs Crown proceedings, and not the common law, the detailed provisions of the Act must be examined. Crown proceedings is an important topic, since central government departments generally act in the name of the Crown. Accordingly, any question as to the liability of a government department in contract or tort will generally fall within the scope of the Act.

7. Background

A feature of the royal prerogative, as has been noted, is the maxim, 'The King can do no wrong.'. Until 1947, this principle was applied not only to the sovereign personally, but also his servants and agents, and to those who exercised authority in the name of the Crown. Thus, the immunity extended to the actions of central government as well, and could not be avoided by holding the Crown vicariously liable for the conduct of (say) civil servants.

Obviously, such a blanket immunity could have been seen to be subject to abuse. Accordingly, the practice developed of allowing an aggrieved person to proceed against an individual for breach of contract or tort. In the case of contract, this procedure was formalised in the Petition of Right Act 1860 which empowered the Home Secretary, at his discretion, to grant a petition of right whereby an individual was given leave to take proceedings for breach of contract in the High Court. As regards tort, an individual could sue the servant or agent of the Crown whose decision led to his loss personally: compensation would, in practice, be paid by the government. However, even where these procedures applied, an individual proceeding against the Crown was not guaranteed success in the courts, since certain principles might prevent it.

8. Principles which might hinder proceedings

(a) *Contract*. Even where a petition of right was granted, an aggrieved individual might be unsuccessful in obtaining compensation from the Crown for breach of contract in certain circumstances.

(*i*) It is an established principle that the government may not levy any charge without Parliament's approval. Any new expenditure, since it inevitably involves such a charge, must therefore be approved. Thus, unless Parliament has previously authorised it, the Crown cannot be compelled to pay money due under any contract it has made with an individual: *Churchward* v. *R* (1865).

(*ii*) In *The Amphitrite* (1921) the principle was established that a court may not 'fetter executive discretion', nor could the government itself commit future governments in that way. Accordingly, a contract which would have such a result could not be enforced against the Crown.

(**b**) *Tort*. The main problem for an individual claiming that he suffered loss as a consequence of tortious conduct by the Crown was (and still is) the fact that, to all intents and purposes, the remedies available to him were limited to damages by way of compensation. A court cannot, for example, award an injunction against the Crown ordering it to act in some way, since that would have the same effect as in **8(a)**(*ii*), above.

Whilst the Crown can now be liable in both contract and tort, these principles still apply, with the result that certain kinds of contract cannot, in practice, be enforced against the Crown, or that tortious remedies may be limited to compensation.

The Crown Proceedings Act 1947

9. The Crown Proceedings Act 1947

This Act came into force on 1 January 1948. It was passed so as 'to amend the law relating to the civil liabilities and rights of the Crown and to civil proceedings by and against the Crown; to amend the law relating to the civil liabilities of persons other than the Crown in certain cases involving the affairs or property of the Crown, and for purposes connected with the matters aforesaid.'

The most significant features of the Act are as follows:

(**a**) Where any person has a claim against the Crown which, prior to the Act, might have been enforced subject to the grant of a petition of right, then an action to enforce that claim may now be brought as of right, without the need for governmental approval: section 1. Thus, a person may bring proceedings against the Crown in contract.

(**b**) The Crown is now liable in tort as if it were a person of full age and capacity, in respect of the following:

   (*i*) Torts committed by its servants or agents;

   (*ii*) Breach of duty owed to its servants; and

(*iii*) Breach of any common-law duty attached to the ownership, occupation or possession of property.

This is so provided that an action would, in any case, lie against the individual (e.g. servant or agent) concerned: section 2(1).

Thus, the Crown is now itself liable in tort. This liability extends to liability for breach of statutory duty (section 2(2)), but such liability may, and often is, excluded by statute (section 2(4)). Certain functions of the Crown are excluded. In particular, no liability shall lie in respect of anything said or done by any person discharging a judicial function (section 2(5)), and until its repeal in 1987 (Crown Proceedings (Armed Forces) Act 1987) section 10 provided that the Crown was not liable for the Acts of members of the armed forces unless the Home Secretary consented to such proceedings.

The following additional points should also be noted:

(c) Nothing in the 1947 Act removed the personal immunity of the sovereign, which is expressly preserved by section 40(1).
(d) Nothing in the 1947 Act has affected criminal liability, so that the immunity from criminal proceedings enjoyed by the Crown and its servants and agents, where they are acting in their official capacity, remains. However, subsequent Acts have made it possible for limited criminal proceedings to be brought against government agencies. For instance, the National Health Service (Amendment) Act 1986 enables prosecutions for breach of Public Health legislation to be brought against hospital authorities (following public concern about standards of hygiene in hospitals).
(e) The principles discussed at 8, above, have survived the Act so that, even now, enforcement of some Crown contracts, or effective remedies in tort, may not be forthcoming.

10. Crown liability since 1948
The modern position can be clearly seen in two post-Act cases.

(a) *Contract*. In *Howell* v. *Falmouth Boat Construction Co. Ltd* (1951), the respondent commenced refurbishing works on ships owned by the Admiralty. The work was authorised orally by a civil servant, and had commenced before the statutory licence (which was a normal requirement) had been issued. Nevertheless, the House held that the Company could sue for payment on completion of the work, since at common law such an oral authorisation could bind a private individual, and the official concerned was a duly appointed officer of the Crown, as required by section 2(5).

(b) *Tort.* In *Home Office* v. *Dorset Yacht Co. Ltd* (1970 The Crown was found liable in negligence when some borstal boys, who had been taken on an outside working party, escaped and damaged the respondents' boats. The House rejected the government's claim that, since such working parties were part of a rehabilitation programme, the public interest demanded that it enjoyed immunity for the negligence of the borstal officers who has allowed the boys to escape.

Public interest immunity

11. Background

Historically, the Crown enjoyed immunity from all legal proceedings, by virtue of the royal prerogative. This was a total immunity and, as a consequence, it followed that the Crown would not be compelled to produce evidence, either as a witness in a trial, or in the form of documents in any proceedings. (Unlike private persons who can be compelled to give evidence as witnesses, or, where they are parties, required to make documents available to the court by virtue of the procedure known as discovery.) This aspect of its immunity was known as Crown privilege, and it applied not only to all proceedings and all documents, so that the Crown could object to the production of documents by either party in judicial proceedings, even though the documents were not in the possession of the Crown itself.

This privilege was not an absolute one, however, and the courts sought to ensure that it was not used arbitrarily. Accordingly, the principle developed that the Crown's objection to the production of documentary evidence in any legal proceedings would be upheld only if it could be shown that production would be injurious to the public interest. A case in which this principle was applied was *Duncan* v. *Cammell Laird & Co. Ltd* (1942). The case arose out of the sinking of a prototype submarine, *The Thetis,* whilst undergoing trials in Liverpool Bay. Relatives of drowned crew-members sought to obtain copies of the submarine's plans, in order to substantiate their claims of negligence against the shipbuilders. The Admiralty objected, claiming Crown privilege. The House of Lords held that in a case of this kind involving a military vessel objection to the production of such documents made by a minister of the Crown should be acceded to, and would not normally be questioned.

12. The effects of the Crown Proceedings Act

Section 28 of the Crown Proceedings Act provides that the Crown is subject to discovery, just like a private person. However, it goes on to state that nothing should affect the common law rule that disclosure of documents may be refused on the ground that it would be injurious to the public interest.

On the face of it, nothing much seemed to have changed with the enactment of the Crown Proceedings Act. In 1953, in *Ellis* v. *Home Office*, the court followed *Duncan* v. *Cammell Laird* and refused to order discovery of documents relating to a prisoner without requiring any detailed evidence from the Home Office (which had objected to disclosure) as to how disclosure would have been injurious to the public interest.

This changed in 1968, however, with the House of Lords' decision in *Conway* v. *Rimmer*.

13. *Conway* v. *Rimmer*

A former probationary police constable (the plaintiff) brought an action for malicious prosecution against a senior officer (the defendant). In order to substantiate his claim, he sought disclosure of certain documents whose existence had come to light during the discovery procedure (by virtue of which each party to judicial proceedings informs the other, on request, of the existence of documentary evidence in his possession; the other party may then apply to the court to have it made available to him for possible use as evidence). These documents included reports made by the defendant on the plaintiff's service. Neither the defendant nor his superiors in the police objected to production of the documents, but the Home Secretary did, and claimed Crown privilege in respect of the documents concerned.

The House of Lords held that the documents should be produced for inspection by the court. If, having inspected them, the court was satisfied that disclosure would not be prejudicial to the public interest, it should order their disclosure.

The House distinguished its earlier decision in *Duncan* v. *Cammell Laird* on the grounds that, whereas the documents in that case had related to a secret military vessel in war time, thus involving security and defence matters, these did not. It was not the law that, wherever a minister objected to the disclosure of documents, then disclosure should be denied. Rather, disclosure should only be denied if:

(a) The documents belong to a class of documents, disclosure of which generally could be regarded as injurious to the public interest (such as secret defence information); or

(b) The court is satisfied that, because of their actual contents, disclosure of the particular documents in question would be injurious to the public interest.

The case is of immense importance, since it establishes the following principles:

(*i*) The question whether documents should be disclosed or not is a matter of substantive law, to be decided by the court on the evidence according to established principles of law. It is not a question which could be decided by a minister simply objecting to disclosure, and is not, therefore, a matter of privilege on the part of the Crown at all.

(*ii*) Whether or not documents should be disclosed depends on a balancing of the likely harm to public interests, namely the public interest in governmental activities (such as defence, or the police), on the one hand, and the public interest in the administration of justice (which incidentally requires an open and fair trial of the plaintiff's claim) on the other.

These two threads have been much developed in subsequent cases.

14. From crown privilege to public interest immunity

We saw at **13**, above that *Conway* v. *Rimmer* established that the question whether or not disclosure of documents is injurious to the public interest is generally one for the court to decide, and that it is not, in effect, a matter of any privilege on the part of the Crown. This point was forcibly underlined in *Rogers* v. *Home Secretary* (1973) in which Lord Person commented, ' . . . the expression "Crown privilege" is not accurate, though sometimes convenient. The Crown has no privilege in the matter.' The true test, according to the House of Lords in that case, was whether disclosure should be refused by the court on the ground that it was necessary to protect the proper functioning of the public service.

The following year in *Alfred Crompton Ltd* v. *Commissioner of Customs of Excise* (1974), the House of Lords held that the fact that information in documentary form had been given to a governmental agency in confidence was not, in itself, sufficient to justify non-disclosure.

In *Neilsen* v. *Laugharne* (1981) the Court of Appeal coined a new phrase to describe the situation where disclosure should be refused. Documents whose disclosure might be injurious to the public interest (in this case details of a police inquiry), they said, were subject to 'public interest immunity'. This phrase has become generally accepted as the correct description of the true grounds for non-disclosure.

15. A balancing of public interests

Two fairly recent cases illustrate the principle that, in deciding whether or not to uphold a claim of 'public interest immunity', the courts are in fact concerned with balancing the likely harm to two (sometimes competing) public interests in an efficient public service on the one hand, and the proper administration of justice on the other.

(a) In *D* v. *National Society for the Prevention of Cruelty to Children* (NSPCC) (1977) H.L., the Society received a report to the effect that D was mistreating his child. In fact, the report proved groundless, as the NSPCC's investigations showed. D, however, wished to bring libel proceedings against the author of the report, and sought disclosure of the report in order to establish the person's identity. The Society, a voluntary body not established by statute, which was unconnected with the government or its agents, objected to the production of the report on the grounds that it relied on the confidentiality of such reports to do its work. If the identity of its informants could be established, it argued, people would be unwilling to report even serious cases of child abuse, for fear of recriminations or legal action.

The House of Lords upheld the Society's claim. Public interest immunity was not confined to the work of central government or other public bodies (in the sense of statutory bodies). The work of the NSPCC could properly be regarded as part of the public service, in which a public interest clearly existed. Furthermore, the House was satisfied that the Society's argument was well founded, and that its work would undoubtedly be inhibited if the confidentiality of such reports was broken. In the instant case, the likely harm outweighed that of the proper administration of justice involved, particularly since the applicant's name (D) had in any case been cleared by the Society's investigations.

(b) On the other hand, in *Campbell* v. *Tameside Metropolitan Borough Council* (1982), on somewhat similar facts, the court ordered disclosure of a confidential report. A teacher was assaulted by a pupil, and had to retire early as a result. The pupil was known by the local education authority to have a record of violence, and reports from the authority's employees to that effect were kept on their files. In order to substantiate her claim that the authority had acted negligently in allowing the pupil to attend her school (as opposed to a special school), the plaintiff sought disclosure of these files. The Council objected, claiming that persons making such reports would be less frank in doing so in future, if they knew that their reports could be made available in this way (rather like the NSPCC's claim in the previous case).

The Court of Appeal were unconvinced by this argument. Although the reports were confidential in nature, it did not follow that those concerned would be inhibited from making them just because there was a possibility that such a report may, occasionally, have to be disclosed. Furthermore, it was the *duty* of such persons (teachers, social workers, etc.) to make such reports on pupils. This was quite a different situation to the NSPCC, whose informants made reports voluntarily.

Regarding the balance of public interest, it was the task of the court to weigh the likely harm to the public interest which would result from disclosure against the likely harm to the public interest in the administration of justice which would result from non-disclosure. In the instant case, the plaintiff contended that, unless she could obtain the reports, she would lack the evidence necessary to support her claim. If that were so, then non-disclosure would lead to a total denial of justice: this would be clearly detrimental to the public interest in the administration of justice.

16. Other grounds for non-disclosure of documents
    In recent years the courts and, in particular the House of Lords, have sought to curb an extension of the use of public interest immunity, and have been at pains to confine it to its proper place. Thus, in a case where discovery of documents is refused by the courts, it should not be assumed that this is always due to a successful claim of public interest immunity, even where disclosure is objected to on these grounds. In *Science Research Council* v. *Nassé* (1980), the House of Lords refused to disclose documents to a man wishing to bring proceedings against his employer for unlawful discrimination. The documents included reports on persons other

than the applicant, and the House was not satisfied that they were a reasonably necessary piece of evidence in support of his case. Accordingly, discovery was refused. As Lord Scarman pointed out, the confidential nature of documents does not, by itself, confer a public interest immunity defence against disclosure. Public interest immunity, according to Lord Scarman, 'exists to protect from disclosure only information, the secrecy of which is essential to the proper working of the government of the State'. For that reason, he regretted the passing of the term Crown privilege, which ' . . . at least emphasised the very restricted area of public interest immunity'.

In the instant case, then, disclosure was refused not on the grounds of public interest immunity but, at the discretion of the court, on the grounds that disclosure was not necessary for the administration of justice.

Thus, even where public interest immunity is inapplicable or not claimed, the court may very well refuse to order the disclosure of documents, particularly ones of a confidential nature. This is perfectly logical, since there is no reason why confidentiality should be breached unless this is reasonably necessary in the interests of justice.

This principle was highlighted in *Air Canada* v. *Secretary of State for Trade* (1983). Here, the House of Lords held (and this applies irrespective of whether public interest immunity is claimed with regard to documents or not) that a person seeking disclosure must satisfy the court that the documents are likely to be necessary for fairly disposing of the case. As Lord Wilberforce put it, there must be some grounds for believing that it goes beyond a mere fishing expedition.

Progress test 19

1. To what extent are public authorities generally liable: **(a)** to civil proceedings in contract and tort; and **(b)** to criminal proceedings? **(1–5)**

2. Outline the main effects of the Crown Proceedings Act 1947. To what extent do any of the old (pre-1947) common law principles, which might have hindered proceedings against the Crown, still apply, and with what effects? **(6, 8–10)**

3. What is (or was) meant by 'Crown privilege'? What were the effects, if any, of the Crown Proceedings Act on this topic? **(11–12)**

4. Outline the decision in *Conway* v. *Rimmer* (1968). How did that decision pave the way for the transition from 'Crown privilege' to 'public interest immunity'? **(13–14)**

5. In what sense are the courts, when considering a claim of public interest immunity, involved in a balancing of public interests? **(15)**

6. On what grounds, other than public interest immunity, might a court refuse to allow disclosure of documents to a party seeking it? **(16)**

Appendix I
Examination technique

Examination technique is something for which a student, wherever possible, should be prepared as part of his course of instruction in a subject. Just as the substance of English law developed largely by virtue of procedural development, so does the student's grasp and understanding of the law develop along with his ability to answer questions concerning it.

The tutorial system is usually geared to this end; however, the student studying alone can still take steps to acquire examination technique as he masters the subject, and, particularly, as he revises. Thus, the process of learning and revising should incorporate practice in planning answers to, and finally solving questions on, the subject.

A suggested scheme is as follows:

1. As you read through your notes and other materials on a particular topic (say a chapter in this book, for instance) make précis notes of the materials containing clear statements of the legal principles involved.

Add only such information as is vital to your understanding of each principle, but do make a note of the important cases and statutes wherein the principle can be found (these should be given in the texts used).

2. Read through these précis notes, making sure you understand the principles given. Memorise the cases and statutes. If necessary, summarise these notes even further.

3. Then, tackle some specimen questions. To begin with, when you are taking the subject one topic (or chapter) at a time, the progress tests at the end of each chapter in this book will be useful. As you proceed, and are learning and revising the subject as a whole, use the specimen examination questions in Appendix III. Use, also, papers which have previously been set in examinations similar to those you intend to sit.

4. When answering the specimen questions make sure you are clear what it is the questions requires of you, and what it is you wish to say. You should plan your answers, making a rough draft of the main points you wish to make before commencing on a full written answer. This plan should contain:

(a) A summary of the legal principles you feel are applicable.
(b) Any cases and statutes which are relevant to those principles.

There are three varieties of questions which might be set in Law examinations: whilst they are, on the face of it, quite different (and, therefore, require a slightly different approach in each case; this is explained further below), it is important to bear in mind that whatever kind of question you are attempting, the most important thing is to demonstrate two things:

1. a good knowledge and understanding of the Law; and
2. adequate analytical skills.

In this context, 'analytical skills' involve, in particular, the ability to assess a factual situation or statement to identify what principles of law are raised in addressing that situation or statement, and the ability to state them clearly, concisely and convincingly. Provided you achieve this, you should not go far wrong, since your argument (the case you are presenting) should emerge naturally and logically. Examiners do not really want to hear a point of view as such, but they do want a reasoned 'argument'. Remember, though, that what that really means is a concise statement of the law as applied to the situation or statement given in the question, leading to reasoned conclusions, no more or less.

The three varieties of questions referred to earlier are as follows.

1. *Problem questions.* These are very popular in Law exams since they come closest to the approach of a practising lawyer, or judge hearing a case. A problem question involves an imaginary factual situation posed by the examiner, which requires the examinee to decide which branch of the Law is involved, and which specific principles are applicable to the facts given. To underline the similarity to the practising lawyer's approach, the question will sometimes require you to 'advise' one of the parties; the following is an example of such a question.

X, a well-known political agitator, calls a public meeting and procession to demonstrate against the Government's policy in overseas aid. Five hundred people attend the meeting, bringing traffic in some public roads to a standstill. Police Sergeant Plod, who is at the scene, decides that the procession should not be permitted in First Avenue, since it is a narrow street, and asks X not to lead the procession down that street. X ignores Plod, and the procession continues in First Avenue. Some of those processing make gestures to pedestrians, including members of the Women's Institute who are present. One of these, Amy, is offended by the gestures, so Inspector Morse, a plain-clothes detective, arrests one of the men making the gestures.

Advise the police.

Clearly, this question is concerned with questions of public order and police power to maintain order. Specifically it involves a number of sections of The Public Order Act 1986 and relevant case law. For example, section 11 requiring advance notification of processions. Does this requirement apply to this particular procession?

Second, Plod's conduct: is he within his powers under sections 12-13 to impose such conditions on the procession? Is X guilty of an offence in ignoring Plod?

By raising these (and the other) issues, and stating the law relevant to them, you can build up your answer, at the same time, deciding what advice you wish to give to the police, in terms of whether they have powers to act as they do, etc.

2.   *'Text-book' questions.* These are usually in the form of a question, e.g. 'Outline the principal conventions of the Constitution and their function'. They are designed to test your memory and understanding of the subject, primarily, and the typical answer to such a question will be a well-presented essay.

3.   *'Quotation' questions.* These are somewhat similar to 'text-book' questions; they are, perhaps, a little more demanding, however. For example: 'The King hath no prerogative save that which the Law allows him'. (*Coke*) Discuss.

You will be required here to decide, first and foremost, what the person quoted is actually getting at. Do you agree with him? Whether you agree or not, it is necessary that you plan your answer, and present a balanced argument to support your point of view. However, be careful to stick to the point of the question in this kind of answer.

Whichever kinds of question you tackle, be sure to observe the following:

(a) Plan your answers before starting to write.
(b) Explain yourself adequately; the examiner can only read your script, he will not know what you wanted to say unless you do so clearly.
(c) Keep to the point, stating the main principles.
(d) Always cite authorities (cases and statutes).
(e) Keep within the time permitted, by apportioning the available time on each question carefully, so as to complete the examination.

Appendix II

Specimen examination paper

Attempt 4 questions.

1. 'The King hath no prerogative save that which the law allows him' (Coke). Discuss this statement, with particular reference to recent decisions involving the applicability of judicial review to the conduct of Government ministers exercising prerogative powers.

2. The Chairman of Cementem Limited offers Brown MP a 'gift' of £1,000 if Brown will vote against the Government in a debate on the economy. Brown accepts. In the course of the debate, Greene MP makes scathing comments about members of the Bossport District Council, at which Grey, MP for Bossport, attacks Greene and has to be removed from the House.

Later, in a televised interview, Greene repeats some of the comments which he made in his speech earlier, and Sam, and Dave, two Bossport councillors, begin proceedings for defamation. In order to expedite their claim, they request a transcript of Greene's speech in the House.

Discuss the conduct of the MPs involved.

3. (Assume that) under the Local Amenities Act 1993, local councils are empowered to compulsorily purchase land for the purpose of providing 'sporting and recreational facilities' for use by members of the public, provided that there is a 'real need for such facilities'. Councils are further empowered to 'impose such charges and conditions' on the use of the facilities as they think fit. Plans must be announced publicly, and affected persons have up to three months to object. The Happydaze Council decide to erect a 'leisure park' in their area and initiate steps for the compulsory purchase of property for that purpose. Pete, the owner of the property earmarked for compulsory purchase, wishes to object. He is told that his objections must be made within one week, since the Minister (whose confirmation of the scheme is required by law) is due to go on holiday and the council wishes to begin building work prior to his return.

When details of the scheme are announced, it transpires that, as well as a running track and football pitch, the council plans to build a supermarket on the site. It also proposes to charge members of the public £10 per day for the use of the facilities, except for councillors and their families who are exempt. Old age pensioners are not to be allowed entry to the leisure park at all.

Discuss the council's plans and conduct in initiating them.

4. What is meant by the Separation of Powers? To what extent does a Separation of Powers exist in the UK and what advantages/disadvantages might accrue from such a system?

5. 'It is often said that it would be unconstitutional for the United Kingdom Parliament to do certain things, meaning that the moral, political and other reasons against doing them are so strong that most people would regard it as highly improper if Parliament did these things. But that does not mean that it is beyond the power of Parliament to do such things. If Parliament chose to do any of them, the Courts could not hold the Act of Parliament invalid.' (Per Lord Reid, In *Madzimbamuto* v. *Lardner-Burke* (1969) 1AC 645)

Do you agree with this assessment of Parliamentary sovereignty? What sort of things might lead some people to regard it as 'highly improper' for Parliament to pass certain Acts?

6. PC Sober comes across Sop and Pop pushing a car. He suspects them of having stolen it, and asks who the owner is. Sop says 'get lost, copper' so Sober answers 'I'm arresting you for theft'. Both men accompany Sober to the police station where they are locked in a cell.

After 7 hours, they are taken to a separate rooms, and asked if they wish to make statements. Sop states that he wishes to see his solicitor, but the sergeant who is interviewing him refuses, so Sop says nothing. Meanwhile, Pop is told by PC Twister that Sop has 'told us everything'. Pop, being feeble minded, 'confesses' to taking and driving the car away without the owner's permission. (This is not correct since Percy, the car's owner, has given his permission to Sop to use the car for a week.)

Advise Sop and Pop.

7. What is meant by:

(a) *Audi alternam partem*; and

(b) *Nemo judex in causa sua?*

In what circumstances might a person aggrieved of administrative action invoke the first of these, and what consequences does breach of the rule have upon the action concerned?

8. Describe the main features of an application for judicial review. What obstacles might an applicant for judical review face, and what criticisms can he make of the current procedures?

9. Answer *both* **(a)** and **(b)**.

(a) In what circumstances is the Crown liable to civil proceedings in contract and tort? Describe any impediments facing a would-be litigant which may result in failure in proceedings against the Crown.

(b) 'I regret the passing of the currently rejected phrase "Crown Privilege". It at least emphasised the very restricted area of public interest immunity.' (Per Lord Scarman in *Science Research Council* v. *Nassé* (1980) AC 1028)

Discuss this statement. To what, exactly, is 'public interest immunity' limited?

Index